AUGUSTINE

AND HIS WORLD

FRANCIS OF ASSISI

AND HIS WORLD

Augustine and His World
For Dianne and Philippa

Francis of Assisi and His World
To Barbara, who exhibits many of Francis's finer qualities

AUGUSTINE
AND HIS WORLD

Andrew Knowles and Luke Penkett

FRANCIS OF ASSISI
AND HIS WORLD

Mark Galli

LION
SCHOLAR

Published by

Lion Hudson Limited
Wilkinson House, Jordan Hill Business Park
Banbury Road, Oxford OX2 8DR, England
www.lionhudson.com

ISBN 978 1 9125 5224 5

e-ISBN 978 1 9125 5225 2

'Augustine and His World': first paperback edition 2004
'Francis of Assisi and His World': first paperback edition 2002

Acknowledgments
'Augustine and His World'

Scripture quotations taken from the *New Revised Standard Version Bible*, copyright © 1989 National Council of the churches of Christ in the United States of America. Used by permission. All rights reserved worldwide.

Excerpts from *St Augustine's Confessions,* tr. with introduction and notes by Henry Chadwick, copyright © 2009, Oxford University Press (Books). Reprinted by permission.

'Francis of Assisi and His World'

Unless otherwise stated, scripture quotations taken from the *New Revised Standard Version Bible*, Anglicized edition, copyright © 1989, 1995 National Council of the Churches of Christ in the United States of America. Used by permission. All rights reserved worldwide.

p. 237 extract taken from the *New Jerusalem Bible*, copyright © 1985 by Darton, Longman and Todd Ltd, and Doubleday, a division of Penguin Random House LLC. Reprinted by permission.

pp. 191–92 (poem from the end of the rule of Francis) and pp. 238–39 ('The Canticle of Brother Sun') from *Francis and Clare: The Complete Works,* tr. with introduction by Regis Armstrong, OFM Cap, and Ignatius C. Brady, OFM, copyright © 1982 Paulist Press Inc (New York/Mahwah, NJ), www.paulistpress.com. Reprinted by permission.

Maps pp. 10–11, 12, 128–29, 150, 166 by Lion Hudson IP Limited

Cover image: © Joris Van Ostaeyen / Alamy Stock Photo

A catalogue record for this book is available from the British Library

CONTENTS

PART 1

AUGUSTINE

AND HIS WORLD

INTRODUCTION

Augustine is one of the giants of the Christian Church. From his birth in North Africa and his days as a relatively permissive young man, through his midlife conversion to Christianity and career as bishop of Hippo, his story has intrigued and inspired every generation for over 1,600 years.

It is as a thinker, teacher, writer and debater that Augustine's influence has proved most strategic. His greatness lay in his ability to relate the philosophies of Ancient Greece and Rome to the precepts of the Christian faith. Augustine also saved the Church itself from disintegrating into rival factions, by forging sound doctrine in the fires of controversy. Not only did Augustine provide a basis for doctrinal unity, but he presented the Church with a vision for its role in the world. Of all the Christian writers from the earliest centuries down to the present day Augustine is not only one of the most prolific but is also one of the most widely studied, remaining as controversial and influential today as he was during his life.

At the beginning of this third Christian millennium Augustine's fame and fascination are largely due to *City of God* and *Confessions,* his two greatest literary masterpieces. But what of the remaining hundred or so books? And what about the man who wrote them?

In 'Augustine and His World' we examine Augustine's life in a series of chapters that look at his adolescence, search for wisdom, conversion, ordination and episcopate. On the way through this life story those influences that most deeply affected Augustine, questions of reason and faith, the interface of pagan philosophy and Christian belief, orthodoxy, and heresy are explored. The final chapter of this account presents aspects of Augustine's significance for subsequent generations.

Augustine also broke new ground in personal spirituality. He probed the depths and recesses of his own heart and mind, memory and motives, to discern the influence of God in his life, and so discovered lessons and insights for every human being. It is not surprising to find, then, that in his own day Augustine was deeply respected not only as a theologian but also as a priest and bishop.

Augustine's ideas are a bridge spanning the gulf between the ancient and medieval worlds, from Aristotle to Anselm. His spiritual quest and ability to express his thoughts reach right to our own day. One prayer in particular that sprang from Augustine's passionate and inquiring soul, 'Our heart is restless until it rests in you', seems to be as pertinent now as it was when it was expressed 16 centuries ago.

As with so much historical study, our work has relied on the research and reflections of many others, and especially on the scholars whose books are listed in the section 'Further Reading'. We freely acknowledge our debt to them and hope that new readers will discover their work through this introductory study. The titles of Augustine's writings and their dates are based on *Augustine through the Ages: An Encyclopedia* (General Editor, Allan D. Fitzgerald O.S.A.); and for quotations from *Confessions* we have used Henry Chadwick's excellent translation (Oxford 2009).

Finally, we would like to express our gratitude to Rosy Baxter, our secretary at Chelmsford Cathedral, who has worked so cheerfully and tirelessly as amanuensis.

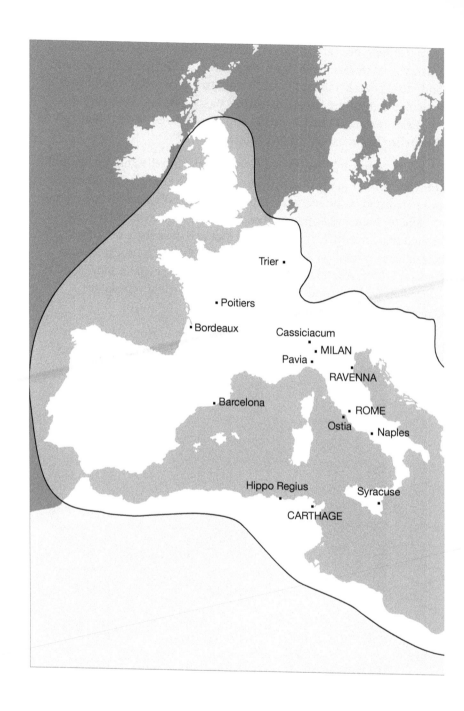

AUGUSTINE AND HIS WORLD – FRANCIS OF ASSISI AND HIS WORLD

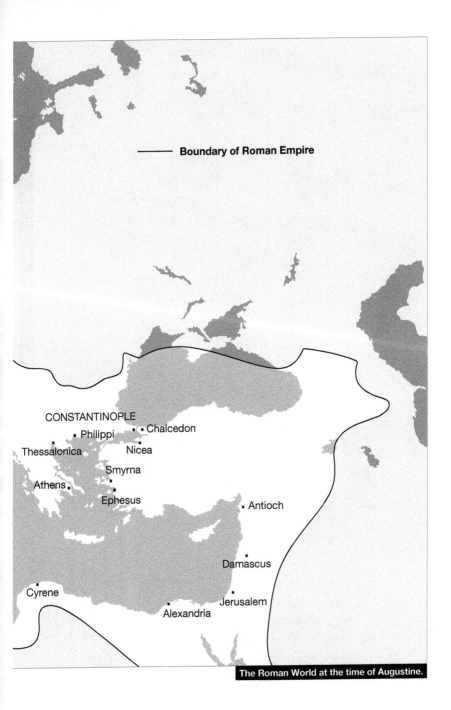

Boundary of Roman Empire

CONSTANTINOPLE
Philippi Chalcedon
Thessalonica Nicea
Smyrna
Athens
Ephesus
Antioch
Damascus
Cyrene
Jerusalem
Alexandria

The Roman World at the time of Augustine.

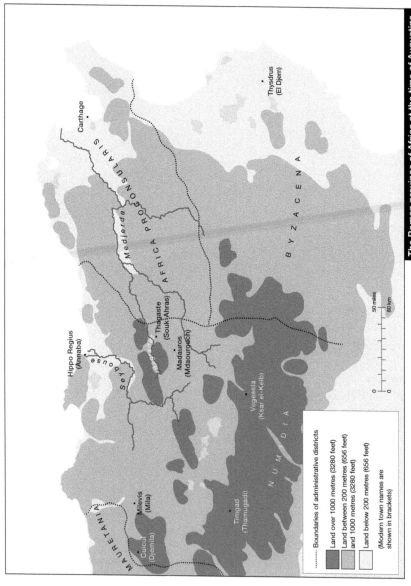

The Roman province of Africa at the time of Augustine.

Land over 1000 metres (3280 feet)

Land between 200 metres (656 feet) and 1000 metres (3280 feet)

Land below 200 metres (656 feet)

Boundaries of administrative districts

(Modern town names are shown in brackets)

Carthage

Thysdrus (El Djem)

AFRICA PROCONSULARIS

Medjerda

BYZACENA

Thagaste (Souk-Ahras)

Madauros (Mdaouroch)

Hippo Regius (Annaba)

Seybouse

Vegesela (Ksar el-Kelb)

NUMIDIA

Milevis (Mila)

Cuicul (Djemila)

Timgad (Thamugadi)

MAURETANIA

0   50 miles

0   80 km

CHAPTER 1
THE WORLD BEFORE AUGUSTINE

The province of Africa was an important and prosperous part of the Roman empire. For the Romans, Africa was not the vast continent that was later discovered, but the area that had been controlled by the main city and sea port of Carthage during the Punic Wars. Today this area is covered by Tunisia and Western Libya. The Punic Wars, waged during the third and second centuries before the birth of Christ, were to decide whether Rome or Carthage should control the sea routes and trade of the western Mediterranean. Despite the genius of the Carthaginian leader, Hannibal, who sprang a surprise attack on Rome by crossing the Alps with elephants, the Romans won the wars and destroyed Carthage in 146 BC.

Roman rule

In the middle of the fourth century AD, the Roman empire had reached the summit of its extent and influence. Its territory extended from Hadrian's Wall, in northern Britain, to Antioch and the eastern provinces, some 3,000 miles from Rome. The north-eastern frontier lay between Germany and barbarian tribes: Goths, Huns and Vandals. To the south, with its seaboard on the Mediterranean, was the province of Africa. It is here, in a town called Thagaste, that Augustine was born on AD 13 November 354.

In theory the Roman empire was a realm of peace, justice and prosperity, founded on Roman law and protected by the Roman army. But the military were overextended in maintaining such long frontiers, and barbarian tribes were pressing on the borders. Security was costly in money and recruits, so that treaties, alliances and compromises had to be made with real or potential enemies. Some barbarian tribes were enlisted as Roman auxiliaries and became as well armed and war wise as the Romans themselves. From time to time, the army commanders themselves attempted to seize power, both in Italy and in the provinces, and it was a period of almost continuous civil war. Meanwhile, the Roman upper class had become complacent and self-indulgent – preoccupied with personal status and political infighting. In short, the peak of Roman supremacy was also the cusp of decline.

Augustine's life would span the decline and fall of the Roman empire. On New Year's Eve 406, a horde of Goths, Huns and Vandals would cross the frozen Rhine to sweep into Gaul and then across the Pyrenees into Spain. In 410, Rome itself would be overwhelmed and sacked by the forces of Alaric the Goth.

Meanwhile, speed of communication was one of the wonders of the Roman world. Straight roads and safe seaways (at least in the summer months), together with the common language of Latin, meant that news and instructions could travel rapidly between the centre of the empire and its provinces. But the emperors were not always at the centre and the centre was not always at Rome. The fastest communication was at the pace of a galloping horse, with riders delivering letters by relay through a series of posting stations. But armies of infantry could manoeuvre no faster than marching sandals and aching legs would allow. 'Rapid response' to barbarian incursions or local riots could take several months. So it was that when Emperor Theodosius I died in AD 395, this vast but unwieldy empire was divided between his two sons, Honorius in the west and Arcadius in the east. The capital of the western empire continued to be Rome, although the administrative centre might be elsewhere. The capital of the eastern empire was Constantinople.

Communication between Rome and North Africa was relatively simple, with a summer sea voyage from Rome's port of Ostia bringing passengers to Carthage in a matter of days. Augustine would be both a student and a teacher in Carthage, and the voyages to Ostia and back (albeit five years apart) would be the only sea journeys of his life.

When the Romans conquered Carthage, they took over the Phoenician cities along the mediterranean coast and developed the towns of the inland plateau. They linked them by roads and bridges to one another and the sea ports, and improved the water supply by building aqueducts, reservoirs and cisterns. As a result, the province of Africa entered an era of unparalleled prosperity, with towns and rural estates alike thriving on commerce and agriculture.

The capital, Carthage, was developed by successive Roman emperors. Augustus, who was the first emperor (from 14 BC to AD 27) levelled the

Byrsa – the high point overlooking the city – and built an esplanade. Hadrian (emperor from AD 117 to 138) constructed an aqueduct 80 miles long to supply the city with millions of gallons of water. His successor, Antoninus, completed the huge baths and a massive basilica. There was a grand amphitheatre, the largest circus outside Rome and a fine palace for the proconsul. Carthage became the second city of the western Roman empire.

From Carthage, merchants traded throughout the known world. The export of cereal crops made North Africa the breadbasket of the empire, and especially of Rome. The region produced olives and olive oil in huge quantities, red-slip tableware and marble of a quality for monumental buildings. Hadrian quarried marble from Africa for his Pantheon in Rome, transporting 50-foot columns over high mountains to the port of Thabraca. During this period of peace and prosperity, educated people built comfortable villas, which they decorated with exquisite mosaics.

Inland, peasant farmers lived in ancient, close-knit communities: the Berber or Carthaginian underclass that had no stake in Roman colonialism. They maintained their Punic cults and language, although in time their fertility gods became identified with the gods and goddesses of Greece and Rome: 'Baal-Hammon' with Saturn, god of time and harvest, and 'Tanit' with Juno, goddess of marriage. But even those who resisted Roman ways could still make their living by growing corn and olives for Italy. Vast olive groves stretched 50 miles further south than their cultivation line today, as the remains of olive presses and the ruins of fine buildings testify. At remote El Djem was a venue to seat 30,000 people: the amphitheatre of Roman Thysdrus, which for a time supplanted Carthage.

A Roman legion was based in Africa for internal security and to help with engineering and agricultural projects. There was also a cohort on duty in Carthage. But the soldiers who assisted with the construction of roads and irrigation could be heavy handed in matters of law and order, and the army presence was an aggravation. The military seized land on which nomadic tribes had for centuries grazed their cattle, causing resentment and outbreaks of violence. They also used indigenous people as migrant labour at harvest time, requiring them by law to give six days' work per year in return for squatters' rights. They often required them to work more, which was another cause of unrest.

The most fertile land was the valley of the Medjerda, where Augustine was born. Much of it was under imperial administration, having been confiscated from senators by Emperor Nero (emperor from AD 54 to 68). Now Roman methods of cultivation and the planting of endless acres of olive groves had altered the terrain. And the ancient towns, with their houses cut into the rock, had acquired arched gates, paved streets, market squares with cisterns and forums with statues. The Romans had come to stay.

Whatever the friction, the Romans were good for Africa. It was not only the land and the towns but the people who had the chance to develop, gain an education and make their way both locally and in the wider empire. Augustine chose this door of opportunity, and was by no means the only African to do so. These were exciting times of mobility and adventure for people from humble backgrounds, with careers in the army or the civil service, which could lead anywhere from Asia to Britain and result in honour, wealth and influence.

> 'May I have joy of the beasts that are prepared for me. I pray too that they may prove prompt with me. I will entice them to devour me quickly . . . if only I reach Jesus Christ.'
>
> **Ignatius, bishop of Antioch, c. 35–107**

Early Christianity

And what of the Church? Three centuries had passed since the life, death and resurrection of Jesus Christ. By the time Augustine was born, in AD 354, Christianity had developed from a novel Jewish cult to a way of life followed by many throughout the empire, east and west. The leading apostles of the Church, Peter and Paul, had recognized that the new faith must break out of its Jewish context to engage with all nations and cultures. The first generation, with this missionary vision, saw the Christian gospel preached and churches planted in such significant centres as Antioch, Ephesus, Philippi and Rome.

> 'Surely I am coming soon. Amen. Come, Lord Jesus.'
>
> **Revelation 22:20**

The early Christians hoped that Jesus Christ would return in their lifetime; an expectation that shines out from the Gospels and Paul's letters. Christ's 'second coming' would vindicate his suffering followers and establish the kingdom of God. In the meantime, life was a struggle between good and evil; but it was a battle that Jesus had already won through his sacrificial death and resurrection. Now the task of his Church was to live with purity and integrity in the 'last days' before God's final judgment. These end times were characterized by human stress, natural disasters and religious persecution – all of which were fulfilled many times over in the unfolding history of the Roman empire.

Jesus did not return, and Christians were persecuted, imprisoned and martyred for their faith. Some survived in secret fellowships like those of the catacombs in Rome, but others met their deaths as sport for the bloodthirsty audiences in the amphitheatres. Christians were law-abiding citizens in every way, except that they refused to sacrifice to idols or worship 'the genius of the emperor'. They openly criticized the sacrificial rites that were used to promote social cohesion or honour the emperor as divine. Like the Jews before them, they acknowledged only one God, whom they held was fully revealed in his Son, Jesus Christ.

> 'If anyone denies that he is a Christian, and proves it in practice by worshipping our gods, he shall be pardoned.'
>
> **Emperor Trajan in a letter to Pliny the Younger, c. 112**

Christian customs

The title 'Christian' had begun as a nickname for those who aspired to be 'like Christ'. They met to 'break bread' in their homes, perhaps on the 'Lord's Day', which was Sunday, the day of the resurrection of Jesus and the first day of the week. They shared a communal meal, known as the *agape* or love feast, which took place in an evening and to which everyone was welcome, rich and poor alike. The 'breaking of bread', however, was different from a meal, in that it formally re-enacted the action of Jesus at the last supper and soon became the more stylized Eucharist (thanksgiving). The early Christians initiated new members by baptism in water after careful and sometimes lengthy instruction.

> 'This food is called the Eucharist, and of it no one is allowed to partake but he who believes that our teachings are true, and has been washed with the washing for the remission of sins and unto regeneration, and who also lives as Christ directed.'
>
> **Justin, c. 150**

The Church's worship followed an annual cycle. The central event was Easter, which was preceded by 'Lent': a 40-day period reflecting the time of Jesus' temptation in the wilderness. The historical events of Christ's birth and baptism were commemorated, and well-known martyrs such as John the Baptist, Stephen, Peter and Paul were remembered. Gradually these special days were integrated into the liturgical year.

In addition to the scriptures, there was a short manual of Christian teaching, known as the *Didache*, or *The Teaching of the Lord Through the Twelve Apostles*. It was discovered in Constantinople in 1873 and probably came from Smyrna (modern Izmir). There were also letters from bishops such as Clement of Rome (c. AD 96) and Ignatius of Antioch (c. 35–c. 107). These give glimpses of the issues and activities of the churches in the first century. The bishops' concerns were for the unity of the Church in the celebration of the Eucharist, for appropriate discipline and properly authorized leadership.

The first century of Christianity saw the Church's mission expand from Jerusalem to Rome. The second century (between 150 and 250) saw the Church facing a series of challenges and potential setbacks. From outside, Christians were persecuted, imprisoned and martyred for their faith. From within, differences of belief and practice led to divisions and the formation of 'sects'. Inevitably, the Church became preoccupied with formulating its core convictions, not least to determine which 'sects' were orthodox ('right') and which were heretical ('wrong'). This period also saw the birth of monasticism, which would grow at a spectacular rate and replace martyrdom as an expression of 'dying to self in order to live to God'.

> 'On Sunday, the Lord's own day, come together, break bread and carry out the eucharist, first confessing your sins so that your offering may be pure.'
>
> *Didache* 14.1

Important theologians appeared in these early centuries. Later known as the Church Fathers, they helped establish church teaching and protect Christianity from heresies such as Gnosticism. These early figures include Irenaeus, Tertullian, Origen, Clement of Alexandria and Cyprian of Carthage. They sought to elucidate orthodox teaching on questions such as the true nature of Christ, the meaning of salvation and the interpretation of scripture. Augustine was not the first Church Father; he followed in a line of brilliant theologians and was, as we shall see, considerably influenced by those who preceded him.

The Roman authorities were suspicious of the Church. The refusal of Christians to worship the old gods was seen as dangerous, because therein lay protection and prosperity. And to deny the supreme authority of the emperor was treason. But Christians had 'another King' in Jesus, and he alone was the Lord who commanded their worship. So Christians were considered to be atheists and their religion 'illicit' or unlicensed. They were also suspected of cannibalism (because they spoke of 'eating flesh' and 'drinking blood') and immorality (because of their 'love feasts').

'If we observe how powerful the gospel has become in a very few years, despite the persecution and the torture, the death and the confiscation, despite the small number of preachers, the word has been proclaimed throughout the earth. Greeks and Barbarians, wise and foolish, have joined the religion of Jesus. We cannot doubt that this goes beyond human powers, for Jesus taught with authority and the persuasion necessary for the word to be established.'

Origen, On First Principles 4.1.2

Persecutions give way to peace

The persecutions of early centuries gave way to a period of relative peace at the start of the fourth century. In 306 a new emperor was proclaimed in York. His name was Constantine, and he was to rule from 306 to 337. One of his lasting achievements was to found the city of Constantinople, which was named after him, and which became the eastern capital of the empire in AD 395. But it was Constantine's conversion through a vision before the Battle of Milvian Bridge, near Rome, in 312, that was to have undreamed-of significance. At the moment he established his authority to rule, by defeating the pagans under Maxentius, Constantine became a devoted Christian and an enormously influential protector and patron of the Church.

In 313, Constantine inaugurated a policy of religious freedom. Christians were allowed to worship freely and all their property was restored that had been confiscated or destroyed in the persecution since 303. Constantine wanted to unite the Christian Church to the empire and concerned himself with the issues that divided the Church. He summoned councils, going to great lengths to ensure that bishops could attend from all over the empire; but he did not control the Church in any legal way, nor was he its constitutional head.

Constantine showed an ongoing commitment to Christian principles. The first Christian symbols appeared on the coinage in 315, and the judgments of ecclesiastical courts became recognized by the State. He reformed the laws on debt and the conditions of slaves, supported the poor and freed celibates and unmarried people from special taxation. In 321 he ordered that Sunday should be observed as a public holiday and generously endowed church building projects in Constantinople, Palestine and Rome. The basilica style of church became commonplace, with 40 in Rome alone.

> 'All judges, city-people and craftsmen shall rest on the venerable day of the Sun. But countrymen may without hindrance attend to agriculture, since it often happens that this is the most suitable day for sowing grain or planting vines.'
>
> **Constantine's legislation for the observance of Sunday 321**

Under Constantine's influence and patronage, bishops became public figures and the Church an institution of wealth and influence. The Church was allowed to inherit property and so began to consolidate power and wield patronage in its own right. By the end of the fourth and the beginning of the fifth century, bishops such as Ambrose at Milan and Paulinus at Nola were a force to be reckoned with in their respective communities, able as they were to play power politics with the secular authorities. Ambrose was an eloquent preacher in Latin who had a considerable and effective following in Milan – enough to confront the imperial power that was then based in the same city.

At Antioch, John Chrysostom wielded enormous influence, although he was not at that time a bishop. His name, meaning 'golden mouth', was earned by the magnificent eloquence with which he stirred Christians to resist the abuses of Roman government. He became bishop of Constantinople in 397 but was exiled in 403 by the empress Eudoxia for denouncing her as a 'Jezebel'.

It must not, though, be assumed that from Constantine onwards Christianity was a runaway success. Persecution had ended and the Church was allowed some economic advantage and political opportunity. Much depended on the personality of the emperor and the quality of the bishops. The court of Theodosius II (eastern emperor from AD 408

Monasticism

The monastic movement grew rapidly from the late third century onwards; the name 'monk' (from the Greek *monachos*) meaning 'one who is alone'. Individuals withdrew to the desert to live a solitary life of prayer, visiting one another or gathering occasionally. The most celebrated hermit was Antony of Egypt (d. AD 356), who gave spiritual counsel to visitors and about whom many inspiring stories were told. A *Life of Antony* was translated from Greek into Latin by Jerome and became immensely popular among upper-class Romans. Meanwhile, Pachomios (d. AD 346) at Tabennisi in Upper Egypt pioneered a rule by which monks could live together in community. He was a founding father of monasticism.

to 450) was so predominantly Christian that some said it resembled a convent. By the early fifth century it was fashionable among the Roman aristocracy to be Christian and attitudes finally shifted from throwing believers to lions to helping them build churches. But pagan beliefs and practices were a long time dying, and even in the middle of the fifth century, Pope Leo the Great (pope from 440 to 460) had to take issue with his congregation for bowing to the sun before entering St Peter's in Rome.

But by the time of Augustine things had certainly greatly improved for the Christian Church. He was to enter a world of fierce debate and controversy, yet also one of relative peace.

CHAPTER 2
THE YOUNG MAN

Aurelius Augustinus – to be known to the world as Augustine – was born in North Africa on AD 13 November 354, in a Roman-style town 200 miles from the sea and 2,000 feet above it. In those days the place was called Thagaste, but today it is the town of Souk-Ahras in Algeria. The wider region was known as Numidia, after the Roman word for 'nomads'.

> *'To praise you is the desire of man, a little piece of your creation.'*
> **Confessions** 1.1.1

A Roman town

In Thagaste there were people of several races and religions. The original Berber population had mixed and interbred with the peoples who had conquered or done business with them: Phoenicians, Romans, Greeks and Jews. The region was also popular with veteran soldiers retiring from imperial service, many of whom settled in North Africa and married local women. But the truth was that the line of 'civilization' ran between the Romans and the rest. Augustine may never have spoken any language but Latin, and all other dialects he grouped under the general term 'Punic'.

The wealthier inhabitants of the town had a strong loyalty to Roman government and Roman lifestyle. They knew and used Latin and lived by the law and order, self-discipline and public service that had made Rome great. In their integrity and high moral values, they were probably more 'Roman' than the Romans, because in some parts of the empire the old order was starting to crumble. Thagaste's public buildings included baths, temples and amphitheatres. The baths were the social centres of the day, while the theatres were the venues for drama, oratory, games and spectacles. Well-to-do estate owners had villas in the surrounding countryside, where they lived in comfort off the land and the labour of exploited peasants. These peasants were poor and marginalized, but armed with a vigorous form of Christianity, which gave them courage and hope in their troubles.

Thagaste

The modern town of Souk-Ahras stands on the border between Algeria and Tunisia. In the nineteenth century it was a French colonial settlement, with a main square and bandstand. Flaubert, in 1858, found it 'atrocious, cold and muddy'. In the twentieth century the working of the mines and the arrival of the railway brought the town some significance and prosperity.

In the distant past, and long before the Romans came, Souk-Ahras was the Numidian town of Thagaste: set in the valley of Medjerda on the uplands of north-east Numidia, and watered by the Bagradas river. The altitude and rainfall were similar to Madrid today: dry and hot in summer, with an uncomfortable sirocco wind. To the east were mountains rising to a height of 3,000 feet.

In Roman times, the people of Thagaste worked the fertile soil to produce corn and olives. In the surrounding hills and forests they snared wild animals such as lions, bears and panthers, to be sent for sport in the amphitheatres of Carthage or Rome.

In Souk-Ahras today, the church is named after the town's most famous son, Augustine; and in the crypt is a small museum dedicated to his memory.

A pagan father . . .

Augustine's father was Patricius, a well-respected member of the town. He was a proud man, holding the office of *decurio,* or town councillor; but he was poor. Augustine describes his father's estate as 'a few acres'. As a leading member of the community, Patricius was expected to support public services and sports with his own money. Many councillors were reduced to poverty in this way and Patricius himself may have fallen on hard times. However, the family were fortunate in having a relative who was willing to help them: Romanianus, a wealthy estate owner and local celebrity. It is he who funded the classical education that unlocked the doors of opportunity for Augustine, and also became his close friend.

> 'I was already a believer, as were my mother and the entire household, except for my father . . . [My mother] anxiously laboured to convince me that you, my God, were my father rather than he.'
>
> **Confessions 1.11.17**

. . . and a Christian mother

Augustine's mother was Monica. She had been married at the age of 12 but was 23 by the time Augustine was born. She had another son, Navigius, and one or two daughters; but it is because of her devotion to Augustine that she became immortalized. Her name is of Berber origin, from a local goddess, 'Mon'. The Berbers were a fair-skinned and fair-haired people who lived in North Africa long before the arrival of the Phoenicians or the Romans. The Romans nicknamed them 'Barbarians' and mimicked their speech as a primitive 'burr-burr'.

When they were first married, Monica had lived with Patricius in his mother's house. Her relationship with her mother-in-law had been difficult at first, because the servants told tales against her. But the young wife had won through with patience and respect. Over the years she was a faithful and loving wife to Patricius, despite his hot tempers and many affairs. And Patricius became a Christian before he died.

Patricius and Monica agreed that their gifted son should have a classical education. Such an education would be expensive and require them to make considerable sacrifices; but it would lay the foundation for a prosperous and perhaps even distinguished career in the Roman civil service. The unusual name they gave their son – 'Augustine', meaning 'little emperor' – signalled their shared ambition.

Darkness and light

In Africa, the native religions were pagan and deeply superstitious. The Berbers worshipped the spirits of the dead and warded off evil with magic charms. The Phoenicians engaged in occult ceremonies, using sacrifices in their attempts to appease the gods and control the forces of nature. Carthage was a major centre for the worship of the Baal fertility gods, Hammon and his consort Tanit, who in extreme circumstances were offered human victims.

Into this sombre and fearful world, Christianity brought the good news of one all-powerful invisible and loving creator God, and a Saviour who could defeat every kind of evil. But the Christians were seen as a threat to the old ways and vested interests, and were persecuted as a

Monica

Monica was a deeply committed Christian with a strict and somewhat superstitious faith. She observed, for example, the local practice of keeping Sabbath fasts, and the very widespread custom of sharing meals with the dead by holding picnics and parties at their tombs. For Christians, death was a birthday and the anniversary was celebrated as such. When Monica attempted to take a basket of refreshments to a grave in Milan, she was told that the bishop, Ambrose, had forbidden it. Monica also believed in divine guidance and paid close attention to dreams as messages from another world.

Monica had received a careful Christian upbringing and wanted the same for her children. She was determined, even controlling, but also affectionate and intelligent. Augustine became the focal point of her life, and she dedicated 20 years of prayers and tears to the cause of him becoming a Christian. As a young man, Augustine's respect for his mother was never in doubt, but his independent spirit chafed against her possessiveness and ambition. In his late twenties, Augustine actually left Monica in Carthage and sailed for Rome without saying goodbye. In her determination she followed him to Rome and went with him to Milan, where she became a much-appreciated member of his household, and shared with him an extraordinary vision of bliss before her death.

result. Emperor Decius (249–51) suppressed the Christians with great brutality, requiring them to offer sacrifices to the ancient gods of Rome. Many African Christians, to save their lives or property, betrayed their faith by handing over their copies of the scriptures and other holy books to the secular authorities. Some of those who refused to compromise were imprisoned or killed. From these contrasting responses sprang a long-running division in the African Church, between the 'Catholic' compromisers and the faithful martyrs, later known as 'Donatists'.

> 'She had brought up her children, enduring travail as she saw them wandering away from you . . . She exercised care for everybody as if they were all her own children.'
>
> **Augustine about his mother, Confessions 9.9.22**

Religion and politics were interwoven. Couples like Patricius and Monica saw themselves as superior to the local Numidian peasants.

Early learning

When he was about 43 and a bishop in Hippo, Augustine told the story of his life in his *Confessions*. He remembered, or at least reflected on, his early years; the process of learning language as an infant, and the anger and jealousy that is inherent in human nature from babyhood: 'The feebleness of infant limbs is innocent, not the infant's mind. I have personally watched and studied a jealous baby' (*Confessions* 1.7.11).

He was intrigued by the stages of human development and the relationship between thought and will and action.

They expressed this in their allegiance to Rome and (in Monica's case) to Catholic Christianity. For them, Rome meant protection and prosperity. Monica's family were Catholic Christians who followed the inclusive approach of Bishop Cyprian, but were regarded as 'worldly' by the more exclusive and hard-line Church of the martyrs and 'confessors'. The common people, including many Numidians, found the Church of the martyrs more popular and exciting. Their numbers grew as the power of Rome and the influence of the Catholic Church began to fade.

Paganism was in decline around the empire, not least because Christianity was giving a sense of value to every human being, irrespective of class, wealth or education. By the time Augustine was in his thirties, imperial edicts were being issued to suppress paganism, ordering idols to be destroyed and temples closed. But Augustine very fairly observed that he knew pagans who lived better lives than he did.

> 'The free-ranging flux of curiosity is channelled by discipline under your laws, God.'
> **Confessions 1.14.23**

Augustine was not baptized as a baby, but rather welcomed into the Christian Church with a blessing, the sign of the cross and a touch of salt. As he grew, he would have gone with his mother to church. Baptism was delayed until late in life, to increase the chances of a sinless death; but when Augustine contracted a childhood illness that appeared life-threatening, preparations were made for an emergency baptism. In the event, he made a speedy recovery, and would not be baptized until Easter 387 when he was over 30.

A divided Church

One of the great 'Fathers' of the African Church, Tertullian, had taught that there was no way back to the Church for those who had betrayed Christ. He had denounced the Catholics for their compromises and himself joined a vigorous and highly spiritual sect called the Montanists.

However, when the Decian persecution came to North Africa, there were some Catholic Christians who suffered for their faith and survived. These were the 'confessors', whose courage and faithfulness might outweigh the failings of the rest. Cyprian, the bishop of Carthage, certainly saw it that way.

By the time Augustine was born in 354, a deep split had developed between those Christians who followed Cyprian, living under the authority of the Catholic Church, and those who became known as 'Donatists', whose faith was a pure, spiritual commitment, unsullied by compromise with a worldly institution.

Schooling at Thagaste

Augustine's early schooling was in Thagaste. As a boy, he learned to read and write, loving Latin, but hating Greek. By his own account, he preferred games to books and was often in trouble with his teachers. He likened the lessons to the labour and sorrow of Adam, and his beatings to the sufferings of the Christian martyrs.

His early prayers included fervent pleas to be spared the rod: 'Though I was only a small child, there was great feeling when I pleaded with you that I might not be caned at school' (*Confessions* 1.9.14).

In *City of God*, Augustine wrote: 'Who would not choose death to beginning childhood all over again?'

> '*I was next sent to school to learn to read and write. Poor wretch, I did not understand for what such knowledge is useful. Yet if ever I was indolent in learning, I was beaten.*'
>
> **Confessions 1.9.14**

Augustine's failure to master Greek was a great disadvantage to him in later life. Greek was the language of the eastern empire and accomplished scholars would be bilingual, as Cicero had been. Although Augustine

Cyprian takes a stand

Next to Augustine, Cyprian of Carthage (d. 258) is the most important bishop in the history of North Africa. He was reluctant to permanently excommunicate those Christians who had lapsed in the face of persecution. He required only that they do penance or wait a certain time before being reinstated. But in Rome, a rigorist by the name of Novatian was attacking his bishop, Cornelius (d. 253), for being too lenient. When Novatian sought an ally in Cyprian, he was rebuffed, the bishop of Carthage preferring restoration to condemnation in the case of his weaker brethren.

Cyprian found support for a policy of rebaptizing those who had split from the Church but now wanted to return. His fellow African bishops agreed that this reduced the risk of independent groups forming to administer the sacraments outside the authority of the Catholic Church. For Cyprian, the sacraments were not efficacious outside the Church, because the Church alone was the body of Christ in which the Holy Spirit resided. It followed that no one outside the Church was authorized to administer the sacraments. This stance led to a rift between Cyprian and Cornelius's successor, Stephen, who had taken much tougher measures to punish schismatics.

would have known some Greek, he was never fluent, which meant that his reading of Greek philosophy was always 'second-hand' through translations.

Augustine was, in fact, a gifted and promising pupil. He developed a love of the theatre, Latin literature and 'rhetoric' – the use of language. The mark of the cultured person was an ability to conjure words and phrases, puns and rhymes, metaphors and irony. Augustine was to have this ability in abundance, and it would pour from him in a lifetime of conversation, debate, letters and sermons. At this stage, his own ambition was to become a schoolmaster himself, but Patricius hoped his son would qualify as a lawyer or rhetorician. At the age of 11, it was decided to send Augustine to a better school for the next stage of his education.

> 'Words are like exquisite and precious vessels.'
> Confessions 1.16.26

Schooling at Madauros

Augustine's new school was at Madauros (modern-day Mdaourouch), a small Numidian city about 19 miles, a day's journey, to the south of Thagaste. Madauros was a university town, larger and more pagan than Thagaste, with two statues of Mars, the Roman god of war, prominent in its centre. One of Africa's famous writers came from here: Lucius Apuleius (c. 125–after 170), an eccentric philosopher whose novel *The Golden Ass* was a scandalous adventure of myth, magic and sex. Augustine became accustomed to the sight of revellers staggering home from their drunken Bacchanals.

At Madauros, the emphasis of Augustine's education was on the rules of language and the structure of persuasive argument. The method was very traditional, rigorous and tedious, aiming to develop a perfect, precise understanding of the meanings and use of words by studying the works of classical Latin writers. He learned by heart extracts of the great Roman orator Cicero (106–43 BC), and was taught the principles of oratory and debate. Here were laid the foundations for Augustine's own speaking, writing and preaching in years to come, and not least in learning how to appeal to the emotions.

> 'Clouds of muddy carnal concupiscence filled the air. The bubbling impulses of puberty befogged and obscured my heart.'
>
> **Confessions 2.2.2**

In addition to Cicero, Augustine encountered the works of Terence and Virgil, Ovid, Seneca and Juvenal. He delighted in the great Latin literature, which moved him to tears on occasion, and he learned to emulate its persuasive skills. He won a prize for his rendition of a famous scene from Virgil, in which Dido, the queen of Carthage, first pours out her grief and then takes her own life as her lover Aeneas sails away to his destiny and the founding of Rome. The class erupted in applause.

> 'All around me hissed a cauldron of illicit loves.'
>
> **Confessions 3.1.1**

Loose living

When Augustine was about 15 years old, his parents decided to send him to university at Carthage. It took them a year to raise the necessary

A waning empire

During Augustine's early years, the glory of the Roman empire was, almost imperceptibly, on the wane. The discipline and dedication of the Roman way of life was giving way to a greater flamboyance of dress, extravagance of lifestyle and specious spirituality. Successive emperors were preoccupied with the defence of their territories against barbarian insurgents from the north and the military threat of Persia in the east. Their centre of government was no longer Rome, but Trier, or Milan, or Ravenna, as they moved with their armies between Gaul, northern Italy and the Danube. Although there was a revival of interest in literature, the main concern was for the might and muscle to preserve the empire at all. Imperial control in the western empire was exercised through crippling levels of taxation and a brutal enforcement of the law.

In these days of slow decline, there was little need for the talents of the North Africans, who were almost old-fashioned in their provincial Roman ways. Although, since Constantine, there was optimism that the Roman empire and the Christian Church would rule the world for ever, a very different underlying trend was revealed in the careers of Augustine and his contemporaries. Many of them, like Augustine, returned to North Africa and their small home towns; some of them eventually becoming bishops. Augustine himself, after standing on the threshold of a distinguished career in Milan, came full circle to Thagaste to settle for the obscurity of a monastic community in his family home.

money, and during this time Augustine was at home in Thagaste. Without a school to attend, and brimming with adolescent energy, he became part of a group of lads who ran wild in the town, proud of their exploits at drinking, theft and sex. For the son of a devout Christian mother, this was the start of a long struggle against the lure of paganism. Perhaps Augustine's famous prayer, 'Grant me chastity and continence, but not yet' (*Confessions* 8.7.17), was born from the conflict of his upbringing, between his mother's piety and his father's permissiveness.

> '*Shame for its own sake.*'
>
> **Confessions 2.4.9**

Shameful memories

In his *Confessions,* Augustine recalled some events from his adolescent years. He remembered the sense of shame when his father caught sight of him naked at the baths. In Roman times there was nothing untoward about nakedness, but clearly there was some embarrassment between father and son. As Patricius smiled knowingly at Augustine's evident emergence into manhood, the young man felt himself exposed and ashamed. In his mind he associated the episode with the story of Adam and Eve, with its suggestive juxtaposition of nakedness and guilt.

On another occasion, the teenage Augustine and his friends stole some pears. They weren't hungry and soon threw them away, but the prank stuck in Augustine's mind as an example of sin. Again, the story of Adam and Eve had centred on fruit stolen from the Garden of Eden. As a bishop, Augustine searched his heart for the motives of such an act. Partly they had desired something beautiful that belonged to someone else. But there was also peer pressure. He would never have stolen the pears without the encouragement of a gang of friends. In the group, he would 'have been ashamed not to be shameless' (*Confessions* 2.9.17). So here was an irony: that two of God's good gifts, the love of beautiful objects and the joy of friendship, could motivate a furtive, pointless and guilt-producing act of theft.

Wrestling with evil

At the end of his teenage years, as a student in Carthage, Augustine became a Manichee. The Manichaean sect was a distortion of Christianity that believed evil was a tangible power to be wrestled with and rejected. But Augustine, on reflection, concluded that evil was a distortion of good. For example, friendship was good. The same power of friendship that had motivated the theft of the pears would be the force that held him in the fellowship of the Manichees long after he ceased to believe their doctrines. But the value Augustine set on friendship found expression in his later experiences of community life and in the community rule he passed on to the world.

Augustine included a further reflection on the theft of the pears in *The Literal Interpretation of Genesis,* which he started writing around the same time as *Confessions.* He believed that, when Adam accepted the stolen fruit from Eve, he knew that he was disobeying God, but he did not want to disappoint his partner. As with Augustine's own escapade with the pears, the sin arose neither from deceit nor hunger, but from misguided loyalty and careless pride. In seeking to please Eve rather than God, Adam committed sin. So, for Augustine, sin is 'love gone wrong'.

It was not until much later in life that Augustine narrated these youthful experiences. Despite its title, *Confessions* does not contain the kind of revelations we associate with tabloid journalism today. They are in fact confessions of faith, as Augustine reflects on God's unfailing love and goodness towards him from the earliest years of his life. Even so he may have been taking the opportunity to warn others against making his mistakes. There is more than a hint of episcopal sermons in some of the rolling phrases. But Augustine wasn't the first teenager to rebel against a pious upbringing, and he may in fact have been one of the quieter and more temperate members of his gang. Monica was evidently aware of Augustine's sexual adventures, and solemnly warned him not to become promiscuous or to commit adultery.

A friend in deed

The wealthy relative Romanianus now began to play a greater part in Augustine's life. He had already helped with financial sponsorship for Augustine's education. Now he and Augustine became good friends. Augustine describes how Romanianus opened not only his wealth to him, but also his heart. There was a benefit for Romanianus in the relationship, as he enjoyed having Augustine's intellectual brilliance on tap. Romanianus owned a library and was himself an aspiring scholar. He hoped that Augustine would eventually settle in Thagaste and become a tutor for his sons. Augustine may have started to fulfil this role during his year at home in Thagaste, before going to continue his studies in Carthage. He would not be the first young teacher to tutor children during the day and run wild with his friends at night.

'Drunk with wine, bloated from overeating and plunged in rottenness and debauchery.'

Salvian, priest of Lérins from c. 424, describing the men of Carthage

Carthage

In 370, at the age of 17, Augustine arrived in Carthage, about 170 miles from Thagaste. The journey of several days brought him to the sea, which he had previously imagined only in a beaker of water. Here was the capital of Africa, the 'Alexandria of the West', with a port that drew traders and travellers from all over the world. Many forms of greed, superstition and vice had washed in with the commerce, and for Augustine it would prove a university of life.

There were some distinguished and influential residents in Carthage, not least the proconsuls who lived in the palace overlooking the forum. These were the people who would be interested in Augustine's skill with words and who might favour him with their patronage. One such proconsul was Symmachus, a man of letters and no mean orator himself, who arrived in Carthage at the same time as Augustine. In future years Symmachus would become urban prefect in Rome and recommend Augustine to his cousin, Bishop Ambrose, to be professor of rhetoric in Milan. Symmachus, although he might not have agreed with Augustine, nor even remembered him, would be an important patron at a crucial moment, especially as the young African had to overcome any Roman prejudice against his provincial accent.

> 'As yet I had never been in love and I longed to love . . . I was in love with love, and I hated safety and a path free of snares.'
>
> **Confessions 3.1.1**

Into the frying pan

Carthage led the world in pagan excesses. The mother goddess was Coelestis, the 'Queen of Heaven', who was attended by effeminate eunuchs and celebrated in public portrayals of sex. At the theatres, the lusty escapades of the god Jupiter were enacted in lurid detail, as were the labours of Heracles and the adventures of Aeneas. In the huge amphitheatre, it was not so long since Christians had met their martyrdom in the jaws of wild beasts. There was also a circus, where Augustine could enjoy the excitement of the chariot races, and public baths in the forum, where he would meet with student friends.

In such a place Augustine was under an avalanche of temptation. The word for Carthage (*Carthago*) sounded like the word for frying pan or cauldron (*sartago*), and Augustine appreciated the pun. He was coming to the boil himself and dived in with enthusiasm.

Monica's spirit was with Augustine, even in the big city. He continued as a Christian catechumen, receiving preparation for his baptism, even though it might not take place until he was on his deathbed with his sinning days over. He occasionally attended church meetings, if only to look out for pretty girls. The young men and women sat together during vigils, with a good deal of teasing and ribaldry between them, not least in putting rude words to the hymns. Augustine recalled such occasions 30 years later, when he preached in Carthage, on the feast of St Vincent in 405.

> 'In those years I had a woman. She was not my partner in what is called lawful marriage. I found her in my state of wandering desire and lack of prudence. Nevertheless, she was the only girl for me, and I was faithful to her.'
>
> **Confessions 4.2.2**

Carthage was also a place of wider spiritual quest. Alongside competing forms of Christianity were the occult arts of mediums and magicians, fortune-tellers and astrologers. Augustine, the possibility thinker, was fascinated to think that one's fate could be discerned in the entrails of a sacrifice or the movement of planets. He experimented with these practices for a while, but concluded that they were a form of demon worship. He later believed it was involvement with the occult that prevented some fine thinkers, such as Porphyry, from coming to faith in Christ.

'God's gift'?

It may well have been at church that Augustine met the woman who became his partner for 15 years and with whom he had a son. Whether they met in Thagaste or Carthage is not known, but the woman soon became pregnant. They called their child Adeodatus, which means 'given by God'. Augustine never divulged the name of his partner. Adeodatus was almost 15 when he was baptized in the spring of 387, so he must have been born in 372, when Augustine was 18. It is possible that the episode at the baths and the theft of the pears in Thagaste are Augustine's

Why didn't Augustine marry his partner?

Augustine and his partner lived together for 15 years and their much-loved son made them a family. Perhaps Augustine doesn't declare the woman's name because to do so would open old wounds, or embarrass her if she was later living in Thagaste. He was unable to marry his mistress because of the difference in their social standing. She may have been poor, or from a peasant or racially different background. Whatever the reason, the culture of the day was against them. While it was quite usual for someone of Augustine's status to take a lover for a while, in the long term he was expected to make a marriage that would improve his position in society and further his career.

Augustine realized the injustice of this situation. In *On the Good of Marriage,* he will commend the faithfulness of a woman who is wronged when her man moves on to make a society marriage. When Augustine's partner was finally sent away from him, she vowed never to go with another man.

way of saying that he was sexually active and that Adeodatus was conceived in the course of adolescent adventures in his home town.

Augustine had longed to be in love. He had visited the theatre and wallowed in plays that portrayed the pain of love and the parting of lovers. Now the loves and losses of the real world were brought home to him. Towards the end of his first year in Carthage, his father died. It was probably around the same time that Augustine made his commitment to the young woman who would be his partner for so many years.

These experiences sobered Augustine. He was scarcely 20 years old and already he felt his life was careering out of control. He had indulged his sexual appetites, but with regrets. With better guidance, he would have preferred to have made a marriage.

As Monica was now a widow she moved to Carthage. She refused to eat with her son because of his Manichaean beliefs, but she continued to

> 'If only someone could have imposed restraint on my disorder. They would have transformed to good purpose the fleeting experiences of beauty in these lowest of things, and fixed limits to indulgence in their charms. Then the stormy waves of my youth would have finally broken on the shore of marriage.'
>
> **Confessions 2.1.3**

pray for him. When she poured out her heart to a bishop, he counselled her to be patient, assuring her that 'the child of so many tears' could not be lost.

Augustine recalls in *Confessions* how much his emotions were in turmoil at this time; that he had 'polluted the spring water of fellowship with the filth of concupiscence'. Looking back, he saw a pure love for God polluted by his passionate quest for human love. With a partner who was now pregnant or with a young child, he found himself caught up in a maelstrom of lust and love, jealousy and joy. He was both a student – wanting the freedom of the libraries and the nightlife of a university town – and a reluctant young father.

> 'Let him be where he is, only pray the Lord for him . . . It cannot be that the son of these tears should perish.'
>
> **Confessions 3.12.21**

Father and son

There was something wonderful and fascinating about baby Adeodatus. Augustine studied his son's development, intrigued by the sucking and sleeping, smiling and crying, physical exertion and mental frustration. For Augustine, who was always as questioning as he was observant, this was a rich seam of discovery and reflection. He could see that 'original sin', in the form of self-seeking and anger, was inherent in human nature from the earliest days of life.

> 'My love was returned and in secret I attained the joy that enchains. I was glad to be in bondage, tied with troublesome chains, with the result that I was flogged with the red-hot iron rods of jealousy, suspicion, fear, anger and contention.'
>
> **Confessions 3.1.1**

Augustine described his own infancy in imaginative terms: 'I would endeavour to express the intentions of my heart to persuade people to bow to my will. But I had not the power to express all that I wanted nor could I make my wishes understood by everybody' (*Confessions* 1.8.13).

When Adeodatus was 16, father and son would collaborate on a book called *On the Teacher*. In it, they would explore the complexities of human learning and language, symbols, signs and memory. Augustine claimed that learning was a process of God-enabled discovery, stimulated by need and best nurtured by the encouragement and understanding of others. In education, he preferred to get the best from a student by reward rather than punishment. He always remembered how counterproductive were the beatings he received in the cause of learning Greek. In Augustine's opinion, learning was best undertaken in an atmosphere of love, which is a reflection of God's dealings with all his creatures.

'Top of the class'

Augustine was a successful student, showing a special talent for public speaking and making lasting friendships. It was true that he continued to yield to peer group pressure and mixed with a wild bunch he called 'wreckers', but only because he was afraid not to belong. They were the sort of students Augustine would find impossible when he himself became a teacher.

'I was already top of the class in the rhetors' school and was pleased with myself for my success and was inflated with conceit.'

Confessions 3.3.6

CHAPTER 3

FROM MANICHEE TO CHRISTIAN

In 373, when Augustine had been in Carthage about two years, he read *Hortensius,* by the greatest of Roman orators, Cicero (106–43 BC). This book is now lost, although enough fragments have survived to give an idea of its contents. It was written in dialogue form and expounded the importance of finding and loving wisdom.

> 'The book changed my feelings. It altered my prayers, Lord, to be towards you yourself. It gave me different values and priorities.'
>
> **Confessions 3.4.7**

For Augustine, *Hortensius* was a revelation. It opened his mind to 'philosophy', which in those days meant a coherent body of teachings that offered a 'world view' of principles and values to live by. For Cicero, 'philosophy' was not a matter of abstruse theorizing, but a highly principled and aesthetically pleasing way of life; almost, in fact, a religion. For the first time, Augustine found himself listening to truth, rather than the mere sound of words. A new stage of his spiritual quest had begun.

Cicero's path to 'wisdom' led through a rigorous programme of self-discipline and self-improvement. The wise man was someone who trained his head to rule his heart and physical passions in order to live a humble and objective life. Cicero taught that by controlling earthly desires and developing reason and knowledge, a person could embark on the way back to heaven. The idea of bringing one's passions under strict control appealed to Augustine, and awakened in him an urgent desire to know God. Like the prodigal son in Jesus' parable, he was coming to himself amid the brothels and circuses of Carthage and realizing how much he was missing the safe haven of Christian faith; but the journey home would take several years.

Cicero's book set Augustine searching for his spiritual roots, a coherent philosophy of life, and a better way of writing. Cicero had abandoned elaborate and stylized rhetoric in favour of plain argument and discussion. His books read as a conversation between people seeking the truth – or between a teacher and his circle of pupils. Plato had also

> 'I longed for the immortality of wisdom, with an incredible ardour in my heart. I began to rise up to return to you.'
>
> **Confessions 3.4.7**

favoured this method, which he learned from his own teacher, Socrates. As Augustine enjoyed thinking through issues in the company of others, the idea of writing in the form of conversation or debate suited him well. It bore fruit in a rich harvest of books, letters, sermons and prayers.

By the time Augustine read *Hortensius,* Cicero had been dead for more than 400 years. In the meantime, 'wisdom' had become an object of religious passion, expressed in a spiritual quest for a pure way of life. Augustine immediately identified 'wisdom' with the Christian God of his upbringing and devoted himself to seek this God by reading the Bible. In the Old Testament, 'wisdom' is the personification of the godly way of life; a theme that the apostle Paul finds fulfilled in Jesus Christ, 'who became for us wisdom from God' (1 Corinthians 1:30).

Although Augustine turned to the Bible with a fresh appetite, he was sharply disillusioned by its style and content. His copy was the rough translation in Old Latin, which had been made for Africans in the second century by uneducated Greek missionaries. Augustine was offended by the crudeness of its style, which compared badly with the eloquence and dignity of Cicero. He also found no virtue in the faults and failings of the people of the Old Testament and was perplexed by the differing genealogies of Jesus in the Gospels of Matthew and Luke.

> '*Augustine was . . . sensual and at the same time spiritual; attracted by the things of this world and yet devoted to the life of intelligence; yielding in friendship on the one hand and yet firm to shake it off on the other. [He was] compounded of excess and restraint, imagination and reason, mysticism and dialect. There is no simple formula that will explain him.*'
>
> **John O'Meara,**
> *The Young Augustine*

Meanwhile, Augustine's circle of friends in Carthage was a great delight to him. The heady combination of love and learning, friendship and the quest for faith, was a foretaste of the Christian communities Augustine would seek to establish in the future. It was at this time that some of the people he found so intelligent and attractive drew him into a radical, exciting and otherworldly form of Christianity, known as Manichaeism.

The Manichees

Augustine was not the only person having difficulty with the Bible. While some of the African bishops had developed Christianity in a legalistic way, with a strict moral code and cramping ritual, some other Christians had broken away from the Catholic Church to live in the true freedom and grace of the gospel. These 'new' Christians argued that they didn't need the Old Testament at all. Instead, they claimed to enjoy a direct and vibrant relationship with the living Christ, who imparted to them his wisdom and power. In Carthage, these neo-Christians formed a gifted, persuasive and fashionable group, which appeared to live out the clear thinking and radical Christianity. They were called 'Manichees'.

The Manichees were named after their founder, Mani (c. 216–76), a self-styled 'Apostle of Jesus Christ'. Mani had received his inspired revelation in Mesopotamia, where he was persecuted and executed by the Persian government in AD 276. His message claimed to be a unique disclosure of the nature of God, humanity and the universe. In effect, it was a Persian adaptation of Christianity, which added in Zoroastrianism, speculative philosophy and superstition. By the time Augustine became a Manichee 'hearer', the founder had been dead for nearly a century. But Mani's mission had been to found the one, true, universal Church.

Manichaeism was taken up with great enthusiasm. It spread throughout the Roman empire and, in later centuries, to the Far East and China, moving from one language to another and adapting to a variety of cultures.

Mani's missionaries arrived in Carthage in AD 297, calling themselves 'The Elect', and living a life of stark self-denial. They spoke of mysteries and secrets, practised strict fasting and abstained from sex. Their holy books were exquisitely inscribed and illuminated volumes of parchment, detailing the secrets and rituals by which fallen human beings could escape from 'darkness' to 'light'.

Those who were attracted to the message of the Manichees (if not to their lifestyle) were called 'hearers'. The movement allowed two levels of membership, whereby someone could make a full commitment or simply join as a seeker or sympathizer. These latter were the 'hearers'.

Augustine was drawn to the Manichees. He was intrigued by their explanation of the existence of evil – that it was due to the invasion of 'the kingdom of light' by 'the kingdom of darkness'. The 'good' or 'light' that is in every human being and in all the world is being ruthlessly invaded by an entirely separate force of 'evil' or 'darkness'. This way of thinking of good and evil as equal and opposing forces perpetually in tension and at war is called 'dualism'.

For the Manichees, 'conversion' took place when a person heard Mani's *Letter of Foundation*. It roused him or her to the terrible plight of being held captive by the forces of darkness. Mani urged his hearers to realize the potential of their divine spark – the little glimmer of God that is within every human being. New believers embarked on a course of study and self-denial that would enable them to escape from the powers of evil and avoid all further wrongdoing and other sources of guilt.

The Manichees had an austere vegetarian diet. Melons and cucumbers, which are light and watery, were thought to be especially rich in 'Soul'. They didn't drink wine, even at communion, because it had been fermented and might lead to loss of self-control. They abstained from sex because they believed everything below the waist was the work of the devil. For Mani, sex was to do with the dark, and the dark was the essence of evil. The aim of all this effort was to enable the tiny spark of goodness that is in every individual to escape and be united with the one Soul.

Augustine joined the Manichees. With his wayward youth behind him, he was an ideal candidate for dedicated study and self-discipline. He was admitted as a 'hearer', which meant that he was allowed to keep his partner and excused the most demanding austerities and rituals. He soon became an ardent evangelist for the cause; confident, eloquent and quick-witted. He could dismiss the arguments of half-hearted and compromised Christians because he had been one himself. Now he was able to feel superior – morally upright and intellectually secure.

Augustine liked the idea of esoteric knowledge and secret paths to salvation; these had already drawn him to dabble in fortune-telling and horoscopes. Manichaeism also appealed to him intellectually as an explanation of the way the world is: split between good and evil. According to Mani, all that is 'good' has emanated from a perfect, pure and innocent god. Unfortunately this 'father of light' is too holy and remote to engage in conflict with 'evil'. This 'good' god was not the same as the God of the Old Testament, who Mani rejected as terrible, violent and immoral. Mani erased all references to the Old Testament from the Christian scriptures. The goal of his religion was not to save the world but to escape from it. In his view all worldly involvement should be avoided for fear of contamination by evil. Jesus, he believed, had been saved by his death, which was passive and unresisting in the face of evil.

Augustine was a Manichee for nine years. He enjoyed the fellowship and sense of purpose, but soon developed doubts about the truth of their beliefs. Manichaeism looked impressive, but it was founded on superstition and myth. It didn't ring true and it didn't work. While it was tempting for Augustine to think that when he sinned it was not his 'pure' self but an evil entity within him, he had to admit that it *was* his real self who was sinning. He questioned the Manichaean insistence that goodness must be passive, and that 'good' was helpless under the onslaught of 'evil'. He couldn't accept that a good God was pathetic and powerless.

Cracks had appeared in the foundation of Augustine's Manichaean beliefs, and the entire edifice would eventually crumble and fall. But the ruin would clear the ground for a much more beautiful and satisfying structure to be built: his Christianity. Augustine's second conversion would be far greater and more lasting than the first.

Return to Thagaste (374–76)

When Augustine had completed his studies in Carthage, he returned to Thagaste and became a teacher. Monica was so opposed to his Manichee views that she would not allow him in the house. We glimpse a stubborn streak in both of them, as Augustine responded by going to live with Romanianus – the patron who had helped his parents to pay for his education.

Romanianus was some years older than Augustine, but the two struck up a lasting friendship. Augustine persuaded Romanianus to become a Manichee, but their life was singularly free of self-denial. They enjoyed eating and drinking, hunting and gambling. Romanianus administered his estate well and was generous with his wealth in supporting the local games and spectaculars. While Romanianus supported Augustine materially, Augustine did much to enrich Romanianus's mind and soul. Augustine began to think of starting

'I had become to myself a vast problem, and I questioned my soul, "Why are you sad, and why are you very distressed?" But my soul did not know what reply to give.'

Confessions 4.4.9

a community of philosophers and Romanianus agreed to put up the money for it.

One of Augustine's old school friends became gravely ill. Augustine had persuaded this friend also to become a Manichee, but on his deathbed he was baptized as a Christian. When, to everyone's surprise, he recovered, he was able to tell Augustine of the extraordinary blessing he had received through baptism, even though he was unconscious at

What did the Manichees believe?

The Manichees understood the created world as a place of conflict between light and darkness. According to Mani, light and darkness are two equal and opposite principles of good and evil. They are eternally in conflict with one another, and neither is ever able to win. Darkness has pulverized light into a myriad tiny fragments, which are scattered throughout the world as the 'divine spark' of life in all living things: humans, other animals and plants. But through Mani's teaching, these particles of divine light could be released and make their way back to reunion with the source of all Good.

According to Mani, the great spiritual teachers, such as Jesus and the Buddha (and Mani himself), had been sent to help human beings free their divine spark and escape to the realm of pure light. By so doing, they could achieve union with God. This God was not the same as the 'god' of the Old Testament, who had made the world and declared it to be 'very good'. Mani taught that 'matter' (the material world of creation) was actually very bad, forming an evil prison from which humans must seek to escape. He wouldn't allow any references to the Old Testament in his version of the Bible because, for him, Jesus was not the fulfilment of Old Testament promises, but a crucified symbol of humanity.

In effect, Manichaeism was a late form of Gnosticism (gnosis meaning secret 'knowledge'). The strictest form of Manichaeism involved self-denial, fasting and celibacy – which enabled people to become members of 'the elect'. But it was also possible to join at a lesser level of commitment, as a 'hearer'. People like Augustine, who were already in sexual partnerships, were allowed to continue as they were, but encouraged to avoid having children. They must do nothing to increase the amount of 'matter' (and therefore 'darkness') in the world.

the time. When the friend became ill again and died, Augustine found himself overwhelmed by passionate anger and grief.

As Augustine describes his feelings, he echoes the Bible story of Cain and Abel. Cain was furious when his brother Abel's offering was accepted by God while his own was not (Genesis 4:2–16). Cain's jealous anger led him to murder his brother, defy God, and become alienated from society. Writing later in *City of God,* Augustine identifies such anger as a great sin. Cain refused to let go of his anger and wandered far from home, eventually founding the world's first city. For Augustine, rage and pride are at the heart of the Earthly City, which is the opposite and enemy of the City of God. Augustine similarly found himself confused and disorientated by waves of passionate emotion, as he first tried desperately to manipulate the faith of his friend and then had to mourn his death. Like Cain, Augustine fled – back to Carthage.

Carthage again (376–83)

In Carthage, Augustine became a teacher of rhetoric. Romanianus may have helped Augustine secure this position, which he was to hold for nine years. It was the first step on a career ladder that, for many Africans, had led to heights of fame and fortune in the Roman empire.

Roman education focused strongly on skill with words and effective argument, with close attention to grammar and the rules of rhetoric. Once developed, these skills were used for both political persuasion and personal flattery – and Augustine excelled in both, as his letters show. In today's terms, he was a master of 'spin'.

Augustine enjoyed his intellectual prestige in Carthage. He was proud of his ability to teach himself from the most difficult books. He read Aristotle's *Categories* in a Latin translation and the 'natural philosophers' such as Cicero on the overlapping studies of astrology and astronomy. He could not help but compare the scientific views of the universe with the superstitions and myths of the Manichees. He also read the works of Varro and Seneca, and had long been familiar with the works of Apuleius, the celebrated author from his school town, Madauros.

Augustine persuaded many of his friends and students to convert to Manichaeism, but he was drawing them into a sect about which he himself had doubts. He later described these conversions as 'self-defeating victories'. He knew now that the Manichees were wrong in their understanding of astronomy and began to probe their teaching on religious matters as well. When Faustus of Milevis, the leading Manichee teacher in Africa, visited Carthage, Augustine was able to meet him. Faustus was a charming personality and a compelling orator, but he was entirely unable to answer Augustine's questions. When he readily admitted his ignorance, the two men became friends.

From this point Augustine's enthusiasm for Manichaeism began to fade. He ceased to practise astrology or make sacrifices to placate demons. And it was about this time that he was impressed to hear a simple Christian called Helpidius argue the case against Manichaeism in a convincing way.

Augustine competed successfully in several speech contests, through which he attracted the attention and friendship of influential people.

Augustine's memory of Faustus

I waited with intense yearning for the coming of Faustus . . . When he came, I found him gracious and pleasant with words. He said the things [the Manichees] usually say, but put it much more agreeably. But what could the most presentable waiter do for my thirst by offering precious cups?

When I put forward some problems that troubled me, I quickly discovered him to be ignorant of the liberal arts other than grammar and literature, and his knowledge was of a conventional kind.

[Manichee] books are full of immensely lengthy fables about the heaven and stars and sun and moon. I wanted Faustus to tell me, after comparing the mathematical calculations which I had read in other books, whether the story contained in the Manichee books was correct, or at least whether it had an equal chance of being so. I now did not think him clever enough to explain the matter . . . He knew himself to be uninformed in these matters and was not ashamed to confess it.

This was an additional ground for my pleasure. For the controlled modesty of a mind that admits limitations is more beautiful than the things I was anxious to know about.

Confessions 5.6.11, 12

The Roman proconsul, Helvius Vindicianus, crowned Augustine with a garland as victor in a poetry competition, and their brief encounter led on to a warm and useful friendship. It was Vindicianus who advised Augustine to abandon the astrology of the Manichees, and through Vindicianus that he was introduced to Flaccianus, a student who became proconsul of Africa in 393. He also met Symmachus (prefect of Rome 384–85), who would help him secure a post as rhetor in Milan and himself had been proconsul at Carthage.

About 380, when Augustine was 26, he wrote his first book entitled *On the Beautiful and the Fitting*. The work has been lost, but Augustine summarizes it in *Confessions* and outlines the basic idea in one of his letters. He argued that the soul within a human being is a spark of the divine nature, so everyone has the potential to progress towards a supreme good. This was the Manichee belief that humans could, by using their reason, win their way to perfection.

> 'That orator was of the type which I so love that I wanted to be like him.'
>
> **Confessions 4.14.23**

Augustine dedicated his first book to Hierius, a famous orator of the day who lived in Rome. He had never met the great man, but hoped the tribute might attract his attention and patronage. The sap of his ambition was rising!

Friends

Despite his doubts about their doctrine, Augustine had continued to enjoy the fellowship of the Manichees. The routine of study, discussion and worship appealed to him, as did the communal reciting of prayers, listening to the reading of the holy books and sharing the discipline of abstaining from food and sex. Looking back on these years, Augustine praised the integrity and goodness of friends such as Alypius and Nebridius. Alypius was a relative of Romanianus from Thagaste who trained as a lawyer but gave up his career to follow Augustine. He eventually became a bishop in his native Thagaste. Nebridius was a highly intelligent and serious-minded young man, who also became one of Augustine's long-term companions. Augustine mentions other friends, including Honoratus and Fortunatus. Most of them followed him into Manichaeism and then into Christianity, but Fortunatus remained a Manichee and would one day take part in a famous public debate with Augustine at Hippo.

In his teens and as a student, Augustine had been influenced by peer pressure, but now he attracted loyalty as a leader. Friendship stirred in him strong and conflicting passions, which he describes as 'less an appetite of the senses than a hunger of the heart'. Always and increasingly, Augustine's heart-hunger fixed itself on God. It was only in God that his consuming restlessness could hope for peace.

Although Augustine was fortunate in friendship and a gifted communicator, he failed to establish his authority as a teacher. His pupils were reluctant to learn and his classes were constantly disrupted by bad behaviour. He had become disillusioned with Manichaeism, without being able to see any other way ahead. In the end he decided to leave Carthage and sail for Rome, having heard that the students there were better behaved.

Augustine seems to have left Carthage in a hurry. Certainly he didn't tell Romanianus, although he was tutor to his old friend's children; and he didn't tell Monica. He may even have lied to his mother, which

Alypius and Nebridius

Alypius and Nebridius were two of Augustine's greatest friends.

Alypius and Augustine had known each other from childhood. In adulthood, Alypius became an administrative lawyer: a man of action and resolve, with a calmness and firmness of purpose that was the very opposite of Augustine – his 'other self'. Alypius enjoyed the bloodshed of the gladiatorial shows and, when finally converted to Christ, walked barefoot on frozen soil through Italy. He travelled to Italy ahead of Augustine.

Nebridius was a gentler, less ambitious person than Augustine, with wealth and freedom enough to accompany his friend on their spiritual and intellectual pilgrimage. He came from a pagan family in Carthage, which is where he and Augustine became friends. In later life, Augustine remembered Nebridius for his diligence in dealing with difficult problems and his indignation when the discussion was shallow or the disputants took short cuts to their conclusions.

indicates that he was seeking to escape her prayerfully determined pleas for his conversion. However it was, at the age of 29 Augustine sailed from Carthage with his partner and their son,

'For a long time the Academics were at the helm of my ship.'
On the Happy Life

together with close friends Alypius and Nebridius. Their destination was Rome.

As Augustine sailed for Rome in 383 he was at sea in more senses than one. Thanks to his education in the liberal arts he had seen through Manichaeism. He was attracted to the thoughtful approach and ascetic lifestyle of the Manichees, but realized that at heart they were deeply misguided. His interview with the Manichaean bishop Faustus of Milevis had confirmed his suspicion that their understanding of the universe owed more to astrology than astronomy; and if they were wrong on that, what confidence could he have that they would be right on anything else?

How to be wise?

Thanks to his reading of Cicero, Augustine was fired with the ideal of living a true and consistent life, guided by wisdom. But where could wisdom be found? His search of the Christian scriptures turned up violence and immorality in the Old Testament and inconsistency in the New. Thanks to his mother's prayers and unfailing support, Augustine was a Christian by upbringing; but he was not so by conviction. There was no bridge between the philosophers and Christ.

So Augustine took his stand on the high ground of scepticism. Cicero had founded an academy where the prevailing view was sceptical – that is, that one had to live life with dignity and integrity despite the absence of God or any assurance that life had meaning. This was a similar view to that of the Greek Stoic philosophers: to live without hope of reward, salvation or afterlife, and yet show a detached consideration, respect and selfless goodwill to all creatures.

Milan and Ambrose

On arriving in Italy, Augustine and his party went first to Rome. Suddenly, instead of being well known for his talent and potential as he was in Carthage, Augustine was just one more hopeful wordsmith in the vastness of the Roman empire. But when a competition for a post as public teacher of rhetoric in Milan was announced, he entered and won. It was 384.

Milan was the main seat of government for the western empire. Here Augustine encountered the formidable figure of Ambrose, who was 14 years his senior and had been bishop of Milan for 11 years. Ambrose was a tough political operator. In 386 he held his ground against the demands of the imperial court that was resident in his city, infiltrated by Arian heretics and supported by Gothic troops. He built a basilica and triumphantly secured its status by interring the relics of two martyrs. But it was as a preacher that Augustine was drawn to Ambrose, first for the eloquence of his sermons and then for their content. This man's mind held the bridge between Cicero and Christ. Ambrose gave Augustine the means of understanding the Old Testament and showed him that it was faith that led to wisdom and not wisdom that led to faith. The key stage of enlightenment was to accept the truth of the scriptures whose authority was guaranteed by the Church. It was the scriptures and the Church together that led to Christ.

> *'I came to Milan, to Ambrose the bishop, known throughout the world as the best of men, devout in your worship.'*
>
> **Confessions 5.13.23**

Ambrose was a highly gifted and influential man who dominated not just the religious but also the political scene in Milan. He had a powerful mind and Augustine was immediately impressed by the quality of his preaching – and this from someone who was an outstanding communicator himself. In Ambrose, Augustine found someone who could communicate at his own intellectual level, confirming his rejection of the Manichees and opening the way for his return to the Christian faith and the Catholic Church of his upbringing.

Neoplatonism

Ambrose and others in his circle were strongly influenced by the writing of Plotinus, the father of Neoplatonism. The Neoplatonists, as they were called, drew together the insights of Christian thinkers from east as well

Ambrose, bishop of Milan

Ambrose (c. 339–97) was born into a noble Roman family and received a classical education. He rose to the position of a provincial governor in northern Italy, living at Milan. When Auxentius, the Arian bishop of Milan, died in c. 373, Ambrose succeeded him by popular demand. He reluctantly agreed to accept the post, although he was not yet baptized or ordained. He then began his study of theology!

Ambrose was a gifted preacher and his fame soon spread. He upheld the orthodox faith against Arianism and was conspicuously successful in maintaining the independence of the Church against the civil power. He was a close adviser of the emperor Theodosius and was one of the first church leaders to use his episcopal office to influence and coerce civil rulers. Augustine had great respect for Ambrose's stature, eloquence and intellect. Ambrose's synthesis of Christian and Platonic thought, and his ability to interpret the Old Testament allegorically, were significant factors in Augustine's conversion to the Christian faith as practised by the Catholic Church.

Ambrose encouraged monasticism in the west. He wrote on asceticism, ethics and the sacraments. He composed many Latin hymns that have survived into modern times, and his letters are of lasting historical significance. Augustine availed himself of Ambrose's knowledge of Greek to introduce eastern theology to the west. He also commissioned a hagiography (a devotional biography in praise of a holy life) of Ambrose from the bishop's former secretary, Paulinus of Milan.

as west to synthesize the revelation of the Christian faith with the insights of the classical Greek philosophers. Like Plato, Plotinus started from the assumption that reality is intimately connected with the process of human thought. He described the structure of things along the lines of Plato's analysis of identity and difference. According to Plato, if we say two things, x and y, are similar, we mean both that they are alike and different. Although they are alike, we can still make a distinction between them; but even as we point up the differences, we are identifying their similarity. From this, Plotinus follows Plato in establishing that there is a unity and permanence that underlies and undergirds multiplicity in

'I was not stable in the enjoyment of my God. I was caught up to you by your beauty and quickly torn away from you by my weight.'

Confessions 7.17.23

Plotinus

Plotinus (205–70) was a pagan Greek philosopher who had been influenced by Christian ideas. He was born in Egypt and studied in Alexandria. After investigating the philosophy of Persia and India (and almost losing his life on a military expedition to Mesopotamia), he arrived in Rome in 244. There he founded a school of philosophy, which became a hub of intellectual activity in the pagan and Christian world.

Plotinus lived an ascetic life with very little food or sleep. He ate only vegetables and never took a bath. His own body and person seem to have been of little interest to him, as though he were living as independently of them as possible. He never celebrated his birthday. He was a progressive, wise and popular teacher who (unusually for those days) taught male and female students together. They sought out his advice on the problems in their lives, much as one might consult a spiritual director.

Plotinus's achievement was to rediscover the authentic teachings of Plato, and indeed many felt that he was a reincarnation of the greatest of Greek philosophers. In old age he even tried to found a model republic in Campania, based on Plato's prescription for an ideal state.

differences we experience and perceive in this world. Even as we talk of change, we imply a permanence that is unchanging.

This concept of changelessness is an aspect of a world of Being that we can grasp only by the use of our mind. We cannot access Being through the usual channels of our senses because they are always engaged with the continuous activity of Becoming that occupies us in the physical world. Those things about the material world that we consider to have special qualities of beauty, goodness or truth, derive their qualities from Absolutes or Forms. But Forms are those constant and unchanging realities that underlie and enable Universal Being. They are invisible to us and undetectable by our physical senses,

'By the Platonic books I was admonished to return into myself. With you as my guide I entered into my innermost citadel, and was given power to do so because you had become my helper. I entered and with my soul's eye, such as it was, saw above that same eye of my soul the immutable light higher than my mind – not the light of every day . . . but a different thing, utterly different from all our kinds of light . . . It was superior because it made me.'

Confessions 7.10.16

yet can be identified through pure mathematical abstraction. They are ultimately real and universally true.

Starting from Plato's perception, Plotinus expounded the divine realm as a great chain or continuum of 'being'. At the summit of this hierarchy of being is the One, or God, that Plotinus called the Absolute, or the Unknowable. All existence emanates from the One in a series of layers or levels – each layer of being taking its existence from the level immediately above it. But because the cause is always greater than the effect, each subsequent emanation is lesser or lower than the level that causes it. The further something is from the source of ultimate Being, the more likely it is to be inferior or imperfect; but this imperfection can be overcome by returning to the source of goodness and truth, the One. Because the One is unchanging, it never loses its virtue and perfection; it is never diminished despite its timeless giving of existence to all that is.

Plotinus, however, rethought many of Plato's concepts and, through his own teaching, established the school of philosophy known as Neoplatonism. Plotinus's theory of existence allowed the Perfect Cause, or God, to be the source and sustainer of a material universe. It offered an explanation of how the One could be both transcendent and involved in the process of existence. It presented a possibility that imperfect or inferior beings might be restored by returning to their absolute and pure source. It accounted for the existence of evil as a loss of perfection as things exist further from absolute goodness.

> 'How unhappy I was, and how conscious you made me of my misery, on that day when I was preparing to deliver a panegyric on the emperor! In the course of it I would tell numerous lies and for my mendacity would win the good opinion of people who knew it to be untrue.'
>
> **Confessions 6.6.9**

Plotinus believed that human beings could retrace the path of emanation to attain reunion with the One and claimed to have experienced this four times during his own life. Christians also speak of similarly being reunited with God; of humanity sharing divinity.

Plotinus discerned a divine trio at the summit and source of all existence: the One, Mind and Soul. The One alone is supremely good. Everything else may demonstrate and experience goodness but will necessarily be less than perfectly good. Mind is less perfect in that it manifests pride and self-seeking. Soul is further still from perfection and has the power to produce matter. Matter is the opposite of Form – evil, formless, non-being. Such evil is of a cosmic, non-moral character. It is better spoken of as imperfection rather than evil. But Plotinus offered two further explanations of evil that address the question of where moral evil in human experience originates. The first was that it originated as a consequence of misused freedom, arising from the potential for weakness in human beings, resulting from their inferior place in the ladder of Being. The second was that it originated from the weakness of the human soul, which tended to lead it to become preoccupied with material things. Because of their imperfection, arising from lessened Being, this human preoccupation with material things becomes the root of moral evil in the soul of a person, causing its fall.

The Neoplatonists enabled Augustine to think through the problems of whether 'matter'

> '*I anxiously reflected how long a time had elapsed since the nineteenth year of my life when I began to burn with a zeal for wisdom, planning that when I found it I would abandon all the empty hopes and lying follies of hollow ambition. And here I was already thirty, and still mucking about in the same mire in a state of indecision.*'
>
> **Confessions 6.11.18**

Porphyry

Plotinus died in 270, but his many long and complex discourses were edited, shaped and published by his disciple Porphyry as *The Enneads*. Porphyry was a Greek from Tyre, less intuitive than Plotinus, but a well-trained academic philosopher. He was the author of a popular work, *The Return (to Heaven) of the Soul*, and has been described as the first systematic theologian in history. Although attracted to Christianity at one time, he wrote a famous – even notorious – work, *Against the Christians*.

While Plotinus was a supremely detached individual, Porphyry was more restless and engaged with the passions and possibilities of human existence. He declined to believe that the human quest for God was purely rational, delved into alternative spiritual paths such as Indian yogi and the occult and – at the age of 70 – married a widow with eight children. Augustine called Porphyry *doctissimus* – 'the most notable pagan philosopher'.

Plotinus and Porphyry laid the foundation and provided the structure for the philosophical quest of the next three centuries. As Neoplatonism was then taken up by Augustine, it was to have a profound effect on the development of Christian theology in the west.

is good or bad and where evil comes from. He read several books by Neoplatonist writers including *The Enneads* and came to see that he had the light of truth within himself – a light that was intelligible, offering insight, reason, understanding and choice.

Augustine came to see evil as the absence, loss or corruption of the good. Evil was the product of fallen humanity. But how could one be delivered from this evil and move towards this good? He was restless and disillusioned with his speech-writing at the imperial court, where his prime task was to flatter the people in power. He despised himself for prostituting his gift with words.

It was at this point that Augustine was ready for the teaching of Paul, that Christ is not just a teacher but the 'saviour' or 'redeemer' of the human race. Paul taught that Christ is the perfect One who entered and embraced the fallen, material world and mediated to it the transfiguring grace of God. The Manichees saw Christ as a teacher but Christianity and Paul recognized Christ as the Redeemer. But Augustine was used to the idea of working hard for salvation, by self-denial and sacrifice. Should he renounce all earthly joys and ambitions? He readily gave up his prospects of a brilliant career in provincial government and with much more difficulty resolved to live a celibate life. It was the beginning of August 386.

'What will this wretched man do? "Who will deliver him from this body of death" except your grace through Jesus Christ our Lord (Romans 7:24) . . . In him the "prince of this world" (John 14:30) found nothing worthy of death and killed him, and the "decree which was against us was cancelled" (Colossians 2:14). None of this is in the Platonist books.'
Confessions 7.21.27

'In the agony of indecision I made many physical gestures of the kind men make when they want to achieve something and lack the strength . . . Yet I was not doing what with an incomparably greater longing I yearned to do, and could have done the moment I so resolved. For as soon as I had the will, I would have had a wholehearted will. At this point the power to act is identical with the will.'
Confessions 8.8.20

'Pick up and read'

Monica joined Augustine in Milan, bringing with her his brother and two cousins. There was nothing to hold them in Thagaste and they were free to share the benefits of Augustine's good fortune. If his career in

Antony of Egypt

Antony of Egypt (c. 251–356) was one of the first Christian hermits. In c. 269 he gave away his possessions and devoted himself to the life of asceticism, retiring into the desert c. 285. He is said to have fought with demons disguised as wild beasts. His discipline and holiness attracted huge numbers of disciples and in c. 305 Antony returned from the desert to organize them into a community of hermits who lived under a common rule.

Antony returned to the desert in c. 310 but was later influential in supporting the Nicene party against the Arians. The *Life of Antony of Egypt,* probably written by Athanasius, was highly regarded throughout both the east and the west for its teaching on Antony's asceticism and as a masterpiece of hagiography.

government was to progress, he now needed to advance his position in society by marrying someone of wealth and social status. Monica negotiated such a marriage to a young girl and with great agony of heart Augustine sent his partner of many years and the mother of his son back to Africa. She vowed she would never take another man and may have entered a religious community. Augustine found to his dismay that he could not live without a sexual relationship and took another mistress until his fiancée should be ready for marriage.

Augustine was torn. Like Paul before him, he found he couldn't do the things he wanted to do and instead did the things he didn't want to do. His philosophy called him to a life of abstinence and self-control, but his physical passions mastered and overwhelmed him. He tried to reconcile this very human battle by praying that God would give him continence – but not yet.

> 'Not in revelling and drunkenness, not in debauchery and licentiousness, not in quarrelling and jealousy. Instead, put on the Lord Jesus Christ, and make no provision for the flesh, to satisfy its desires.'
>
> **Romans 13:13–14**

Ambrose had shown Augustine how to understand the Old Testament in terms of allegory. He now turned to the Bible with a fresh appetite, no longer put off by the poor Latin translation.

One day Augustine received a visit from an African Christian, Ponticianus, who was surprised to find the professor of rhetoric reading the letters of Paul. Ponticianus told Augustine and his friend Alypius the story of Antony of Egypt, who had lived a life of supreme holiness as a hermit in the desert. He was surprised that they had never heard of the Desert Fathers or the monastic communities that had become so popular among those seeking a closer devotion to God.

Hearing about Antony filled Augustine with a great sense of shame. How far he was from this kind of devotion to God! On the contrary, despite his high ideals he was a slave to self-indulgence and lust. Going into a garden with Alypius, he was in an agony of inner conflict. He felt his will 'pitting myself against myself'. Why couldn't he simply desire and do what was best?

In the garden, as he wept beneath a fig tree, Augustine heard the voice of a child somewhere nearby. It was chanting the rhyme of a game: *'Tolle lege, tolle lege'* ('Pick up and read, pick up and read'). Running into the house, Augustine picked up the copy of Paul's letters that he had been reading earlier, and opened it at random. His eye fell on some words from the letter to the Romans, chapter 13, which were to change his life.

'I neither wished nor needed to read further. At once, with the last words of this sentence, it was as if a light of relief from all anxiety flooded into my heart. All the shadows of doubt were dispelled.'

Confessions 8.12.29

He told Alypius what had happened. His friend took the book and read on, finding the words 'Accept anyone who is weak in faith' and applied them to himself. Together they found Monica, to tell her that her prayers had been answered – and to share in her joy.

CHAPTER 4

THE ROAD TO ORDINATION

Augustine had been converted to Christianity, but his struggle had been as much over lifestyle as belief. As he described it later, he was yielding finally and completely to a way of discipline and self-denial, which he had always believed was the authentic path of discipleship, but never been able to embrace.

> 'The nub of the problem was to reject my own will and to desire yours . . . Already my mind was free of "the biting cares" of place seeking, of desire for gain, of wallowing in self-indulgence, of scratching the itch of lust. And now I was talking with you, Lord my God, my radiance, my wealth, and my salvation.'
>
> **Confessions 9.1.1**

Cassiciacum

Augustine's first action was to gather Monica and some like-minded people around him to form a kind of monastic community. A friend Verecundus, who was a grammarian in Milan, lent him a villa about 19 miles north-east of the city, at Cassiciacum (probably modern Cassago-Brianza) near Lake Como on the foothills of the Alps. They lived there for nearly a year. The villa was large and surrounded by fields, with baths where they could meet together when the weather was bad. In the event, the weather was often beautiful, though cold.

There were ten of them altogether – a mixture of relatives (Monica, Adeodatus and Navigius), cousins (Lartidianus and Rusticus), friends (Alypius and Nebridius) and pupils (Licentius and Trygetius). If Augustine was still doing work for the court, there may have been some additional staff of servants and secretaries; but part of the exercise was to live in community and to share the daily chores. This was 'leisure' – the freedom and space to think and learn. In the context of this shared life, Augustine wanted to teach, discuss and reflect. He wanted to digest and integrate the insights of Neoplatonism and Christianity, and to draw together the intellectual and religious strands of his life as he, Alypius and Adeodatus prepared themselves for baptism.

> 'In nothing shall I depart from the authority of Christ, and reason will find truth with the Platonists, and this will not oppose our sacred mysteries.'
>
> **Against the Sceptics 3.41–43**

Revelation and reason

In the *Cassiciacum Dialogues,* Augustine explores his newfound conviction of a harmony between faith and reason. He had repudiated and rejected Manichaeism and turned to the scepticism of Cicero and the New Academy. But scepticism, while being intellectually satisfying, did nothing to slake his spiritual thirst. Now Plotinus and the Neoplatonists had opened up for him a philosophy that embraced the life of the spirit, giving him confidence in the philosophical quest for wisdom. And Ambrose had given him confidence in another exhilarating area: the revelation of Christ in the scriptures.

Augustine celebrates the marriage of reason and revelation, although the union was never consummated by Plotinus or his disciple and successor Porphyry. While Augustine was glad to check the revelation of Christ against the assured conclusions of reason, there was not much traffic coming in the opposite direction. The incarnation of Christ that is central to Christianity was passed over in silence by Plotinus and scorned by Porphyry. Some scholars feel that the *Cassiciacum Dialogues* show that Augustine is still not thoroughly converted, and that the dialogue form allows him to explore the problems and doubts with which he continued to struggle.

In the days before diaries and autobiographies, the *Cassiciacum Dialogues* are Augustine's own aide-memoire of his spiritual and philosophical quest: a period of emotional, intellectual and religious upheaval. He will revisit these memories in *Confessions,* which, although in the form of a prayer, will be the first autobiography ever written.

Augustine was recreating something of the fellowship he had enjoyed with his Manichee friends in Carthage, when they had spent time studying the Bible, discussing Cicero and Virgil, and praying the Psalms. This experiment in Christian community was an ideal he would pursue for the rest of his life. He might be ascetic, but he was never solitary.

The community at Cassiciacum was celibate. Verecundus was unable to join them because he was married. Augustine's partner had been sent back to Carthage, although their son Adeodatus

> 'Myself reflecting with myself for some time on various things, and persistently for many days quizzing myself over what I should seek, what avoid, I suddenly addressed myself.'
>
> **The Soliloquies 1.1**

stayed with his father. When Augustine had heard of the example of Antony, he had been shamed to think that someone who wasn't even a philosopher had attained such heights of spiritual purity. In those days it was the philosophers who were expected to achieve control of mind over matter. 'Self-control' meant abstinence from sexual activity in particular, as it was regarded as the prime behaviour of the 'lower' nature. Even the wise and objective Marcus Aurelius (121–80) had dismissed sexual intercourse as 'the release of slime' (*Meditations* 2.15), while the emperor Julian the Apostate (332–63) likened lust to 'a crazed and ruthless despot' (*Ammianus* 5.4.2).

> 'Alone with each other, we talked very intimately . . . We asked what quality of life the eternal life of the saints will have . . . While we talked and panted after it, we touched it in some small degree by a total concentration of the heart.'
>
> **Confessions 9.10.23, 24**

Because the idea of progress from evil to good and from darkness to light had more than a dash of the old Manichaeism in it, some have concluded that Augustine remained a Manichee all his life. But with Christianity, self-denial was no longer an end in itself, but the means of focusing his devotion on God. In place of the old frustration and self-loathing, Augustine found release into freedom and peace. He was no longer a Manichee, fighting the entrapping evils of the material world, but saw all the good things of creation as God-given; only to be handled with care, lest they be loved or desired more than the Giver. Asceticism and dedication belonged together as two sides of the perfect freedom: a single-minded devotion to God.

The insights of Neoplatonism would continue to exercise a profound influence on Augustine's thinking as a Christian theologian and bishop, particularly in his understanding of the nature of evil and his exposition of the Trinity.

At Cassiciacum, Augustine began to write with vigour and freedom. Until now (he was 32) he had written only *On the Beautiful and the Fitting*. In the course of a few months at the villa, he produced four books in dialogue form. They were presented as the outcome of the daily discussions and are known as the *Cassiciacum Dialogues*: *Against the Sceptics, On the Happy Life* and *On Order,* and *The Soliloquies.*

Augustine evidently felt that he had discovered a guiding principle that could be expounded in many directions: education, the arts, philosophy and religion. In this he seems to have been following Manlius Theodorus, from whom he had borrowed books in Milan. Theodorus had retired from his position as consul to devote himself to philosophical writing. Augustine now dedicated *On the Happy Life* to him. Although Theodorus was a Christian when Augustine had first met him in the Neoplatonist circle at Milan, he later reverted to paganism.

As he dedicated one book to Theodorus and another to Romanianus, Augustine began to narrate and comment on his own life story. In effect, he stumbled on a way of talking to himself that became autobiography, resulting first in *The Soliloquies* and eventually in the *Confessions*.

But Augustine was not merely talking to himself; he was testing, challenging and probing his own attitudes towards the issues that preoccupied him. He called the exchanges *Soliloquies* to distinguish them from monologues. Important, too, were the many incidents and conversations that took place within the little community – and the connections Augustine was able to make between everyday happenings, the workings of philosophy and the life of the soul.

Baptism at Milan

Augustine returned to Milan in the spring of 387, ready for his preparation for baptism. Along with the other candidates, he went unwashed through the Lenten period and wore a hair shirt as a sign of penitence. Instruction in the Christian mysteries was given by Bishop Ambrose, the Creed and the Lord's Prayer were committed to memory, and the candidates were baptized by Ambrose himself – after an all-night vigil – at sunrise on Easter Day. It was 25 April.

> 'We were baptized, and disquiet about our past life vanished from us.'
>
> **Confessions 9.6.14**

After his baptism, Augustine remained in Milan for a while, resuming his philosophical friendship with the Neoplatonists, Simplicianus and Theodorus. His immediate interest was to prove that the soul is immortal and he wrote about this in *On the Immortality of the Soul*. He then conceived a project to produce a series of books that would lead people from the liberal disciplines to the higher perceptions of the spirit. To this end, he made a start on the first two volumes: *On Music* and *On Grammar*.

Ostia and the vision with Monica

Augustine was now committed to living in a community. In the summer after his baptism he journeyed south, with Monica and a few friends, by way of Rome to the seaport of Ostia. Their intention was to return to Africa and form a community there for prayer, study and the service of God. At Ostia their voyage was delayed by the outbreak of war between the emperors of east and west and the usurper Maximus. In a house overlooking a garden, Augustine and Monica were talking of the joys of eternal life when they experienced a shared vision. Augustine describes how they were caught up beyond all earthly concerns, to touch wisdom 'in some small degree' in a moment of 'total concentration of the heart'.

Monica confided in Augustine that she was now content to die, having seen her prayers answered that her son should become a Christian. In the event she contracted a fever and died nine days later. She was buried at Ostia but her remains were later interred beside the high altar at Augustine's church in Rome. A part of her epitaph was discovered at Ostia in 1945.

Tribute to Monica

Augustine paid affectionate tribute to his mother. From his formative years he had been profoundly aware of her Christian faith and lifestyle in contrast to his father's paganism. It was she who had created a loving home, its harmonious atmosphere hallowed by prayer. Augustine recognized that his independence of mind and life had caused her much heartache, but she had never ceased to desire and pray the best for him.

Many questions have been asked of Monica's obsession with Augustine – after all, she had other children to consider as well. Her prayers and tears seem to indicate a controlling nature that could barely let her favourite son out of her sight. But Augustine had by no means been tied to his mother's apron strings. From the age of 12 when he went to school in Madauros until he left to take up his studies in Carthage, he was only at

'There is no nature, and absolutely no substance, which does not possess in itself and manifest, first that it is, then that it is this thing or that thing, and thirdly that it remains as much as possible in the very thing that it is.'
Letters 11

home in Thagaste for a year – and much of that was spent in burgeoning independence as he stayed with Romanianus and took up with the young woman who became his partner.

In Book 9 of *Confessions,* which deals with the time at Ostia, Augustine includes a brief memoir of his mother. It may be that his appreciation of her had only flowered during the months at Cassiciacum, as Neoplatonism challenged Augustine to be more open to the education and opinions of women. Although Monica lacked a formal education, she was observant, intelligent and witty; and she shared her son's ability to make connections between the everyday world and abstract concepts.

In their vision at Ostia, Monica and Augustine, mother and son, were able to transcend such barriers of intellectual or emotional difference that were between them, and 'enter the joy of their God'. Plotinus claimed to have had 'out of the body' experiences, but attributed them to his ascetic

For Romanianus

Augustine wrote *On True Religion* before his ordination in 391. In it, he seeks to persuade his old friend Romanianus away from Manichaeism to a contemplative form of Christianity.

In the prologue, Augustine writes warmly of Platonism and remarks how compatible it is with Christianity. Augustine believed that if Plato had lived in the Christian era he would have embraced Christianity. Augustine then presents a range of solutions to the problem of evil other than that proposed by the Manichees, and deals at length with 'the ascent of the mind to God' – a theme that dominates so much of his early thinking. He examines the relationship of faith and reason, and the role that carnal desire, pride and curiosity play in human spirituality and development. He concludes with an epilogue in which he exhorts the reader to adore the triune God – the 'Holy Trinity' of Father, Son and Spirit.

On True Religion is a short and masterly work. Augustine explores the concept that vice is a false imitation of the divine. For him, both philosophy and religion are a quest for happiness: the happiness of truth that is desired, discovered and lived. Vice might offer self-knowledge through immoral behaviour, but this would lead to guilt and regret rather than freedom and joy. Only in true religion is found true happiness, because it is centred on the worship of the one true God.

lifestyle and exalted thoughts. Augustine could see that, in Monica's case, there was no such determination to 'ascend' to ecstatic experience. Their vision was entirely 'of grace' – a gift. And it was shared.

A year in Rome

As the port of Ostia was under blockade, Augustine and his group were unable to sail for Carthage as they had planned. Instead, they returned to Rome. When Augustine had first arrived there from Africa, he was a fledgling orator moving freely in the influential circles of his Manichaean friends. Now he was a Christian, intent on expounding answers rather than speculating questions. His ambition was to write books.

The political atmosphere in Rome was volatile. One pope had died and his successor had been driven out of town. Augustine's mentor Ambrose was lending his weight to a new pope, Siricius, to curb the aggressive persecution of Christians by the usurper Maximus. Much as Augustine admired Ambrose, he did not involve himself in the bishop's power-broking.

Augustine stayed in Rome until after the death of Maximus in summer 388. During this time he was entirely focused on the monastic life and the task of writing books. He continued to use a dialogue approach – this time in conversation and debate with his friend, Evodius, who had left his post with the imperial secret police in Milan to travel with Augustine to Africa. Augustine completed a dialogue entitled *How to Measure the Soul* and began work on the two-volume *On Free Choice* – which would remain unfinished for nearly a decade. He also wrote prepared short answers to questions raised by friends that, along with others added at Thagaste and Hippo, would eventually appear as *On Eighty-Three Different Questions.*

Community at Thagaste

By the autumn of 388 the blockade was lifted and Augustine and his group sailed for Carthage before winter closed the sea routes. Arriving in Africa, Augustine and Alypius stayed with a former official named Innocentius, who was miraculously healed of a painful fistula. It was while visiting Innocentius that Augustine met a local deacon, Aurelius, who was to become bishop of Carthage and be his senior colleague for 35 years.

Augustine also visited his young friend Nebridius, who was in poor health, but living in a grand manner with his mother near Carthage. The two corresponded 'of Christ, of Plato, of Plotinus' and Augustine declared the letters of his friend 'the apple of my eye'. Nebridius must have thought of joining the community at Thagaste – but his poor health and the cost of sacrificing his comforts made such a move impossible. Their enforced separation stimulated a fascinating and valuable correspondence, which has survived. Nebridius put so many questions to his learned friend that Augustine complained that the answers were beyond the intelligence and time of anyone to provide. Even so, they explored the nature of knowledge and the characteristics of imagination, memory and enlightenment. They also continued a discussion about the incarnation and the nature of the Trinity that had begun at Cassiciacum.

Arriving in Thagaste, Augustine and his friends set up a lay monastery in the old family home. Most of the property was sold and the money given to the poor. They settled into the daily routine of a contemplative life, which had 'leisure' in the true sense of the word – time and space to seek God and become like God.

The reading and discussion within the community inspired Augustine to further intellectual endeavour. With Adeodatus he wrote a dialogue work called *On the Teacher,* in which they investigated the nature of words and the causes of learning. Augustine praised Adeodatus for his brilliant answers, but sadly the young man died the following year. He was 17. If his mother had come from Thagaste and returned there, it is possible that she would have been able to be with him in the last weeks of his life.

> 'We associated with us the boy Adeodatus, my natural son . . . I contributed nothing to that boy other than sin. His intelligence left me awestruck.'
> **Confessions 9.6.14**

Anti-Manichaen writing

Augustine deeply regretted the part he had played in persuading friends and colleagues to join the Manichees. In 388, the year after his baptism, he began to write and publish arguments against Manichee beliefs – a running battle that would last some 15 years. He knew at first hand their elaborate myths and superstitions and was able to expose their scientific ignorance of the nature of the universe. He also had evidence (perhaps from Constantius himself) of their hypocrisy.

At Rome he had begun to set the record straight with the first of many written works against the Manichees, entitled *On the Catholic and Manichee Way of Life,* which included a graphic description of a so-called 'self-denying' Manichee who enjoyed a superb standard of living. It was started in Rome and finished in Thagaste.

Because the Manichees claimed to be reasonable, Augustine set out to argue reasonably with them. He defended the Old Testament scriptures against the Manichee criticism that its patriarchs and God were primitive, coarse and immoral. For the first time, he engaged in comparing the Old Testament with the New, to demonstrate the coherence and integrity of the Bible's message. He also argued that the asceticism that was found among Christians in Egypt and Italy was superior to that of the Manichees. In *Against the Sceptics* (written in autumn 386) Augustine wrote that true happiness is not to be found in virtue alone but in loving the transcendent goodness of God. Asceticism must give way to a higher authority, which is the teaching of the scriptures.

> 'By his conversations and books he taught both those who were present and those who were absent.'
>
> **Possidius, c. 370–440,** *Life of Augustine*

Augustine upheld the Catholic and Orthodox Church as the custodian of these scriptures and therefore the institution that guaranteed and commended the values that held family, society and state together. He compared the inconsistency of Manichaean morality with the stability and depth of the Church, which was centred on and formed by love. The books proved popular and were circulating widely in Africa by the following year.

Augustine also addressed the problem of evil. He argued that evil is in fact a *lack* of something that a thing or being ought to have. The supreme good is God, who alone lacks nothing and will never decrease in essence. Augustine attacked the Manichee elect by exposing the hypocrisy and decadence of their much-vaunted asceticism. In condemning matter as evil, they denied the goodness of creation – but they didn't object to partaking of 'sacred' food when it was offered!

The first five commentaries on Genesis were written in the context of the community at Thagaste in 389: *On Genesis Against the Manichees.* Augustine was attempting an exposition of the accounts of creation in Genesis. It was a theme to which he would return many times. He wanted to write a Catholic commentary on the book of Genesis, which would also serve to oppose the Manichees; but in fact he found it very difficult to interpret Genesis literally and had to resort to explaining it as allegory. He rebutted the Manichaean objections to Genesis, but not without some selective reading of the text himself. His view begins to emerge that the world is not a spiritual obstacle to be despised, but a creation to be used for attaining the enjoyment of God. Around this time Augustine also wrote his first ecclesiastical pamphlet. Returning to his home town and realizing his identity as an African Christian, he wanted to defend the faith against the myths of the Manichees. As an African to Africans in Africa, he wrote in a simple and accessible style.

> 'Let us put off all empty duties and put on useful ones. As for exemption from care: I do not think that any can be hoped for in this world.'
>
> **Letters** 18

A public role

The community at Thagaste was rather different from that at Cassiciacum. At Cassiciacum, Augustine had wanted privacy and the company of friends. At Thagaste his reputation and therefore his life was more public. Augustine and Alypius were 'servants of God' – dedicated, well-educated Christian laymen who mixed with the leaders and patrons of the Church. In addition, Augustine was now a distinguished intellectual in his own right and his advice was sought not only by friends and acquaintances, but increasingly by correspondents. The 'servants of God' were a resource for the Church, objects of interest to pagans, and role models of perfection to their weaker brethren. In the next generation, it was Pelagius who would cash in on the Roman preoccupation with the 'perfect' life.

Getting involved

When writing to Nebridius, Augustine had spoken of the ideal of 'growing god-like' in retirement – in other words, envisaging a secluded life of prayer, reflection and self-improvement. But with a person like Augustine such a state of spiritual equilibrium couldn't and didn't last. His sense of identification with, and responsibility for, his fellow Africans was strong. As we shall see, the African Christians were struggling for survival against the Donatist schismatics as well as the Manichees. Augustine the man of action must interrupt the contemplative retirement of Augustine the man of leisure. Nor could he be the uninvolved observer of affairs that he was as a foreigner in Milan or Rome. In Thagaste he was a local.

In an age when suitable individuals were seized and compelled into ordination by the acclamation of local congregations, Augustine already knew to beware of ecclesiastical ambush, as he remembered what had happened to Ambrose in Milan. Augustine began to avoid visiting places that were without a priest, or where the bishopric was vacant, in case he was also called. But in his own mind he was abandoning the systematic exposition of the liberal arts on which he had embarked. He completed the sixth chapter of the text *On Music* at Thagaste, but the rest of the series was given up. Instead, he began to write material that would defend and commend the Christian faith in this African setting.

> 'By no means did I seek to be what I am . . . It pleased the Lord to say "Rise up".'
> **Sermons 355:1, 2**

In the course of five years, Augustine's life had undergone great changes. By 390, when he was 36, he had said farewell to his partner and suffered the deaths of his mother and son. His friend Nebridius also died. But in that time he had become a Christian, started to write and establish his reputation, and founded a monastery where he was regarded as a spiritual father. He emerged from this spiritual and emotional upheaval with a strong resolve to use the rest of his life to good effect.

Call to ordination

Augustine was strongly committed to the monastic life, where individuals submitted themselves to each other out of Christian charity, united by their love of God and their commitment to the authority of a superior. In 391, he visited Hippo Regius, partly to visit a Christian friend who was a member of the imperial secret police; but also with the

Hippo Regius

Hippo Regius (modern Annaba in Algeria) was a major and prosperous port in Augustine's time, situated on the coast about 34 miles from Thagaste. It had been a Roman city for 200 years, and was the principal city of 'Proconsular Numidia', where today Tunisia borders eastern Algeria. It was governed by a deputy or 'legate' of the Roman proconsul in Carthage.

Hippo provided a natural harbour for the grain fleet that transported wheat and other cereal crops across to Ostia to feed the population of Rome. The river Seybouse afforded natural landing places and access to the agricultural plains of the interior where the crops were cultivated. Archaeologists have unearthed a huge Roman forum, a large theatre, an imposing temple and impressive public baths. The remains of villas fronting the sea, with vestiges of beautiful mosaics and statues, indicate a wealthy and cultured society; albeit one that had peaked and was losing its vigour.

As time and tide silted up the ruins of Hippo, Arab traders assumed it was the baths that had once been Augustine's cathedral. In fact his bishop's 'quarter' – church and chapel, house, monastery and garden – lay between the main hill and the harbour, well away from the pagan and political centre of the town: the temple and the forum. While Roman institutions were underfunded and becoming dilapidated, there was plenty of private wealth on show in the features and furnishings of individual houses. The sea gave access to a wider world and enabled the flow of visitors and letters; but Augustine was not himself a traveller in the usual sense.

It was the emperor Nero who had decided to take grain from Africa rather than Egypt. To this end he commandeered large estates to secure the necessary food supplies for an empire that was always hungry; but in so doing he created an underclass of marginalized and disaffected peasants. These landless seasonal workers were recruited by religious groups, especially the Donatists, to provide an intimidating rabble of supporters in the doctrinal disputes of the day.

idea of establishing another monastery. While there, he was suddenly called by the local church to be its priest.

The elderly bishop of Hippo, Valerius, was a Greek-speaker who was unable to understand the Punic language of his flock. He was also ineffective against the Manichaen presence in Hippo, which was headed by the popular 'bishop' Fortunatus (a friend of Augustine's in Carthage days), and the Donatist schismatics, led by their bishop Faustinus. The Donatists were so influential that they were able to forbid the bakers to provide bread for the Catholic community. Valerius needed a gifted assistant with immediate effect – and there, walking into his church, was Augustine! Like Elijah calling Elisha, he gave the younger man little room for refusal. Augustine was acclaimed by the congregation as God's choice and hauled before the bishop for ordination there and then.

Augustine would recall how he had wept at his ordination – not out of joy or frustration, but because he had previously thought so little of such people; their faithfulness, desires and needs. Possidius adds that he was even then aware of his inevitable advancement to the episcopacy, with its huge pastoral, intellectual and physical workload. To be called was a privilege, but Augustine only agreed to be ordained if he was allowed to build a monastery near the church.

Augustine would live at Hippo – in a house with a garden, near the cathedral-church – for the next 40 years. In a letter to Valerius after his ordination as priest, he requested study leave – 'a little time' – so that he could increase his understanding of scripture in preparation for his ministry. He also needed to adjust his mindset from contending with fellow intellectuals to communicating the faith to simple people.

Books

Augustine's output of writing is astonishing. He produced some 5 million words in books, pamphlets and sermons. This was achieved, no doubt, because he was accompanied by secretaries – a practice that would have started in his days as a professor of rhetoric in Milan and certainly continued when he was a bishop preaching around his diocese.

Books were copied by hand and circulated by the author and his readers. Entire manuscripts were parcelled up and sent with messengers to fellow scholars and interested groups. One hindrance to the progress of a publication was any lack of copyists; another was a shortage of suitable *carta* – the antecedent of paper.

Letter to Honoratus

The Manichees had a strong presence in Hippo and among them was Honoratus, another friend of Augustine's from Carthage days. Augustine wrote Honoratus a long letter, which became a small book entitled *On the Advantage of Believing*. He urges Honoratus not to dismiss the Bible without at least understanding it better. They would not have dismissed the writers they admired in their youth, Virgil and Terence, in such a way. He distinguishes between a faith that is produced for the ulterior motive of attaining happiness and a faith that is based on trust in the one true God attested by the authority of the Church. For this he quotes Isaiah: 'Unless you believe you will not understand' (Isaiah 7:9). For Augustine, faith is a step on the way to knowledge.

Knowing that Honoratus is a sophisticated thinker, Augustine delicately tries to argue for the primacy of faith over reason. He distinguishes faith from gullibility and identifies it more with 'trust' in a wise person, of whom Christ is the supreme example. At his simplest, Augustine will say, 'If you cannot understand, believe in order to understand; faith precedes, understanding follows'; but Honoratus may have found that short cut unconvincing.

In later works, Augustine changed his mind about *On the Advantage of Believing*. He came to believe that humans cannot in fact attain ultimate happiness – that is, the permanent vision of God – in this life. Rather, he agreed with the apostle Paul that in this earthly and temporal existence humans are unable to see God clearly ('for now we see in a mirror, dimly' – 1 Corinthians 13:12). He also criticizes himself for saying that humans can only be wise or foolish. In the course of his arguments with Pelagius (which we will cover in Chapter 6), he realized that children are born with original sin but are hardly guilty of personal sin; they are neither wise nor foolish.

In 391 Augustine followed up his letter to Honoratus with a more general letter to all the Manichaean friends of his youth. He called it *On the Two Souls* – by which he meant the two 'natures' of body and soul that the Manichees

'Sin is the will to keep or obtain what justice (in the sense of a morally reproachable act) forbids and from which one can freely abstain.'

Reconsiderations 1.15.4

Paulinus (c. 353–431)

Paulinus was born into a noble and wealthy Aquitaine family and educated at Bordeaux. He trained as a magistrate and served as a governor of Campania. On retirement, he married Theresia, who was herself from a noble family, and settled on his family estates in Aquitaine. He became a convert to Christianity and was baptized sometime before 390. The couple went to live in northern Spain.

When their son died, Paulinus and his wife took a vow of continence and began to distribute their possessions to the poor. On Christmas Day c. 393 Paulinus was ordained priest in Barcelona. In the following year he and Theresia left Spain to lead a monastic life at Nola in Campania. Paulinus became bishop there sometime between 403 and 413.

Paulinus had personal dealings with many of his famous contemporaries, including Martin of Tours, Ambrose, Jerome and Augustine. He left a large collection of letters, some of which have survived to shed valuable light on events at the turn of the fifth century. He was also one of the foremost Christian Latin poets of the early Church.

believe are at war within each individual. Augustine argues the impossibility of this psychic duality by denying that evil has any positive reality. For him, each human has a single soul that enjoys free will – and it is from free will, not 'matter', that evil arises. Augustine considers that evil could actually be attracted to good, although it is an absolute opposite and has nothing in common with it. He explains how he was taken in by the Manichees and flattered by his own success at persuading others to join them. He had been ignorant of some of their implausible beliefs about the nature of evil and their path to freedom and light. He now believed that sin was an act of will.

In 395 Augustine sent a copy of his book *On Free Will* to Paulinus of Nola. Paulinus and Augustine never met in person but they corresponded for a quarter of a century. Because Augustine was restricted by his episcopal duties in Africa, he sent his books to Paulinus for distribution in Italy.

The debate with Fortunatus

In August 392 Augustine took part in a two-day public debate at Hippo. His opponent was Fortunatus, whom he had known in Carthage and who was now the Manichee 'priest' of Hippo.

Augustine famously opened the debate with the words: 'I now regard as error what I formerly regarded as truth. I desire to hear from you who are present whether my supposition is correct.' He then offered a devastating critique of Manichee beliefs. Fortunatus's defence was that the Manichee beliefs might be misguided, but their moral behaviour was exemplary. Augustine steered the debate towards doctrine rather than morals, and found the audience on his side. Fortunatus proved a clumsy and evasive disputant, quoting scriptures out of context and sidestepping Augustine's questions by posing others. The audience adjourned in uproar to continue the discussion in small groups.

On the second day, Fortunatus outlined the Manichee belief on the origin of evil, insisting that it had nothing to do with God. Augustine agreed, but then explained his belief that moral evil is a necessary consequence of humankind being given free will. Fortunatus replied that if God had given humans a free will that enabled them to sin, then in some measure he was a party to evil and colluded with it. The debate reached stalemate, as neither could present a logical account of the origin of evil. Augustine then found a way forward by comparing the Christian God with the God of the Manichees. While the Christian God takes a loving risk in creating human beings with free will, the Manichee God crushes the spiritual potential of humankind by imprisoning the soul in evil 'matter'. Fortunatus was unable to answer this point, conceded defeat and left the town.

Augustine had taken centre stage in a form of public debate that was as entertaining as it was instructive. He had a talent for this kind of encounter and would soon be called on to defend the faith against other opponents as well.

CHAPTER 5
LEADER AND BISHOP

As priest of Hippo, Augustine had the pastoral care of a congregation and community that had its fair share of superstition, bad habits and laziness. He was obliged to admit the limits to human perfection, not least in himself, which was a far cry from the idealism of his Neoplatonic conversion.

Just to persuade Africans not to swear oaths (for example) required the breaking of a habit as strong as the use of language itself. Indeed, it was compulsive force of habit (*consuetude*) that Augustine now identified as the seat of the struggle with sin: the fact that the memory had hoarded a store of wicked experience that continued to excite, seduce and entrap the soul in a state of spiritual death. Augustine began to realize that perfection in this life was only ever going to take the form of fleeting glimpses.

The dilemma led Augustine to a deeper engagement with the letters of Paul and especially the letter to the Romans, on which he was lecturing and hoped to write a commentary. Until now, he had assumed that Paul advocated the idea that the Christian individual is 'a new creature': 'If anyone is in Christ, there is a new creation: everything old has passed away; see, everything has become new!' (2 Corinthians 5:17).

Now, however, he discovered that the 'new' life was not so straightforward. Paul himself wrote to his readers in Rome: 'I am of the flesh, sold into slavery under sin. I do not understand my own actions. For I do not do what I want, but I do the very thing I hate' (Romans 7:14, 15).

Augustine discovered Paul teaching a life of conflict between 'flesh' and 'spirit' that would only be resolved in death and a share in the ultimate victory of Christ. His image of spiritual progress was now no longer an 'ascent' but a long and arduous journey, of travelling rather than having arrived. The realization humbled him in some degree, and sensitized him to the failures of others to some extent.

Augustine refused to despair. As a way forward, he reflected on 'delight' as a true motivator of the human will, alongside the intellect. But 'delight' is not subject to human control: it can appear surprisingly and disappear depressingly. As to those whom God delights in, Augustine had to admit he had lost his former certainties. God does not judge by human goodness, intelligence or education; so in all probability the scholarly idyll at Cassiciacum had not been a taste of heaven after all.

The tombs of the martyrs

There was a widespread custom in the African Church of honouring the departed, and especially the martyrs, by sharing *agape* meals and other celebrations at their tombs. These occasions, which were not restricted to anniversaries, were often the excuse for parties with excessive drunkenness and carousing.

> 'Sometimes you cause me to enter into an extraordinary depth of feeling marked by a strange sweetness. If it were brought to perfection in me, it would be an experience quite beyond anything in this life. But I fall back into my usual ways under my miserable burdens. I am reabsorbed by my habitual practices. I am held in their grip. I weep profusely, but still I am held. Such is the strength of the burden of habit. Here I have the power to be, but do not wish it. There I wish to be, but lack the power. On both grounds I am in misery.'
>
> **Confessions 10.40.65**

Augustine was anxious to tackle this blasphemous and licentious behaviour and wrote to his acquaintance, the deacon Aurelius who was now bishop of Carthage and primate (most senior bishop) of Africa. The outcome of their correspondence was the calling of a council at Hippo on 8 October 393 – the first such council to be held outside Carthage and an indication of the high regard in which Augustine was already held among his peers. The council prohibited the banquets, but it was still left to Augustine to handle the local celebration of Leontius (the *Laetitia*) at Ascensiontide in 395. By dint of sermons comparing the fruit of the Spirit to the fruits of drunkenness, and the behaviour fitting to Christians compared with that of the Donatists (who could be heard partying in their basilica), he succeeded in carrying the day – but not without contemplating his resignation during the tense hours when defeat loomed.

Augustine becomes bishop of Hippo

Augustine became bishop of Hippo soon after he turned 40, probably in the summer of 395. As bishop, he had the care of the churches in

The demise of paganism

On 8 November 392 the emperor Theodosius had banned attendance at pagan temples throughout the empire and sacrifices even within private homes. The decree, which was published in the east, had little immediate effect in Italy. In Africa, Count Gildo also sat lightly to imperial directives until he was deposed in 398. In 395 Theodosius died and was succeeded by his son, Honorius, who was able to impose his religious policy through his regent Stilicho.

On 1 January 399 Flavius Manlius Theodorus took office as consul of the west. He was the Christian dignitary whom Augustine had met in Milan in 386 and to whom he had dedicated *On the Good Life.* On 29 January 399 a new law was promulgated at Ravenna, banning pagan cults. On 19 March, the counts of Africa, Gaudentius and Jovius, acting on the emperor's orders, dismantled temples and destroyed idols. In Carthage, the Christians, led by their bishop Aurelius, seized the temple of Juno Caelestis, the patron goddess of the town. But although paganism died politically from this point, it could not be so easily erased as an influence in the popular culture.

his diocese, as well as the immediate supervision of the monks in his monastery, some of whom were training for ordained ministry and would themselves become priests and bishops. As chief pastor, he was concerned for the poor, orphans and widows in his area, the visitation of the sick, and the protection of his people in the face of oppression by the civil authorities. As a bishop he presided over an ecclesiastical court that heard civil cases. As custodian of the churches, he was responsible for their maintenance and administration – a task he found difficult to delegate to suitable lay people.

Augustine usually preached twice a week, on Saturday and Sunday, but this would increase to every day if he was travelling through an area, or spending some weeks in a centre such as Carthage, or preaching during the Lenten season. As sermons were one of the main means by which Christians were taught, they were akin to a lecture or 'teach-in' and could last for an hour or more. Court cases often required his attention every day – sometimes for whole days at a time. And he involved himself in the councils and controversies of the wider Church, both in Africa and further afield. This meant that he (reluctantly) undertook long journeys and engaged in extensive correspondence with adversaries and colleagues. As always, there were secretaries on hand to take the dictation of his letters or note the words of his sermons.

As an advocate of the orthodox faith and a defender of church unity, he worked ceaselessly to counter the influence of heretical groups such as the Manichees, the Donatists, Pelagians, Arians and pagans. These opponents did not raise their heads conveniently in sequence, to be dispatched one at a time, but presented a combination of challenges and distractions throughout his episcopacy. Paganism, at least in theory, was a spent force; but in reality continued to hold sway in society and in the hearts and behaviour of many people.

Against the Donatists

In the spring of 397, the struggle against the Donatists in Carthage was at its height. After the Manichees, the Donatists presented the second great challenge of Augustine's polemical career.

The Donatists were zealous and passionately committed Christians who broke away from the Catholic Church in North Africa between 308 and 311. The occasion of the split was a disagreement over the election of a new bishop of Carthage, but the causes went back to the years 303 and 304, when the Church was cruelly persecuted by order of the emperors Diocletian and Maximian. Some church members had compromised or renounced their faith in order to survive, while others had held fast and been imprisoned or killed. The bishop of Carthage, Mensurius, substituted heretical books for the scriptures and handed them over instead; but a neighbouring bishop, Felix of Thibiuca, refused to do any such thing and was imprisoned and beheaded. So a split emerged in the Church between 'confessors' and 'traitors', which often ran along the racial, economic or geographical fault lines between groups, such as the Carthaginians and Numidians.

The Donatists (as they were to become known) identified with the martyrs. They were fiercely critical of their fellow Christians (Catholics) who had collaborated with the persecutors by committing *traditio* – that is, 'handing over' copies of the scriptures to be confiscated or destroyed.

When the time came to elect a bishop, these radically committed Christians rejected the Catholic candidate, Caecilian, because one of the bishops who consecrated him (Felix of Abthugni) was suspected of betraying the scriptures during the Great Persecution. Instead, they elected their own bishop, Majorinus. It was Majorinus's successor, Donatus, whose name was given to the new movement by the authorities and other opponents; but the Donatists referred to themselves simply as Christians.

On becoming emperor, Constantine upheld the status of Caecilian, but the supporters of Majorinus demanded a hearing in Rome. This was held at the Lateran in October 313, when Donatus appeared for the first time as the leader of the schismatics. Although his appeal was rejected, this was only the first of many such battles. In 317 the imperial government ordered the dissolution of all Donatist communities and the

'The lusts of the flesh and the pride of life'

On his conversion to Christianity, Augustine had renounced lust, greed and ambition; but he was still troubled by dreams! He blamed this on those past experiences that had furnished 'the vast halls of memory' and over which his subconscious had no control. He was reluctant to enjoy food and treated it as a necessary medicine, except for the occasional feast. Nor was he tempted to overindulge in drink, as he remembered his mother's warning of how she got into the habit of tippling when she was a young girl.

Augustine was a keen observer, and tried to discipline the lustful gaze of his youth into an appreciation of the natural world. For him 'inner light' was all-important and he seems to have been wary of giving full rein to his senses. Scents did not attract him, but he found some music enchanting – especially that which reminded him of the church in Milan. For him, it was the words that were important in acts of worship. Catholics in general had a reputation for rather lacklustre singing – certainly in comparison with the more exuberant Donatists.

As to worldly ambition, Augustine had long since renounced a 'successful' career; but he was now a prominent, even distinguished, person in his own right. He admitted that vanity was the hardest of sins to avoid, to be countered only by grace.

The roots of the Donatist schism

The Donatist schism was rooted among the nomadic farm workers and poor landed peasants of North Africa. Before the arrival of Christianity, they worshipped 'Saturn', a cosmic god to whom they offered animal sacrifices. This in turn had its origins in the older worship of a Punic god Baal-Hammon and his partner Tanit who were worshipped in human sacrifice. There was a tradition of mobility among these people, with passionate feeling, violence and bloodshed in their religion. They could be fanatical to the point of committing ritual suicide.

At root, the Donatists were expressing an African tradition of thought and spirituality. Their members were the older Berber and Punic peoples of the region. Their form of Christianity had posed no problems in the third century, as it was orthodox in local terms. But with the arrival of Roman government, with its imperial structures, wealthy landowners and military might, the local people found themselves marginalized. Those of Donatist persuasion retreated to the remoter, less developed, less affluent areas, and the highlands of Numidia. There they asserted an authentic faith and vigour, which didn't depend on worldly status or wealth. They were the 'original' Christians of North Africa and they cared little for the Roman determination to bring African worship and structures into line with European practice and create a universal Church.

In 250 the Christian Church had been persecuted by order of the emperor Decius. When forced to offer sacrifices to the gods of the empire, Christians had reacted in contrasting ways. While some had killed themselves, others had bought certificates to vouch that they had complied. In the spring of 251, Cyprian the bishop of Carthage had to handle the fallout between Christians – the hard-line 'confessors' and the soft-edged 'lapsed'. After the councils of 251 and 252 Cyprian decided to pardon those who had compromised, but barred them from being ordained as priests. When a further question arose as to whether those who had renounced their faith should be rebaptized, Cyprian believed they should. By contrast, the Church in Rome was content with penitence and the laying on of hands to restore lapsed believers to the fellowship. In September 258, Cyprian himself was martyred in Carthage during the fierce persecution of Valerian.

transfer of their basilicas to the Catholics. The Donatists were brutally suppressed and several were martyred, but the predictable effect was that their numbers grew. Constantine was obliged to become more tolerant towards them and by 336 they were able to assemble 270 bishops for a conference in Carthage.

Donatus was bishop of Carthage from 313 until about 355. The split, or 'schism', between Catholic and Donatist Christians lasted over a hundred years, until the Vandals invaded North Africa in the early fifth century. The Donatists were a divisive and distracting feature of church life in North Africa throughout Augustine's time as a bishop.

The Donatists had two gifted leaders, first Donatus and then Parmenian. On the Catholic side, Optatus, the bishop of Milevis in Numidia, wrote some spirited criticism of the Donatists, but his six books did not appear until 366 or 367. His writings, together with those of Augustine, are a major source of information on the Donatist church. Some documents of the Donatists themselves also survive, celebrating the martyrs and recording the Donatist councils. One of their own authors was Tyconius, an orator and lay theologian, whose writings impressed Augustine. Tyconius was unusual for a Donatist, because he argued that the Church must necessarily include a mixture of people, both bad and good. With such views, Augustine was surprised that Tyconius remained a Donatist and did not join the more tolerant and inclusive Catholics.

When Constantine became emperor, the Donatist schism meant there were two groups of Christians in North Africa, both claiming to be the official Church. The Donatists accused the Catholics of political intrigue and compromise and established a wide area of influence through their zealous and enterprising evangelism. The hostility between the Catholic and Donatist communities became a long-running feud. In 340, the Circumcellions began to roam the countryside, posing as a holiness movement but in fact stirring up a peasants' revolt, attacking landowners and freeing slaves.

In 347, Constantine's son, the emperor Constans, appointed two commissioners, Paulus and Macarius, to investigate the Donatist schism. Their approach was reasonable, offering help to the Donatist communities, but rejected by Donatus as interference by a persecuting government. At Vegesela (Ksar el-Kelb) in the province of Numidia,

The Circumcellions

'Circumcellion' comes from the Latin *circum celliones,* meaning 'those who prowl around homes'. The Circumcellions were violent, superstitious and even debauched, but they saw themselves as 'warriors of Christ', intent on conflict and welcoming martyrdom. Although they sided with the Donatists, they were an embarrassment to the Donatist bishops, who were unable to control them. They brought the Donatists' cause into disrepute, while at the same time defending the Donatist churches against Catholic persecution. According to Optatus of Milevis, the Circumcellions were so far out of control in 343 that the Donatist bishops requested military intervention to suppress them.

Macarius arrested and flogged a delegation of ten bishops. One of the bishops, Marculus, was either executed or committed suicide by a fall from a high rock. He was venerated for this sacrifice and his story added to the many similar 'passions' that strengthened the Donatist claim to be 'the church of the martyrs'.

Taking on the Donatists

Augustine, through his writings, is one of our main sources of information about the Donatists. He traced their beginnings to the election of the two rival bishops for Carthage, and noted that the Donatists were the party claiming purity by rebaptizing Catholics.

Augustine believed Donatism arose from selfish ambition and lack of understanding and love. It wasn't a split about doctrine so much as the need of a particular group to assert its superior faith. The Donatists, for example, refused to recognize baptisms that had taken place outside their own 'true' church. They insisted that Christians joining them from the Catholic Church should be rebaptized; and they rejected the authority of the Catholic bishops whom they believed were tainted with the compromises of the *traditores.*

The beliefs of the two groups, Donatists and Catholics, were much the same, but the Donatist controversy raised questions about what it actually meant to be the Church. The Church in North Africa was the heir of Cyprian (bishop of Carthage, d. 258), who had insisted on rebaptizing Christians who came into the larger Church from small unorthodox sects. He had taught 'separateness' – that is, that the 'world' and the 'Church' were incompatible: the 'world' was contaminated with sin while the 'Church' was morally pure. For Cyprian, the Church was a holy and separate enclave for Christian saints in the midst of a wicked and demonic world. This meant that the Church's sacraments (baptism and communion), together with its bishops and ministers, must all be 'pure' – among other things, guarding against foreign influences from 'across the sea' (a favourite Donatist phrase).

Cyprian was a spiritual giant who had been first exiled and then executed for his faith. His influence continued in North Africa for several generations after his death. This gave a strong local identity to the Christians in North Africa, in the face of the empire-building tendencies of Rome and Europe. The native North Africans might be poor and ignorant in the eyes of the world, but they were pure and faithful in the sight of God.

Augustine disagreed with the sectarianism of the Donatists, but never lost his respect for the African tradition and the teaching of Cyprian. He learned from the Donatist theologian Tyconius that the Church must contain sinners and therefore be a mixed body of people. This in turn affected the way he thought about the nature of the Church and its

A popular song

Augustine realized that he must counter the Donatists at the level of popular sentiment even before he tackled the task of theological debate. Towards the end of 392 or 393, he wrote a popular song, a 'Psalm Against the Donatists'. It had none of the classical form and metre of his Latin education, but was designed to lodge in the mind and on the lips of ordinary, uneducated people. It told them the story of the Donatist split and argued the case for reunion with the Catholics.

A sequence of 20 verses beginning with the letters of the alphabet were followed by a chorus of 'You who delight in peace, now judge what is true.' It closed with 'Mother Church' inviting the Donatists to return to unity with the Catholics. Augustine may have written this song in response to similar efforts by Parmenian, the Donatist bishop of Carthage.

sacraments, as well as themes such as judgment and the identity of the Church in the world.

Augustine's understanding of Donatism was helped by Optatus of Milevis who had written a history of the controversy. Augustine found a letter of Parmenian against Tyconius, a lay theologian in his diocese. Tyconius had taught that the Church was diffused throughout the entire world and that the sins of one Christian do not contaminate others in the Church. Although this controversy had taken place at the start of the 380s, Augustine used Parmenian's letter as a springboard for his own attack on contemporary Donatists. He wrote his *Against the Letter of Parmenian* in 400.

In the first of three books Augustine criticized what he saw as an inconsistency in Donatist ecclesiology: that Donatists did not rebaptize those returning from schisms in their own church but did rebaptize those coming in from the Catholic Church. In the second book Augustine wrote about the attributes of the Church. He claimed that the Donatists could not be the one true Catholic and Orthodox Church because they had broken communion with the churches outside Africa. He also critiqued the Donatist claim to purity: their priests were as

Augustine's health

In general, Augustine seems to have enjoyed good health. As a boy, he was taken ill with an attack of breathlessness that almost precipitated his baptism in case he was about to die. As an adult he suffered a fever when he first arrived in Rome; and some kind of pulmonary complaint gave him the excuse to resign his professorial chair in Milan. Towards the end of 397, he was unable to walk, sit or stand because of haemorrhoids. But overall he was able to exercise his exceptional capacity for work, both physical and mental.

As he grew older, Augustine complained that he was less able to do all that he wanted to do. Long journeys, in particular, were demanding of his energies, and he avoided travelling in cold weather or high winds. The coastal climate of Hippo sometimes had a penetrating dampness that got into his bones. When he was 75 he excused himself from attending the dedication of a church explaining, 'I could come, were it not winter; I could snap my fingers at the winter, were I young.'

sinful as any other and their people took part in the violence of the Circumcellions.

Augustine argued that the ministers of the sacraments could not contaminate other members. The validity of a sacrament did not depend on the minister but on the action of the Holy Spirit. If a person did not lose the sacrament of baptism or holy orders by sinning or schism, he could continue to administer baptism in schism. The efficacy of the sacrament, however, would be impeded until the recipient returned to the true Church. This is the first explicit distinction of validity and effectiveness in sacramental theology.

> 'Nothing in you do we hate, nothing detest, nothing denounce, nothing condemn, except human error.'
> **Sermons 359.5**

In the last book, Augustine connected the unity of the Church with charity and recommended mutual correction. He argued against excommunication and in favour of uprooting the evil from within the individual. This first major work against the Donatists established the fundamental thesis that in the unity of the Catholic Church and in the communion of the sacraments evil does not contaminate the good.

It wasn't until the 390s that support for the Donatists began to wane – beginning in Carthage, where the Catholic bishop Aurelius and the recently ordained Augustine presented them with vigorous opposition. In 405 the Edict of Unity established sanctions against the Donatists, making them liable to punishment as heretics. In 411 a huge convention was organized in Carthage, which tried to limit and even ban their activities.

'Assembly' at Carthage

In 410 the tribune Marcellinus was sent by the emperor Honorius to deal with the rising tide of violence from the Circumcellions. The Catholics had requested that the peasant bands should not be allowed to take refuge in the sanctuaries of Donatist bishops after committing such crimes.

Marcellinus brought the bishops of both sides together for a *collatio* or 'Assembly' at Carthage. He dealt with them very fairly. He restored to the Donatists the churches that had been taken from them under the terms of the Edict of Unity. He also guaranteed them safe passage on their journeys to and from the conference. In advance of the Assembly, he established an agreement that the Catholics would surrender their churches and offices if they were found to be heretical. For their part, if the outcome was that the Donatists should be reunited with the Catholics, they would still be allowed to keep their churches and offices.

> 'The clear winner of the Assembly was Augustine, the verbal technician of his age, impassioned, wary, discriminating and deadly.'
>
> **Paul Monceaux, *Histoire litteraire de l'Afrique chrétienne* 4.425**

The Donatist bishops turned out in considerable numbers, to make a show of strength. Once there, they challenged the validity of the consecration of some of the Catholic bishops, including Augustine whom they reproached with his distinguished record as a Manichee. The Catholics were fewer in number and later in arriving, but in the end the Assembly was between 284 Donatist bishops and 286 Catholics.

Marcellinus told each side to nominate seven speakers, seven advisers and four recorders. The Donatists not only insisted that they should all be present, but refused to sit down with the Catholics. Marcellinus patiently accommodated their demands. Because of these and other procedural wrangles, the atmosphere was very tense. Augustine advised Catholics to stay away from the area to avoid being drawn into violence.

When the debate finally began and the history of the *traditores* was laid out, the Donatists continued to be obstructive. Augustine argued the case for a 'mixed' Church, citing the parable of the wheat and weeds growing together. The Donatist bishop Emeritus of Caesarea replied with a bombardment of scriptures to the effect that an evil world was in rebellion against a holy God. Augustine had plenty of ammunition on God's *love* for the world, which he offered in the face of much heckling from the Donatist side. All in all, in the company of some fine speakers, it was Augustine who carried the day.

> 'If you accuse, accuse from love. If you correct, correct from love. If you spare, spare from love. Let love be rooted deep in you, and only good can grow from it.'
>
> **Sermon on 1 John**

The Assembly ended on 8 June, and Marcellinus ruled that it was the Donatists who were in breach of the heresy laws. In an edict of 26 June, the Donatists lost their churches, were forbidden to hold meetings,

Marcellinus

Marcellinus was a tribune after Augustine's own heart, and Augustine dedicated the first volume of *City of God* to him. Sadly, Marcellinus was himself caught up in a purge after an attempted coup and executed in 413. Augustine tried to save him but, as we have seen before, the bishop of Hippo was no Ambrose of Milan when it came to imposing his will on the civil power. The episode was deeply disillusioning of any hope Augustine may have had that Church and State could work in partnership for good.

and fined for not attending the Catholic Church. The enforcement of the edict was inevitably patchy, but some Donatist leaders lost their churches, some Circumcellions committed suicide, and there were random and gruesome acts of terrorism. Augustine preached reconciliation, begged for mercy for the terrorists, and shared his basilica at Hippo with a Donatist bishop. Even so, there is little evidence that the stand-off between Catholics and Donatists eased. The schism dragged on through the lifetime of Augustine and the Vandal occupation of North Africa that began in 430. But the Vandals brought a much stiffer challenge to the Catholic Church – that of Arianism. By the time North Africa came under Byzantine rule, a hundred years later, the rival communities of Catholic and Donatist Christians had somehow merged. In due course, the term 'Donatist' came to mean any rebellion or dissent against orthodox faith and practice.

CHAPTER 6

CONTROVERSY NEVER FAR AWAY

Although Augustine had routed the Donatists in debate, the heresy continued to blaze throughout the African Church during his lifetime. Further controversies awaited Augustine's attention as he sought to articulate the Christian faith and defend the authority of the Church. From his ordination as a priest in 391 to his death in 430, a vast amount of writing was devoted to this end.

Against Pelagius

Pelagius was born in Britain and learned his theology in Rome. He was a big man, committed to an ascetic life, who believed that human nature was basically good. Augustine read Pelagius's work *Nature* in 415 and was immediately alerted to the danger of believing that humans can achieve the good life by their own efforts. For him, this was a threat to a true understanding of human nature, divine grace and the need for salvation through the death and resurrection of Christ.

About 400 there was controversy in Rome concerning death, sin and the purpose of baptism. There was hesitation in Rome concerning the doctrine associated with Cyprian and North Africa that infants are baptized not for their own sins but for the inherently sinful nature they had inherited from Adam. But was this true? How could a newborn baby be guilty of anything? Many in Rome preferred to think in terms of sinful tendencies rather than an inherently sinful nature. In North Africa the doctrine of original sin was held as the authentic tradition and would soon become orthodox belief. It could seem almost Manichaean in its pessimism about the condition in which human beings are born.

When Alaric captured Rome in 410, two of the refugees who escaped across the sea to Africa were a British monk called Pelagius and his assistant Caelestius. They arrived in Hippo at a time when Augustine was away from the town because of illness, but the absent bishop communicated with Pelagius in a kindly and courteous letter.

From Hippo, Pelagius continued on his way to Carthage, where Augustine claimed to have caught sight of him (he was a conspicuously big man) in May 411; but Augustine was too preoccupied with preparations for a conference to have time for a meeting. By June, when Augustine was free, Pelagius had left for Palestine. It was ironic that the two men did not meet face to face when they had the opportunity, because they were to engage in a long-range disagreement for the next 20 years.

Having been born in Britain, Pelagius went to Rome about 380, perhaps as a student of law but also to learn theology. He dedicated himself to an ascetic life, but kept in contact with the world, and is the first British-born author whose writings have survived into modern times.

Pelagius denied that human sin is inherited from Adam or that death is a consequence of Adam's disobedience. Rather, he believed that humans have a free choice to act righteously or sinfully. According to Pelagius, Adam introduced sin into the world only to the extent that he was a corrupting example. Pelagius did not attribute human sinfulness to the descent of the race from Adam, as though it were genetically inherited. He also claimed that it is possible to live a sinless life, although he admitted that not many people have done so.

In Pelagius's view, God predestines no one to righteousness or damnation, although because he is omniscient, he foresees who will believe and who will reject his grace. God forgives all who have faith in him and, once forgiven, humans have power of themselves to live lives that are pleasing to God. For this reason, Pelagius found no need for the special enabling power of the Holy Spirit. His idea of the Christian life was practically the Stoic one of ascetic self-control.

Pelagius's beliefs were particularly attractive to the wealthy aristocrats of Rome, one of whom was Caelestius who became a leading supporter. The movement also flourished among the estate owners of Sicily. Some of Pelagius's followers held convictions rather more strongly than he did himself among them Rufinus the Syrian, Caelestius and Julian of Eclanum.

By emphasizing human freedom to choose good by virtue of a God-given nature, Pelagius defended Christian asceticism against the charge of Manichaeism. Pelagius himself was not concerned with the doctrine of original sin, but the concept was introduced to the movement by Rufinus, who in turn influenced Caelestius.

Augustine disagreed sharply with Pelagius's view of human nature. His own experience had given him a deep sense of human sin and hence the greatness of God's salvation. He felt that nothing less than the irresistible grace of God could have saved him from sin, and only the constant inflowing of God's grace could sustain him in the Christian life. His Christian ideal was not Stoic self-control but love for righteousness infused by the Spirit of God.

Caelestius stayed in Carthage after Pelagius had left. He argued publicly that the baptism of infants was for sanctification in Christ rather than the remission of sins. When he offered himself for ordination to the priesthood, Paulinus of Milan (a deacon who was also a refugee from Italy) summoned him before an episcopal tribunal in the autumn of 411. Caelestius's defence provides a good outline of Pelagianism as it was emerging. He claimed that Adam died because he was mortal, not because he sinned; that human death is not the fault of Adam; nor can humans be raised to life by being identified with Christ. Caelestius's views were condemned in Carthage and he left for Ephesus where he was accepted for ordination to the priesthood.

The following year, Augustine began to preach and write against Pelagian doctrine. His first effort was prompted by an enquiry about infant baptism from the tribune and notary Marcellinus. It was Augustine's letter in reply to Marcellinus, 'On the Baptism of Infants', which he revised and issued as *On the Merits and Forgiveness of Sins and on Infant Baptism*.

Augustine had thought long and hard about the issues of infant baptism. How was baptism efficacious for a child who was unaware and unconcerned of its spiritual situation? What was the pastoral need of parents to know that their child would go to heaven? How was baptizing a child who was unconscious different from baptizing an adult who was oblivious? Ten years earlier, in *On Baptism*, Augustine had argued the importance of the faith of the parents who brought a child for baptism; now he added the need for the supporting faith of the Christian congregation, the Church.

Augustine's arguments against Pelagianism took him deep into the nature of sin. He agreed with Pelagius that it was possible for a human being to live a sinless life, but marshalled scripture and experience to deny that it had ever happened, except in the case of Jesus. Augustine argued that Jesus was unique and had assumed the appearance of sinful flesh 'for our salvation'. The rest of humankind sins because it wants to, and is inherently sinful by its physical descent from Adam.

In the early years of the debate, Augustine treated Pelagius with respect, praising him as 'a Christian of eminent virtue'. Both Augustine and Pelagius were brilliant exponents of scripture, both seeking to discern the great underlying truths and realities of the spiritual life. Augustine didn't question that the Pelagians were true believers who lived in chastity and did good works. His only criticism of them (but it was a serious one) was that they had dismissed the justice of God and substituted their own.

This was a debate about the nature of sin and its influence on human beings. For Augustine, Adam's sin was a catastrophe that rendered the human race spiritually dead. In his view the whole human race was 'in Adam' and therefore corrupt and incapable of goodness. Pelagius, in sharp contrast, believed that God had created humans with a good nature, free from sin. Sin, when it occurred, was merely an individual act or accident. It had no power to corrupt the good nature and was certainly not transmitted genetically. For Augustine this meant that Pelagius was diminishing the impact of sin and therefore the need for, and reality of, Christ's salvation.

In 412 Augustine wrote in response to a further enquiry from Marcellinus. This work was entitled *Of the Spirit and the Letter* and contrasted the Old Testament law (which worked by threat) to the New Testament 'law' (which worked by faith). Pelagius had already attacked a famous phrase of Augustine's in *Confessions,* where he says to God, 'Grant what you command, and command what you will' (10.29.40). Such a sentiment implied that God's grace is paramount, in partnership with the faith of the believer, if one is to live a life without sin. Augustine was defending the centrality of grace in God's salvation, as opposed

Jerome

Jerome, Eusebius Hieronymus, was born around 345, in Strido in Dalmatia (now in Croatia). He studied Greek and Latin in Rome, was baptized at the age of 19 and became a hermit near Antioch in Syria, where he learned Hebrew and Aramaic.

Jerome's scholarship and grasp of languages made him the most learned scholar in the early Church. His urgent task was to produce a reliable version of the Bible in Latin, but the Old Testament alone took him 15 years. The result was the Vulgate version of the Bible, so called because it was in the 'vulgar' or 'common' language of Latin. Completed in 404, it was a breathtaking achievement.

Jerome had a complex personality, notorious for his bad temper and vitriolic turn of phrase. Garry Wills, describing him as 'a testy grump', says 'It was as rare for Jerome to keep a friend as for Augustine to lose one' (St Augustine, page 85). When he engaged in correspondence with Augustine (and on one occasion it took him nine years to reply), Jerome was sarcastic about Augustine's status both as a bishop and as a scholar.

to the efforts of humans to attain godliness by legalism and ascetic practices. In God's plan of salvation, Jesus was the supreme mediator of God's grace, not merely an example of a good life.

In 415 Pelagius was accused of heresy by a young Spanish priest, Paulus Orosius, who had been sent by Augustine to Jerome at Bethlehem. Jerome had been in dispute with Pelagius for over 20 years. Pelagius succeeded in clearing himself at a diocesan synod at Jerusalem and at a provincial synod at Diospolis (Lydda), but the African bishops condemned Pelagius and Caelestius at two councils at Carthage and Milevis in 416. They persuaded Pope Innocent I (410–17) to excommunicate them.

Caelestius went to Rome and so impressed Innocent's successor, Zosimus (417–19), that he reopened the case. The Africans stood firm and at the Council of Carthage on 1 May 418 they issued a series of nine canons in support of Augustine's doctrine of the Fall and original sin. On 30 April, the emperor Honorius (395–423), perhaps under African pressure, had issued an imperial decree denouncing Pelagius and

Caelestius. Soon afterwards Pope Zosimus decided against them and by his *Epistola Tractoria* (418) reaffirmed the judgment of his predecessor. By 419 the Pelagians were banished by imperial decree. Caelestius followed Pelagius to the east, where churches were more receptive to their teaching; but in 431 they were condemned by the General Council of the Church meeting in Ephesus.

The debate with Julian

Augustine encountered more Pelagian views in a fierce and often unpleasant debate with Julian of Eclanum. Julian was confident in his convictions and dismissive of his opponents. He claimed to find the commentaries of Jerome laughable and emphasized the cultural gulf between himself as a pedigree Italian and Augustine as an African donkey. His task was to repel the African influence that was being imposed so heavy-handedly in Italy – a Punic War for theologians.

Julian suggested that Augustine's view of sin was little different from his old Manichaeism – the believer was plunged into a lifelong struggle between good and evil. Augustine held the contrary view, that Catholic Christianity avoided both the mistaken negativity of the Manichees and the false optimism of the Pelagians. Julian focused on the goodness of human nature, maintaining that those aspects of life that so concerned Augustine – such as sexual desire and death – were in fact quite natural. For Augustine, sexual desire was sinful (although it could be legitimately channelled into marriage) and the difficulties of life (and death itself) were a punishment for sin.

Julian was young enough to be Augustine's son; he was abrasive, scornful and provocative in his arguments. Augustine was an experienced controversialist, but a good deal busier than Julian – and tired. Julian was a philosopher at heart, specializing in dismissing the Manichees; whereas Augustine had moved on to the faith certainties of old age. A debate that, if conducted with more courtesy, could have yielded useful outcomes, was in the event bad-tempered, clumsy and inconclusive. Julian in his clever scholarship was a forerunner of the Christian humanism that would reach its finest expression in Thomas Aquinas (1225–74).

Julian of Eclanum (c. 380–454)

Julian was born in Apulia, where in 416 he succeeded his father as bishop. He came from a cultured family and was well educated, having the Greek Augustine lacked. He married a priest's daughter and was bold in his positive statements about their sexual relationship.

Julian became an enthusiastic supporter of Pelagius and attacked the *Epistola Tractora* ruling of Pope Zosimus, which had condemned Pelagius and Caelestius. In 418, at the age of 35, he led the resistance of 18 Italian bishops. As a result, he was deposed from his see and banished from Italy. He travelled in the east and was received by Theodore of Mopsuestia and Nestorius, but was expelled from both Cilicia and Constantinople.

Juliar of Eclanum represented the younger generation of Pelagian believers and became the leading academic exponent of Pelagianism. Returning to the west, he settled as a teacher in Sicily. He spent half his life in exile. Three of his letters and 12 of his books are referred to by Augustine. They date from the years 418–26.

Sex

Augustine has a reputation for having permanently marred the western Church's view of sex. As we have seen, Augustine as a young man had his share of sexual adventures and his mother warned him against committing adultery. As a student in Carthage he wrestled with sexual desire, seeing it as in conflict with a holy life. The Manichees required celibacy of their 'elect', but Augustine was already committed to his partner and remained a 'hearer'.

As a professor in Milan, Augustine separated from his mistress but felt the draw of 'an even deeper whirlpool of erotic indulgence' (*Confessions* 6.16.26). When he was converted in the garden in Milan, it was through reading Paul's exhortation to renounce 'debauchery and licentiousness' and 'make no provision for the flesh, to gratify its desires' (Romans 13:13, 14). From that moment he lived as a celibate, either with friends or in a monastic community.

During Augustine's debate with Julian over Pelagianism, Julian accused Augustine of wanting to destroy the institution of marriage, making his charges to the emperor Valerius, who was himself a married Christian. Augustine wrote to Valerius immediately, to deny that he was opposed to marriage and to dissociate himself from the views of Jerome, who had written vehemently of celibacy as spiritually superior to marriage.

Unfortunately, our impressions of Augustine's views on sex are shaped by his replies to Julian's sharp attacks and taunts. Augustine is forced into defensive and negative statements in order to refute his young, intellectual and witty adversary. As a result, he comes across as pessimistic about human nature, burdened with the struggle against evil and memories of sexual activity as an undertow against the stream of godliness.

In fact both Julian and Augustine shared the assumption of their age that celibacy was desirable for wholehearted consecration to God. Pelagius taught the high-minded aristocrats of Rome and Sicily that a 'sinless' life was desirable and achievable – and this entailed celibacy. Pelagius himself never married, and Julian and his wife became celibate once their marriage proved childless. By contrast, Augustine was very lax in his views that human sin is inevitable. His admissions in *Confessions* of temptation, weakness and failure were a shocking betrayal of the ascetic ideal. For Augustine, the intervention of God's grace was the only hope of holiness – hence the prayer that so outraged Pelagius: 'My entire hope is exclusively in your very great mercy. Grant what you command, and command what you will' (*Confessions* 10.29.40).

Augustine was rare among theologians in asserting that Adam and Eve would have enjoyed a sexual relationship in Eden: sex was a God-given part of creation, not a regrettable consequence of the Fall. Augustine agreed with Julian that if Jesus was perfect in every way then he was certainly sexually virile. The issue was not whether one had a desire and capacity for sexual activity, but how one submitted to the higher demands of holiness and godly love.

Augustine, along with many other philosophers and saints, believed that there was something chaotic and disintegrating about sex. Sex overwhelmed the soul's attempt to ascend to God by means of a disciplined, reflective and balanced life. Lust was at war with the intellect: the sex act 'throwing a man's mind from its tower' (*The Soliloquies* 1.17). Sexual arousal, unbidden and uncontrollable, is evidence that body and soul lack integrity of will and action. Impotency is equally evidence of an inner dividedness, as the body is unable to perform what desire and imagination demands. As all this is embarrassing, our very sense of shame is also a result of the Fall.

It should be said in Augustine's defence that he was not obsessed with sex. He was engaged in a frank and direct argument on the issue with a frank and direct critic. So far as his other writings, sermons, letters and pastoral advice are concerned, there is no evidence that he was unhealthily preoccupied with sexual misdemeanours. He expelled a monk for a deception over the handling of property, but not for homosexuality. His own life experience meant that he was sympathetic to the struggles of others. While Pelagius and Julian made claims to perfection, Augustine was only too ready to admit human weakness in himself and his people. In his opinion, Julian was too full of youthful arrogance, but at the end of the day this was an epic debate about the very great questions of nature and grace. Like opposing boxers, Augustine and Julian traded heavy blows, but both were agreed that the fight was worthwhile.

> 'Man's maker was made man that He, Ruler of the stars, might nurse at His mother's breast; that the Bread might hunger, the Fountain thirst, the Light sleep, the Way be tired on its journey; that Truth might be accused of false witness, the Teacher be beaten with whips, the Foundation be suspended on wood; that Strength might grow weak; that the Healer might be wounded; that Life might die.'
>
> **Sermons 191.1**

Far from being negative about the human body or the 'lower' orders of creation, Augustine was full of affirmation and wonder for everything God has made. He eulogized about the shape and movement of the earthworm and was somewhat 'earthy' himself. He observed that the human passing of wind was 'like making music from the other end'. It was central for Augustine that God 'became flesh' in Jesus and so expressed the divine favour towards the human body with its orientations and appetites. The arduous path of bodily self-denial to achieve the soul's enlightenment was replaced by the parabola of the incarnation, whereby God reached down in Christ to restore the human race to his divinity.

Against the Arians

Another heresy that concerned Augustine was Arianism, which took its name from Arius (d. 336), a presbyter in Alexandria during the early fourth century. Between 315 and 318, Arius took issue with the sermons of his bishop, Alexander. Arius argued that Jesus was not eternal but created before the ages by the Father out of nothing. Jesus was not God but one of God's creatures, and therefore susceptible to change. Jesus was different from other creatures, and the Father bestowed dignity on him as the Son of God because of his righteousness.

Arius's ideas quickly took root and spread. In effect, he denied the eternal nature of Jesus Christ as the 'Logos' of God. In his view the Son was subordinate to, and not coequal with, the Father. The Synod of Alexandria excommunicated Arius and the Council of Nicea condemned Arianism in 325. However, the Arians achieved a wide popularity after the death of Constantine in 337, because Constantine's son and successor Constantius favoured them.

It was Athanasius, the young deacon to Alexander, who argued against Arius. Arius claimed that if Christ was 'begotten', he must have had a beginning and was therefore not eternal. Athanasius countered that to say that a father begets a child is one thing, but to say that 'the Father begat the Son' is another. One is physical and temporal, the other is eternal; one is from human will, the other from divine 'Being'. Christ, 'begotten of the Father', could not have had a beginning such as we imagine in human terms.

The questions raised by Arianism struck at the heart of the orthodox doctrines of creation, redemption and the Trinity. The Council of Nicea agreed that the Lord Jesus Christ is of one substance with the Father from eternity, as testified in the Gospel of John (John 1:1–3, 14). After Athanasius, Christ could no longer be thought of, in the Greek way, as God's intermediary in his work of creation and redemption. Athanasius insisted there is no room in Christian thought for any being of intermediate status between creator and creature. Redemption is an act of divine right and grace, so only God-in-Christ, and not some intermediate being, could redeem.

Athanasius carried the day and Arius was banished to Biliria. He returned to Alexandria in the closing years of his life, but was never restored to the fellowship of the Church.

Augustine's writings against the Arians are concerned to defend and clarify the trinitarian theology of the Council of Nicea. Augustine had met with Arian theology in the writings of Hilary of Poitiers and Ambrose, and in the reports of the Church councils of the late 350s. Some of his *Eighty-Three Different Questions* address Arian issues and he revisits them in his commentary on the Gospel of John and books on the Trinity.

In 418 or 419 Augustine received a copy of a collection of anti-Nicene arguments, which, although referring to Jesus Christ as Lord, emphasized his subordination to the Father. The Son was born, it was argued, in order that humanity would not despair or regard itself as worthless. Augustine wasted no time in replying. In *Against an Arian Sermon* he argues the consubstantial nature of divine Persons and defends the orthodox doctrine of the incarnation – Jesus the Son 'in the form of a servant' (John 14:28) and 'in the form of God' (John 10:30). This work was to make a distinctive contribution to the Council of Chalcedon in 451.

Almost a decade later, the Goth Sigiswulf sent an Arian bishop Maximinus to Hippo to seek peace between the two sides in the trinitarian debate. Maximinus invited Augustine to a public debate, arguing that the Father alone is the true God and that the Son, although a god, is not the true God. Augustine argued that the Son shared the same attributes as the Father. Like the Father, the Son is 'incomparable, immense, infinite, unborn, invisible'. The debate is recorded in the *Debate with Maximinus: An Arian Bishop.* When Maximinus returned to Carthage from Hippo he boasted of having won the debate. This prompted Augustine to write *Against Maximinus: An Arian* in an attempt to refute his opponent's points and strengthen his own case. In truth, Augustine's debating powers were on the wane due to his advanced age, but he still managed to refine some of the doctrinal points he had already stated in *On the Trinity.*

The Arian debate was a lengthy one, involving the exchange of many complex documents. Thanks largely to the efforts of Athanasius, the force of Arian teaching was eventually dissipated, and the Nicene ruling was confirmed at the Council of Constantinople in 381.

Against heresies

Augustine wrote other works to counter heresies. In 415 he published a treatise against some of the doctrines of the Priscillianists and the Origenists, where he considered them in error on the concept of 'creation from nothing' and 'eternity of punishment'. In the spring of 418 he wrote *Against Adversaries of the Law and the Prophets* to refute the old Marcionite argument that the God of the Old Testament is 'the author of war and fury' while Christ is 'the father of peace and charity'. Augustine emphasizes that the same God is revealed in the New Testament as in the Old.

In *Against the Jews* Augustine argues that the prophecies of the Old Testament have been fulfilled in Christ and the Church. He urges an attitude of humility and charity towards the Jews, but believes they are blind and stubborn and culpable for the crucifixion of Christ. He is more negative about the Jews and Judaism here than he is elsewhere, holding that the Christian Church is the new Israel and the only hope for the Jews is to convert to Christianity.

Augustine wrote a book *On Heresies* in response to a request for guidance for clergy. The request came from Quodvultdeus, a deacon and later bishop of Carthage, who wrote to Augustine in 427 or 428. Drawing on existing works and adding information from Eusebius and Jerome, Augustine discussed the nature of heresy and schism. He distinguished schism from heresy by arguing that it is persistence in schism that leads to heresy. Although the work was incomplete at the time of Augustine's death, its list of 88 heresies from Simon Magus in the Acts of the Apostles to Pelagius and Caelestius was valued by the African clergy as an authoritative work in the early Middle Ages.

CHAPTER 7

GREATEST WRITINGS AND OLD AGE

In 386, during the happy interlude of living in community at the rural retreat of Cassiciacum, Augustine had devised a new kind of writing. Part personal exploration and part prayer, he penned *The Soliloquies*. Many years later, as a bishop looking back on his life (and to some extent protecting his reputation), he embarked on a unique journey of the soul – the story of his life, as told to God, that is *Confessions*. In what is effectively the first autobiography, he explores the mystery of himself as an expression of the mystery of God. This, in turn, led him to write another great book about the nature of God: *On the Trinity*.

The *Confessions*

The *Confessions,* one of Augustine's greatest and most original works, was written between 397 and 401, that is, soon after the author had become bishop of Hippo and when some of his critics were concerned about his Manichaean past. The title betrays the dual nature of the work. In one sense confession is the avowal of sins, and Augustine's *Confessions* is the first work to examine in detail the interior state of the mind. The Donatists accused Augustine of remaining a crypto-Manichaean and the first nine books are autobiographical, describing Augustine's loss of faith, the ten years of adherence to Mani, succeeded by deep scepticism and a conversion to Neoplatonism that led to the recovery of his childhood faith and baptism. The facts of Augustine's boyhood and youth are better known perhaps than any in late antiquity.

Much of *Confessions* is expressed in terms of the utmost praise to God. Augustine exults that he was so graciously turned from his futile and tortured way of living when he read from Romans in the Milanese garden. He rejoices in the vision he shared with his mother at Ostia before her death. Having turned the corner from paganism to Christianity, Augustine then proceeds to write about creation, memory, time and the Trinity. The key to the entire work, which includes

Augustine's past and his move towards God, may be found in the first few lines of the work: 'You have made us for yourself and our heart is restless until it rests in you.' The work in its entirety is a description of the theme of return to and rest in God. The *Confessions* may be interpreted as a Christian counterpart to the pagan *Odyssey* of Homer. In this work on past faults, conversion and salvation, we may find a variety of themes and interpretations. Many of these find their roots in the pagan past. The fall and return of the soul to God is found in Plotinus and Porphyry and in the parable of the prodigal son. The search for and the discovery of truth are found in both Cicero and the Gospel of Matthew. It is, perhaps, the grounding of one man's ascent to God that has made the work so engaging to such a variety of readers throughout the ages – a patristic everyman.

By revisiting his past, sometimes with great wrestling and difficulty, to capture the truth of a situation, Augustine believed he would discover the mystery of God within himself. This in turn led Augustine into an exploration of the nature of memory, which gave him an analogy for God's creation of time out of eternity. The whole creation was present in God's eternity and only became a physical reality when it was pronounced in time by his 'Word'. Time, in turn, is a processing of the future into the past, moving through a point that is immeasurable, for no sooner is it present than it is gone. Yet we only know the past as a present memory and the future as a present anticipation!

> 'For you are the abiding light by which I investigated all these matters whether they existed, what they were, and what value should be attached to them. I listened to you teaching me and giving instructions . . . I can find no safe place for my soul except in you.'
>
> **Confessions 10.40.65**

In these abstruse reflections, Augustine was exploring the mystery that was himself as a clue to the nature of God in whose 'image' he was made. He finds himself both 'in' time and somehow outside it. In these and other speculations he shows himself a forerunner of disciplines as diverse as psychology and particle physics. The ideas tumble onto the page, so agog is he with the joy of exploration and the wonder of discovery.

As the century turned, Augustine's thoughts focused in three main areas: the human mind, time and eternity, and the triune God. He devoted separate books to each at the end of *Confessions*: Book 11 on time and memory; Book 12 on Genesis; and Book 13 on the Trinity. The three works form a meditation on the Persons of the Trinity: the Father creating time, the Word articulating the world and the Spirit binding all together in love. From this perspective, the first ten books of

> 'Love is the act of a lover and the love given the loved person. It is a trinity: the lover, the loved person, and the love itself.'
>
> **On the Trinity 8.14**

Confessions were a preface to the three at the end, as Augustine explored his own Genesis and Fall in autobiographical episodes of theft, nakedness and grief.

In the course of his writing, Augustine was forging an understanding of the will that was new to philosophy. In Neoplatonic thought the highest human faculty was the intellect, and wrongdoing was explained as a mistaken self-interest. Now Augustine introduces the will as a force to be reckoned with – in the case of Satan, a high intellect lacking love. By contrast, in Augustine's trinitarian theology, God's free will is 'loving love'.

In the light of his developing thought, Augustine recast the account of his conversion. In *Confessions* it becomes less an intellectual transition to a higher plain of thought, as in the *Cassiciacum Dialogues,* and more a triumph of God's grace over his pride. In retrospect, Monica's prayers have a more significant role to play than the philosophical arguments of Manlius Theodorus.

In *First Meanings in Genesis,* Augustine explores a 'fundamental' meaning of the text – not in terms of a literal interpretation, but in terms of its primary, foundational sense. The 'light' that God creates on the 'first day' is not that of the sun (which was created on the fourth day) but something more subtle. Terms such as 'light' and 'day' in the Genesis narrative are to convey divine realities to human minds. The 'light' of the first 'day' is the beginning of the process of intelligibility whereby human beings may eventually apprehend the works of God. One day 'the true light, which enlightens everyone' will come into the world (John 1:9). We know God because the mystery of our intellect reveals God's mystery.

In *On the Trinity,* Augustine draws on his own perceptions of himself as 'trinitarian'. For example, he can perceive time and memory in three ways: as past, present and future. He finds that his soul has three distinct and complementary faculties: the will (to act), the intellect (to articulate reality) and the memory (to establish continuity and identity). These, for Augustine, are glimpses of the mystery of God, who is Father, Word (or Son) and Spirit. Augustine's perceptions were to shape western theology for a thousand years – not only in their conclusions, but in their observant, reflective and astonishingly honest quest for truth.

The fall of Rome

In 410 Alaric the Visigoth captured Rome. For 620 years the city had been impregnable, but now the invading hordes swept in – the first since Hannibal's surprise invasion across the Alps.

Alaric was an Arian Christian who spared the Church's treasures. The wider empire continued to function, as the emperors of east and west ruled from their courts at Constantinople and Ravenna respectively. But in truth the conquest was a profound shock – and compelling evidence that the old order was disintegrating.

> 'Rome, capturer of the world, fell captive.'
> **Jerome, c. 345–419**

The fall of Rome was not just a crisis for pagans, but also for Christians. They had thought of their faith redeeming the empire and establishing Rome as 'the eternal city'. Now they found themselves blamed for Rome's fall, because they had offended the pagan deities who had protected the city for so long.

Many Christians fled to Africa as refugees. Augustine welcomed those who arrived in Hippo and listened to their questions and doubts. Why had Rome fallen? Did its ruin mean that civilization itself had failed and the end of the world was at hand? He turned the issues in his mind and began to formulate an answer.

The City of God

Augustine's finest apologetic work, *City of God,* is also one of the great masterpieces of Christian literature. It was begun in 412 and not completed until 427, although books from it were published at intervals during this period. The work as a whole follows a clear structure. It is divided into two main parts. The first ten books are a refutation of the full teachings of the pagans. Books 11–22 are a demonstration and defence of the truth of the Christian faith and are presented as a positive counterpart to the negative criticisms voiced in the first part of the book.

In the first part, Augustine refutes the worship of pagan gods, whether for personal happiness, imperial supremacy or hope of an afterlife. He demolishes pagan religion as it is variously presented – 'mythical', 'civil' or 'natural'.

In the second part, Augustine expounds the idea that all humanity lives in one of two cities: the city of God, symbolized by Jerusalem, or the earthly city, symbolized by Babylon. In three sections, he deals with the origin, development and end of these two cities. They are not like earthly cities with geographical locations and boundaries. Rather, they are mystical cities, whose citizenship is not determined by birthplace or family line, but by the object of a person's love or the goal of their actions.

Augustine was concerned to dethrone Rome from its idealized place in the popular mind. It had been defeated many times in its history, and there was no reason to lay the blame for its most recent fall at the Church's door. Christianity had not undermined its sense of citizenship or its will to resist enemies. Far from subverting patriotism, the Church reinforced it – both the Old and New Testaments command allegiance to civil authority and the laws of one's country. Similarly, by censuring pagan practices, Christianity had strengthened the moral fibre of the community and promoted the peace and prosperity of the city.

The fall of Rome was a time for prophetic insight. Augustine was saying that Rome was never the city that could satisfy human hearts. Only the city of God could do that.

The dream of a 'Christian era' had been dashed, but Augustine offered a greater perspective, an enduring identity. He addressed the bewildered refugees in Carthage as 'God's own people, the body of Christ' – the 'citizens of Jerusalem' who belonged to a better place.

Because the two 'cities' of human belonging and loyalty, 'Jerusalem' and 'Babylon', are inextricably mixed in this world, Augustine encouraged Christians to demonstrate their distinctiveness. They should long for God's future and perceive in the changes forced upon them an opportunity for growth. Of those who had been killed, injured, assaulted or dispossessed, he emphasized that no physical accident could affect the security of their souls; no material loss could rob them of their eternal inheritance in heaven. He especially urged

The bishop as judge

As bishop of Hippo, Augustine was required to rule on many issues. In 411 a particularly difficult episode centred on a man called Pinian who was a wealthy refugee from Rome. The congregation at Hippo wanted to seize on him to make him their priest – perhaps because he had considerable landholdings locally. Pinian escaped only by promising to live in Hippo and not to accept ordination elsewhere. But the promise was made under duress and he fled. Augustine's task was to deal justly with both sides. He told his congregation he would resign if they forced ordination on Pinian; but he also felt strongly that Pinian should have kept his promise!

Augustine was becoming accustomed to wielding a weighty opinion. In his ecclesiastical court, he upheld sound principles and took the opportunity to demonstrate a quality of mercy that he felt the Romans often lacked. Since Constantine's conversion, the legislative functions of Church and State had begun to overlap – bishops presided in civil courts and emperors summoned ecclesiastical councils. As religious intolerance was the order of the day,

> 'Let the heretics be drawn from the hedges . . . use compulsion outside, so freedom can arise once they are inside.'
>
> **Sermons 112.8**

Catholics, Donatists and Arians took it in turns to oust each another from positions of privilege, depending on the views of the emperor in power or the local group in political ascendancy.

Despite his desire for leniency in some civil cases, Augustine developed a justification for religious suppression. He declined to punish the conscience of others with torture or execution, but nevertheless felt that the law should 'compel' heretics to arrive at an orthodox faith for their own good. Had not the beggars in the highways and hedges been 'compelled' to come in to the Master's banquet in Luke's parable (Luke 14:23)? Augustine may have been using the law for the purpose of love, but in so doing he placed a cruel legal precedent in the hands of his successors – not least the perpetrators of religious persecution in future generations.

those women who had been raped not to take their own lives because of their shame.

Augustine had been raised on the heroic story of Virgil's *Aeneid*, in which the gods ordain that Rome will model the divine order of justice. Now he counters that Rome could never do such a thing. Only the city of God is perfectly ordered and at peace. The human state, like the Church, contains a mixture of good and bad, saints and sinners. In saying this, Augustine sails close to the old divisions of Manichaeism, where good and evil are continuously at war. But he explains that the earthly city is not all bad, as even wicked people display virtues of courage and have good motives to care for their own. To resolve this, he borrows from the Donatist theologian Tyconius, to explain that the conflict is moving towards a final resolution – the harvest and judgment of God at the end of the age.

Augustine challenges the classical theory of Cicero (and Plato before him) that a state is based on mutual self-interest and an agreed standard of justice. Instead, he emphasizes the primacy of the will over the intellect and of love over justice. He formulated a view of the earthly city that admitted, and worked with, imperfections such as unjust regimes and criminal elements. Even in an imperfect setting, he urged Christians to be good citizens and required officials to be impartial.

In answer to the question 'Who then belongs to the City of God?' Augustine admits we don't know. Only God knows – indeed, in Augustine's opinion, God *foreknows*. In this world, as in the parable, wheat and weeds grow together. Unlike the parable, by God's grace, 'weeds' can become 'wheat'. Augustine's image here is not of an indissoluble boundary between Church and State, but rather a fluid, changing, dynamic process of spiritual transaction and transformation.

Miracles

One unexpected development of Augustine's later thought was his conversion to the reality of miracles. At one time he had tended to deny them as part of his adamant opposition to the cults of the martyrs that were centred on eucharistic feasts and prayers at their tombs. But when there was a fresh wave of miracles in Africa in the 420s, Augustine came to admit that such divine interventions were possible. A God who could take on human form could surely make creative intrusions in human lives. In taking this position, he was also making a concession to the charismatic faith and fervour of the Donatists, who were now 'officially' reunited with the Catholic Church and for whom the miraculous was a normal expectation.

Reconsiderations

As Augustine moved into his seventies, he realized that his energy and time were beginning to run out. After his old friend Severus died, who had been bishop of Milevis (Mila) for 30 years, Augustine began to put his own house in order. He nominated his colleague Eraclius as his successor and delegated to him some of his episcopal functions, such as the hearing of court cases. He used the time thus gained to put in hand a review and revision of his own writings.

Augustine recognized that his thought had developed over the course of his lifetime and that he did not now necessarily agree with some of the views of his younger self. He had taken care to retain copies of each of his books in the library of the monastery at Hippo, and he now sat down to reread, amend and place in chronological order, the complete works. He also wrote a reflection on them that he entitled *Reconsiderations*, by which he meant a reconsideration rather than a withdrawal of his opinions. He also intended to do the same with his letters and sermons, but he was interrupted by a fresh avalanche of correspondence from Julian of Eclanum. One unexpected benefit of this huge and unprecedented task was the discovery and completion of his great work *On Christian Doctrine*, which had lain unfinished since 397. Shortly after Augustine's death his friend and pupil, Possidius, also made a catalogue that included the letters and sermons but he, too, was aware that even his catalogue was not complete. It is a measure of Augustine's reputation and standing that in the Middle Ages many works were falsely attributed to him. Modern scholarship has, to a large extent, determined those works that are authentically Augustine and others that are pseudo-Augustine. In the second half of the last century many additional letters and sermons that were written by Augustine were discovered and these have now been added to the catalogue.

Talking to Boniface

In 417 a Christian official called Boniface was appointed as commander ('Count') of the Roman army in Africa. Remembering, no doubt, his close co-operation with Marcellinus, Augustine first wrote to Boniface and then journeyed 120 miles to speak with him.

Augustine urged Boniface that war should only be waged when it was necessary to secure peace, and with the minimum force necessary for success. In dealings with an enemy, it was appropriate to act with truth and mercy, and without resort to the death penalty.

For his part, Boniface confided in Augustine his intention to become a monk. The bishop went to great lengths (hence the 120 miles) to dissuade the army commander from relinquishing the godly vocation of protecting a Christian peace.

To a large extent Augustine's works are the product of a man who was converted first to philosophy and second to Christianity, a man who was ordained bishop within a century of Christianity being recognized by the emperor, and a man who was a teacher and a monk. Augustine's early interest in philosophy is mirrored in his first works. His dissatisfaction with the Manichees led to many polemical writings against these and other heretics. His desire to defend the faith against pagans resulted in his apologetic works and within a few years of beginning these he naturally turned to teaching and producing dogmatic writings. As a newly consecrated bishop Augustine wrote a short series of moral and pastoral books. His turning away from Manichaeism to Christianity and, thereafter, his continual study of the Bible resulted in his exegetical writings. As a monk Augustine wrote some of the earliest monastic rules in the medieval west. Reflection on his early life in his mid-forties resulted in one of the earliest autobiographical works in Christian literature. For over 40 years (from the winter of 386 until his death in 430), Augustine also was an extremely productive letter writer and some 300 letters have so far been discovered. As a priest and then bishop Augustine delivered over 400 sermons and these, together with

> 'So numerous are the works that he has dictated and published . . . that a studious man could scarcely read them in their entirety.'
>
> **Possidius, c. 370–440, Life of Augustine**

the letters, reflect not only Augustine's own life and teaching but also the world in which he lived and worked.

Last days

As Augustine laboured in the library at Hippo, the storm clouds of war gathered around Roman Africa. Boniface, the 'Count' with whom Augustine had previous dealings, had now become sadly corrupted by his power and distracted by political machinations in Italy. He had allowed the soldiers under his command to become brutal and undisciplined, and left the province vulnerable to marauding tribes from the Sahara. Augustine wrote, carefully and confidentially, to rebuke him.

But there was another threat to the security of Africa. In May 429, the barbarian Vandals – 80,000 men, women and children, swelled by Alans and Goths and led by the Arian chief Gaiseric – crossed from Europe by the Straits of Gibraltar. They moved slowly east towards Hippo, meeting with little resistance. Roman rule in Africa was in a state of collapse. As successive Numidian towns fell to the invader, Boniface attempted to strengthen the fortifications of Hippo and there decided to make his stand. The Christian bishops and their congregations came for refuge as Gaiseric set up a blockade from the sea and embarked on a lengthy siege. In the third month of the siege Augustine fell ill, and on 28 August 430, he died. He was almost 76.

One of Augustine's last pieces of pastoral advice was that pastors who were able to flee the invading Vandals should stay with the helpless members of their churches.

Augustine was probably buried in his cathedral, the Basilica Paci. His remains were later transported to Sardinia and from there, around the year 725, to Pavia, where they rest in the basilica of San Pietro in Ciel d'Oro. As to his precious books, it seems that when Hippo eventually fell to the Vandals, it did so without too much damage to the town or Augustine's library. Possidius, bishop of Calama, had spent the remaining months of the siege cataloguing the works, which were transported in later years to the apostolic library in Rome.

> 'Those who have need of others must not be abandoned by those whom they need.'
> **Letters 228.2**

As far as Augustine could guess, his life's work might be dying with him. The Roman order that had held sway throughout Africa during his lifetime was being swept away. The structure and continuity of the Church's worship, churches, services and sacraments were in ruins. In the face of such a demolition, he drew deeply from the dispassionate perspective of Plotinus.

'He is no great man who thinks it a great thing that sticks and stones should fall, and that men, who must die, should die.'

Enneads 1.4.7

CHAPTER 8

LEGACY

Augustine died in 430, having lived all but five years of his life in Roman North Africa. For the last 34 years he was bishop of Hippo, a port that is now Annaba in Algeria. His town was not significant, nor was his office (there were 500 bishops in Africa), yet his influence has been monumental on all subsequent generations. He is well called a 'doctor of the Church' – a learned, sound and saintly defender, exponent and propagator of the Christian faith. The other 'doctors' of this age in the western Church are Ambrose, Gregory the Great and Jerome; but Augustine stands head and shoulders above them in his intellectual influence, which continues to the present day.

Augustine is remembered in the popular mind for his dramatic conversion to the Christian faith. Along with Saul on the Damascus Road and John Wesley in the church in Aldersgate Street in London, Augustine in the garden hearing a child's voice calling, 'Pick up and read, pick up and read', has lodged in the Church's memory as a classic example of an individual turning to God. Other enduring images, of his devout mother, Monica, his riotous youth and his years living with a mistress and child, have also struck chords, both censorious and sympathetic, in the hearts and circumstances of subsequent generations. Here, in Augustine, is a real person struggling with real life.

But Augustine's life and circumstances would be of little enduring importance were it not for the extraordinary greatness of his intellect and the quality and influence of his writing. Augustine's questing, enquiring mind, was central to his achievement. Nothing seems to have been outside the scope of his interest and observation, from the kicking of a baby to the origins of time. Today he might have been a professor of philosophy, a research psychologist or a particle physicist and, in his spare time, a newspaper columnist or spin doctor.

Long before the advent of the printing press (to say nothing of electronic communication), Augustine produced and distributed dozens of profoundly influential books and wrote hundreds of letters. In addition, nearly 400 of his sermons were recorded by the shorthand writers who attended him. His output of more than 5 million words is greater than that of any other ancient author; two of his works, the *Confessions* and *City of God* must rank among the all-time 'greats' of world literature.

Augustine's work constitutes a vital stage of development in western thought, integrating the insights and principles of Greek philosophy with Christian theology, and establishing the orthodox faith in the face of several vigorous heresies. What were the key aspects of Augustine's thought?

A modern man

We know more about the life and character of Augustine than of anyone else in the ancient world. He profoundly shaped the western way of thinking about humanity and God. In this we find him speaking across the centuries with an almost contemporary voice. His *Confessions* not only constitute a new form of literature (really the first autobiography), but begin to chart the unseen continent of the 'subconscious' mind, which is now the province of psychology. Here, with a startling degree of honesty and self-awareness, is an ancient stretch of a road that leads to Descartes, Pepys and Freud.

He wrote over a period of almost half a century, addressing a wide range of issues, and often responding to the controversies that raged in his time. It is not surprising to find that his ideas changed and developed. Augustine himself learned as he wrote; he was, in his own words, 'a man who writes as he progresses and who progresses as he writes'.

Good and evil

A key issue for Augustine was the origin and nature of evil. At first Augustine accepted the dualistic beliefs of the Manichees, that there is a battle raging between good and evil, and that pure 'spirit' is entombed in the degraded substance of 'matter'. Later, he came to believe that 'matter' is part of the One God's good creation, affirmed and dignified in the incarnation of Christ (the 'Word made flesh'). He came to see evil as the consequence of humans wrongly using their God-given free will.

Augustine's ideas were often forged in the heat of debate. Not only the Manichees, but also the Donatists and the Pelagians engaged him in lengthy and testing controversy. But long-term his heart was in the questions of the great philosophers, concerning the nature of happiness, knowledge and choice, or seeking a definition of God and the human condition. Here he engaged his own great intellect with the giants of classical thought. (It is interesting to note in passing that even the word 'heart' used in this way was coined by Augustine.)

A Christian Platonism

Augustine came to a settled conviction of his own beliefs through encounters with Neoplatonist thinkers in Milan, especially Ambrose. Neoplatonism opened up the dimension of spirit beyond space and time. This, together with the extraordinary story of Antony of Egypt's devotion to God and the challenge of Paul's letter to the Romans, liberated Augustine into an informed and spacious faith, secure in mind and morals. He himself then became the key thinker in forging a synthesis between Christianity and the classical philosophy of Plato and Aristotle. Plotinus had done the foundational work for this (although he was not himself a Christian), which Augustine both critiqued and developed. Augustine's work effectively forms a bridge between the ancient, medieval and modern worlds.

Augustine liked the 'dialogue' form of writing, which reflected the question and answer of conversation and debate. In this he carried the enquiring style of Plato and Cicero into Christian education. Augustine's *Christian Teaching* is a supremely influential work, in which he outlines a Christian approach to learning and study, with permission both to draw on secular insights and to explore scripture as allegory. It is the first work of its kind, in east or west, to set out a Christian approach to meaning, exposition, understanding and persuasion. In writing it, Augustine shaped the way in which the Christian faith has been taught ever since.

Original sin

Augustine concluded that sin is a wilful misdirection of love. For him, love should be properly and completely offered to God, and all human desires (which are accessed through the physical senses and worldly ambition) are to be rigorously subjected to the higher love of God.

For Augustine, evil is a subversion or corruption of the original order of creation. This corruption has resulted in the disease and death that are now an inescapable part of human experience. Although God can use these afflictions to curb human pride and punish wickedness, the fact is that without sin there would be no need for such discipline. While the Manichees had located evil in 'matter' (the stuff of which we are made), Augustine identified the crucial role of the 'will' (our essential desire and motivation). From this he developed a profound and enduring psychology of sin.

If sin is essentially a turning away from God to love lesser things, then Augustine saw no need to look further for an origin of evil. The experience of stealing pears as a youth had led him to distinguish between sin and a crime. A crime was the form sin might take, but sin itself was the desire for something other than the love of God: in thieving pears, this was nothing more than the compulsion to be accepted by his friends. Augustine traced this tendency back to the Fall, when Adam preferred the companionship of Eve to the company of God. This tendency, inherited by all descendants of Adam and Eve, means that sin is 'original' to human nature.

> 'The fault is not in our stars but in ourselves.'
> **William Shakespeare,**
> *Julius Caesar* II.134

Augustine developed his doctrine of original sin in response to Pelagius, who held that a person can live a good life by his or her own effort. Augustine believed, on the contrary, that humans have no choice but to sin, because their sinful disposition is inherited from Adam and Eve. Adam and Eve had choice and therefore the freedom not to sin, but their descendants can change only with a special dispensation of God's grace. It was Augustine's prayer of complete dependence on God ('Grant what you command, and command what you will', *Confessions*) that stirred Pelagius to argue for human free will and moral responsibility. This did not mean that Pelagius viewed human nature as perfect, but he believed that humans have a capacity to change themselves with the help of the God-given grace with which they are born. His stance was in line with the classical Stoicism that had given dignity, courage and self-reliance to the Roman age.

But Augustine disagreed. Instead, he drew on his own experience of God's special grace. Without such grace he was sure he could never have been saved from his sinful life. Without God's grace, a person can never make even the first move towards a change of life. The ongoing life of faith and goodness is likewise dependent on a continuous outpouring of this same divine grace. For Augustine, God's grace must be both 'prevenient' (to enable one to turn to God in the first place) and 'concomitant' (to enable one to continue in a Christian way of life). In an age when those who had been martyred were praised as the 'elect', Augustine wanted every Christian to know the grace of God, whether they were male or female, celibate or married.

Augustine pointed to the Church's practice of infant baptism as evidence of original sin. Why baptize an innocent child, unless it already has an inherently sinful nature? This, he argued, indicates that sin springs not from human choice but from the fallen nature inherited from Adam.

The Church has followed Augustine in asserting the necessity of supernatural grace to overcome the inherent resistance of human nature to the love of God. Augustine went further, to argue that God's grace is irresistible – a doctrine that found a valued place in Calvin's doctrine in the sixteenth century, but not in the wider orthodoxy of the Church.

Salvation

Augustine's understanding of salvation centres entirely on Christ. Jesus Christ is the God-man, who is the perfect mediator because he is both human divinity and divine humanity. He is the perfect mediator because he is both priest and sacrifice. Christ mediates between a holy, just and immortal God and sinful, unjust and mortal humans, to bring them from death to life, from disintegration to unity, from sin to salvation. This is the reason Christ came – to save human beings from sin and death. There is no other Saviour or way of salvation, but Christ alone who reconciles the whole world back to God.

It is because Christ came to reconcile humankind to God that Augustine deduced there has been a separation from God through sin. And because Christ died for all, Augustine deduced that all are tainted by this 'original' sin. With Paul, Augustine can say that sin has come through Adam and salvation has come through Christ.

Grace

For Augustine, God's grace is all-important for God's work in the world and in spiritual creatures (by which he means angels and humans). It is by grace that humans are moved to know and love God.

Augustine followed the Neoplatonists in thinking of God's power and love being emanated from the highest orders of being to the lowest. Adapted into a Christian frame of reference, angels and humans are enlightened and empowered by turning towards the Word of God, Jesus Christ. To turn away from the Word is to lapse into sin and futility. Again, it is by the continuing work of God's grace that angels and humans can live and move and have their being in the light and love of God.

In Augustine's understanding, grace is not something God has created, but rather the very presence and action of God in human life. The Spirit of God is constantly, eternally, proceeding from the Father and the Son, and being bestowed on God's creatures in time and place. Even devils and the damned receive this emanation, which is manifested in such light, sound judgment and desire for fulfilment as they have. Without the grace of God, which is the sustaining life-giving power and love of the Word, creation would collapse into nothingness. The struggle Paul describes as taking place within him, between the good he wants to do and the evil he actually does, is an example of the Holy Spirit drawing the individual to a higher life.

Sex

Augustine is widely suspected of disapproving of sex, except in the context of marriage and for the necessity of having children. He has long been blamed for a range of mistaken attitudes to sex, from denial or rejection to guilt and shame. In fact he was a moderate voice in the context of his time, when both pagan philosophers and ascetic Christians were advocating celibacy as the way to a higher life.

Of Augustine's ascetic contemporaries, Jerome likened marriage to a tangled thornbush (confusing, uncomfortable, but occasionally fruitful) while Gregory of Nyssa thought sexuality was an unfortunate bestial addition despoiling humanity's originally 'angelic' nature. Augustine, by contrast, was ready to affirm human sexuality in its physical, psychological and spiritual dimensions. He challenged Julian of Eclanum to contemplate the wonderful sex Adam and Eve must have enjoyed in the Garden of Eden. Sex and sexuality were not results of the Fall, but a vital part of God's original and perfect creation.

As a writer and pastor, Augustine treated sex with caution. He knew something of its complexities and pain in his own life. He advised that sexual relations should take place within the discipline of marriage and for the purpose of having children, but he declined to make sex for pleasure a very great misdemeanour. For him, sexual relations were disappointing in the sense that the Fall had spoiled and diminished every aspect of human life. Everything could have been so much better as God intended.

Scripture

Augustine approached scripture as God's truth, even if he had to begin by correcting the translation or challenging the accuracy of a manuscript. He worked his theology from scripture, seeing in it the authority of Christ himself, backed by the consistent witness of the Church. He argued for the unity of the Bible's message through themes such as original sin and redemption, grace and free will.

Over the years, Augustine expounded scripture in a variety of ways, never bound by any one formula in his approach. As a bishop, he was first and foremost a preacher and teacher, and invariably he started from the scriptures. In the letter to the Romans Augustine found God's justice, mercy and predestination. In the Gospel and first letter of John he found an emphasis on God's love. But his first and favourite explorations seem to have been in the book of Genesis, the Psalms and Paul's letters, and it is these to which he returned time and again.

If Augustine enjoyed an allegorical approach in illuminating the Bible for a mixed congregation of listeners, he always addressed the literal sense intended by the original authors when he came to his doctrinal studies and commentaries.

The mystery of God

Much of what Augustine wrote was in response to the controversies of his day. An exception to this was his work *On the Trinity*, which he wrote in 15 volumes, starting in 399 and continuing over some 20 years. In it he laid the foundation for trinitarian theology.

> *'It is better that you should understand me in my barbarism, than that you should be flooded by my fluency.'*
> **Explanations of the Psalms 36.3.6**

The Council of Constantinople in 381 had rejected two extremes of understanding of the Godhead: the Arian view that the Son is subordinate to the Father, and therefore not God in the same sense as the Father is; and the one taught by Sabellius, that the terms 'Father', 'Son' and 'Spirit' are merely descriptions of three modes in which we perceive the activity of the indivisible One. The orthodox doctrine of the Trinity took its stand between these poles, asserting that God is both one and three at the same time.

Augustine understood God in terms of a triple nature – supreme Being, first Truth and eternal Love. To him it was obvious that a 'trinitarian' nature is part of everyday experience, for human beings are themselves a complexity and unity of body, mind and spirit. Augustine discerned three aspects in particular – believing, knowing and willing – that are united in a single personality. But he found several others: memory, intelligence and will; mind, knowledge and love; the lover, the beloved and the love that binds them.

Establishing that 'three-in-one-ness' as part of every human's self-understanding was relatively straightforward. But this still understood the Trinity in terms of a metaphor of human personality. How, then, to understand the idea of division within the Godhead? Augustine found the talk of three 'persons' unhelpful, and preferred to think in terms of *relationships*. Within the Trinity, the Father is the fount or principle of Godhead, the Son is eternally begotten and the Spirit eternally proceeds.

Augustine identified the Holy Spirit as proceeding from the Father and the Son as from a single principle. We see again the influence of

Platonism on his thought. But the Father, who is the fount or origin of the divinity, has conceded it to the Son to emanate the Holy Spirit. The Spirit emanates or proceeds as love, which is an inclination and gift of communion. Here Augustine draws a model from psychology: 'the will (love) proceeds from the intellect but not as the image of the intellect' (*On the Trinity* 15.27.50). He distinguishes between 'generation' and 'procession', with the example that 'it is not the same thing to see with the intellect as to desire and enjoy with the will' (*On the Trinity* 15.27.50).

> 'God is everything which He has except for the relations by which each person is related to another. There is no doubt that the Father has the Son, but the Father is not the Son . . .'
>
> **City of God** 11.10.1

Augustine's writings on the Trinity are original, daring, brilliant and profound. He closes the chapter on Origen's influence, which had made the Son and Spirit subordinate to the Father, and opens instead a relational understanding, subtle, mutual and reciprocal, which has been taken up by all the great Christian traditions.

The mystery of humanity

At the centre of Augustine's understanding of humanity is that we are created in the image of God. For Augustine, the image of a person comes from within – from the mind rather than the body – and is inseparable from the immortality of the soul. This image of God in us is deformed through sin, but can be restored by grace. Humans have been made for God and are being restored to fellowship with God. This is the foundation of Augustine's Christian self-understanding.

Humanity is not only created in God's image but is also enlightened by God's truth. 'Our illumination is a participation in the Word, that is, in that life which is the Light of men' (*On the Trinity* 4.2.4). God is not only the source of our being but the light of our understanding, which Augustine describes as 'the sun of the soul'. For Augustine, a happy life is one that enters into the joy of God's truth, which is God's wisdom. This introduces an important sense of development, journey and hope into human existence that is distinctively Christian, both for individuals and the Church. We are held

> 'You have made us for yourself and our heart is restless until it rests in you.'
>
> **Confessions** 1.1.1

together and our lives move forward in the love and providence of God; our sense of history derives from this faith.

The elect

Augustine was clear that only a proportion of the human race would be saved. Part of the evidence was that while some believers joined the 'elect' by martyrdom, others were clearly damned by taking the side of the persecutors. Again, many people were passing through life without being baptized, which in the African Church was considered essential for salvation. Augustine followed Cyprian in insisting that 'outside the Church there is no salvation'; but even so he claimed no certain knowledge as to who was saved and who was damned.

The Christian Church is a mixture of saints and sinners, some being led to salvation and some being tolerated until they are separated out and thrown away. Augustine was all too aware of the danger of damnation, which he saw as a reflection of God's justice. But God is also loving and merciful, and Augustine believed that he has predestined some people to salvation and the life of heaven. He did not make clear what it is about predestination that leaves the damned in hell, but insisted that the words of scripture must be taken 'as speaking the truth' and not merely 'as a threat' (*City of God* 22.1–28).

Augustine saw church membership as a supportive and helpful context in which to live a godly life, and from which to pray for and call others to become children of God. When Augustine speaks of the Church, he sometimes means the gathering of the faithful who trace their origins to the apostles, and sometimes the pilgrim people who have lived by faith since Old Testament times. Sometimes he means the blessed company known only to God, who are predestined to immortal bliss. Whatever the image, there is a sense of identity and process in his thought.

The Church

For Augustine, the task of the bishop was to call people into the Church, baptize them and administer communion to them. A bishop was an expression of the unity of the Church and its continuity since the time of the apostles. Apostolic authority was important to Augustine, who looked to Rome as the senior see in the west, probably not least because the apostles Peter and Paul were buried there. On occasion, Rome would be asked to give a ruling on a contentious issue, but as often as not the African bishops decided matters among themselves.

Throughout Augustine's lifetime there were two churches in Africa, the Catholic and the Donatist, each with its own bishops and clergy. This raised the question as to which church was true, who were the true believers, and whose administration of the sacraments of baptism and holy communion was effective.

The African Church owed its distinctive identity to Cyprian. Augustine, particularly through the challenge of the Donatists, was forced to think again about what defined the Church in terms of its sacraments, membership and boundaries. As a result, he noted four characteristics: unity, holiness, catholicity and apostolicity. For Augustine, the unity of the Church was to be found in its communion of faith, administration of the sacraments and loving service. To this end he opposed heresy, schism and sin (which was lack of love) as the enemies of the true Church. The authority of the Church was expressed in its Catholic doctrine and councils, and in the 'seat of Peter', which is the primacy of apostolic teaching.

Both Catholics and Donatists had believed that the Holy Spirit was only active in the lives of those who received the sacraments. Augustine argued vigorously that those who were in rebellion against the true Church were outsiders to the faith and no different from pagans and unbaptized infants. In their fallen state, humans have no power to avoid sin, or to will and do good.

Augustine differed from Cyprian in believing that a person who is ordained to the priesthood cannot subsequently forfeit that ordination or the ability to administer the sacraments effectively. Augustine drew a careful distinction in the sacrament between the visible sign (bread, wine, water), the invisible grace that it represented and the benefit enjoyed by the faithful recipient. A sacrament is always 'valid' wherever it is administered, but it is 'fruitful' only within the Church. For Augustine, the effectiveness of the sacrament depended neither entirely on the faith of the priest administering it nor on the faith of the person receiving it;

Augustine's spirituality

The story of Augustine's spiritual journey is told in his own words in *Confessions*. From the complex mythology and strict asceticism of the Manichees, he discovers a way to God that is not centred on intellect or self-denial, but on love. This is a Christian life that is expressed in actions, motivated by the love of God, which has been revealed for each individual and for the whole world through his Son Jesus Christ. We hear a passion for God in Augustine's reflections and prayers, which indicates a heart open to intimate communion with the divine. Here is someone who delights in God, knowing that he has become a child of God, not by effort, but by God's amazing grace.

It is central to Augustine's spirituality that humans are made in God's image (Genesis 1:26), but an image that has been defaced by sin. It is this 'image' that enables humans to remember, understand and love God. The image of God was marred at the Fall, but the capacity for friendship with God remained. From Plotinus he learned the idea of the inner spiritual journey, first from the exterior world of appearances to the interior world of the soul, and then to the superior realm of the divine. At baptism, the Holy Spirit enters the soul, bestowing his gift of grace and making it the dwelling place of the Trinity. For Augustine, the goal of the spiritual life is to have restored in one's self, and in community, the image of God. This is received by loving God and fellow humans, and by living in harmony and mutual regard.

That all this is the journey of a lifetime is expressed in Augustine's prayer at the end of *On the Trinity:* 'Lord God, Trinity, may I be mindful of you, understand you, love you. Increase these gifts in me until you have entirely reformed me' (15.28.51).

but he emphasized the importance of the Church as the only place where the unity of the Spirit is to be found. 'Those who do not love the unity of the Church do not have the charity of God' (*On Baptism* 3.16.21).

Augustine taught that the head of the Church is Christ, who is always present and active in the Church, which is his body. This body has the Holy Spirit as its soul, and as such cannot be divided. From this he argued that the Holy Spirit could not be active outside the Church, and least of all in those who were wilfully in rebellion against it. The visible

Church, too, is imperfect, but within it are the saints who are eternally part of the kingdom of God. The Holy Spirit draws all the saints into a community with the faithful people of Israel and the blessed angels in heaven. When all is complete, this will be the kingdom of God in its fullness.

Summary

Although Augustine did not write systematically, his work has proved foundational to Christian thought and practice in every subsequent age. His *Confessions* have informed awareness of the inner life; his engagement with the Donatists shaped the identity and government of the Church, and his doctrine of grace and the elect identified a spiritual conundrum that is with us to this day.

Monasticism

From his first experiment at living in community, at Cassiciacum, Augustine never lived alone. On their return to Thagaste, the friends formed a fellowship of 'the servants of God' committed to contemplative philosophy. At Hippo as a bishop he founded a monastery, turning the episcopal house into a clerical monastic community, a nursery that produced many African bishops.

This 'religious' life was a corporate reflection of Augustine's ideal of the whole Church: a witness to the future kingdom of God. The Rule associated with Augustine, and the monastic orders of monks and nuns that bear his name or follow his tradition, emphasizes 'Living in freedom under grace'. It seeks that a monastic community be a microcosm of the city of God, longing for mystical union with God, but also firmly rooted in the love and service of others, both within the community and in the wider world.

There is no mention of Augustine's Rule, in his own *Reconsiderations* or Possidius's *Catalogue,* but there is evidence of a monastic rule attributed to Augustine a century after his death. Benedict of Nursia (c. 480–547) knew of it and was influenced by it, as were several other founders of religious orders. The origins of Augustinian Canons (also known as 'Black', 'Regular' and 'Austin' Canons) are connected with the reform movement of Pope Gregory VII's time (c. 1021–85). Such canons did not belong to a single order but were organized into various houses, which in turn subdivided into congregations. Thomas à Kempis and Gerhard Groote belonged to Windesheim, and Erasmus was an Augustinian Canon. Canons Regular of the Lateran and the Premonstratensian Canons still survive, and two famous teaching hospitals in London, St Bartholomew's and St Thomas's, owe their origins to the Augustinian movement.

Through the ages

Interest in Augustine has been continuous during the 15 centuries since his death. Boethius (480–527) acknowledged 'the seeds sown in my mind by Augustine's writing', while Benedict of Nursia owed much to Augustine's template when drawing up his Rule for western monasticism. Gregory the Great (540–604) put Augustine's principles into practice in both his spirituality and his churchmanship.

The list of Augustine's debtors is long: Anselm and Aquinas among the scholastics, Luther among the reformers, Pascal among the mystics, and Kierkegaard and Wittgenstein among the philosophers are only a few of the famous names. And Petrarch was never without Augustine, for he carried a copy of the *Confessions* in his pocket.

Some 20,000 books have been written about Augustine, as well as a vast number of scholarly papers and articles. His works are available on disk, and websites are devoted to him. As long as we human beings ponder our own nature, the nature of the divine and the relationship between the two, Augustine will continue to inspire and instruct.

CHRONOLOGY

13 November 354 Augustine is born at Thagaste (Souk-Ahras, in Algeria).

361 Attends first school in Thagaste; becomes seriously ill.

366–69 At school in Madauros.

369–70 Returns to Thagaste; has a year of idleness.

370–73 Studies in Carthage; has a mistress.

c. 371 Augustine's father, Patricius, dies.

372 Augustine's son, Adeodatus, is born.

373 Augustine reads Cicero's *Hortensius* and is converted to philosophy; becomes a Manichee.

373–74 Teaches rhetoric in Thagaste.

376 Teaches rhetoric in Carthage.

380–81 Writes first book, *On the Beautiful and the Fitting.*

381 Council of Constantinople.

383 Meets Faustus of Milevis and begins to have doubts about Manichaeism; leaves Carthage and teaches in Rome.

Autumn 384 Appointed official orator in Milan.

Spring 385 Monica arrives in Milan.

Spring 386 Augustine reads some Platonic books and studies Paul's letters.

August 386 Visited by Ponticianus; converts to Christianity.

September 386 Retreats to Cassiciacum; writes the first *Dialogues.*

March 387 Returns to Milan.

Easter 387 Is baptized by Ambrose in Milan on 24 April; shares vision with Monica at Ostia; Monica dies.

387–88 Returns to Rome; begins anti-Manichaean writings.

388 Returns to Africa, to Carthage, then settles in Thagaste and begins monastic life there.

388–90 Adeodatus and Nebridius die.

Spring 391 Augustine begins monastic life in Hippo and is ordained priest there (Hippo Regius, Annaba, in Algeria).

392 Debate in Hippo with Fortunatus; Augustine begins writing the *Explanations of the Psalms.*

October 393 Speaks at Council of Hippo.

June 394 Council of Carthage.

395 Consecrated bishop of Hippo.

396 Rereads Paul; develops theology of grace.

June and August 397 Takes part at Councils of Carthage; preaching campaign at Carthage; begins writing the *Confessions*.

April 399 Council of Carthage; begins writing *On the Trinity*.

June and September 401 Councils of Carthage.

August 402 Attends Council of Milevis.

August 403 Council of Carthage; preaches regularly at Carthage.

June 404 Council of Carthage.

August 405 Council of Carthage.

406 Begins writing *Tractates on the Gospel of John*.

June 407 Council of Thubursicum.

June and October 408 Councils of Carthage.

June 409 Council of Carthage.

410 Alaric enters Rome.

May–September 410 Visits to Carthage.

June 410 Council of Carthage.

Winter 410 Retreats to villa outside Hippo because of ill health.

411 Preaches regularly in Carthage and Cirta against the Donatists.

June 411 Plays a decisive role in the Assembly (*Collatio*) debate between Catholics and Donatists; beginning of debate with the Pelagians; develops doctrine of original sin.

411–12 Has connections with aristocratic refugees from the sack of Rome.

412 Begins writing the *City of God* (completed in 427).

June 412 Synod at Cirta; preaches regularly in Carthage.

413 Fails to prevent the execution of Flavius Marcellinus at Carthage.

September and October 416 Attends the Councils of Milevis.

September 417 Preaches at Carthage.

May 418 Council of Carthage.

September 418 Augustine at Caesarea in Mauretania.

May 419 Council of Carthage; debate with Julian of Eclanum begins.

June 421 Council of Carthage.

426 Augustine visits Milevis, leaves Hippo; again suffers from poor health; begins *Reconsiderations*.

428 Debate with Maximus at Hippo.

429–30 Vandals enter Africa and lay siege to Hippo.

28 August 430 Augustine dies in Hippo.

PART 2

FRANCIS OF ASSISI

AND HIS WORLD

INTRODUCTION

Everyone loves Francis. His statue (usually with a bird on his arm) is found in gardens all across the world. His example is touted as much needed in our day. Francis, the patron saint of ecology. Francis, the peacemaker. Unfortunately, in our attempt to make Francis relevant, the man we have come to love resembles only a distant relative of the real Francis.

Francis was less interested in ecology and peacemaking than we are. And when he did focus on these themes, he did so for unmodern reasons. His were medieval reasons. This can be a problem for modern people. If someone today wants to condemn an idea or practice, few one-liners do a better job than, 'That's so medieval.' Everyone nods and chuckles. No one has to say what everyone thinks: 'Indeed. How irrelevant.' What is surprising, though, is that, in Francis's case, it is those medieval reasons that make him both relevant and vital for our day.

This account, then, is an attempt to understand the modern medieval Francis. First, it tells the story of Francis. It does not try to tell the reader what scholars think of other scholarly opinions of Francis. Nor does it weigh scholarly arguments about the facts of Francis's life. The careful reader will see that a great deal of scholarship has been consulted in the writing of this account (see 'Further Reading'). But scholarship has been used to enable the author to tell Francis's story concisely, and to tell it in an engaging way.

Too many biographies of Francis get bogged down in scholarly debate. Others tell his story without any historical distance, so that Francis comes across as someone who walked about a foot above the ground. Here, I attempt to keep the narrative moving while employing (usually behind the scenes) the best scholarship available to help bring detail and life to the story.

Second, the account is about Francis's world. It is not a social history. It will, hopefully, pique the reader's curiosity to explore the medieval world even more. Here, the reader will get only a glimpse of life in the Middle Ages – but enough of a glimpse to set Francis's feet firmly in his world.

As the narrative progresses, the reader should gain a deeper understanding of who Francis really was, and why he taught and acted as he did – as a medieval man living in a medieval world. It is only then that readers will see his real relevance to modern world. And, just in case I have not been clear enough in the narrative, I have outlined my conclusions in chapter 21.

As I have noted, many books have helped me to navigate Francis and his world. The most helpful have been Omer Englebert's classic *St Francis of Assisi: A Biography*, and the more recent *Francis of Assisi: A Revolutionary Life* by Adrian House. Anyone familiar with these books will see my debt to these fine scholars.

Nearly all of the quotes from Francis or his early biographies come from the volumes of translated Francis documents: *Francis of Assisi: Early Documents*, edited by Regis J. Armstrong, J.A. Wayne Hellmann and William J. Short. The work of these and other scholars was a continual source of awe and thanksgiving for me. Their patient labours on matters of the closest detail freed me to concentrate on simply telling Francis's story in an economical and, I trust, engaging way.

Finally my wife, Barbara, my daughters, Katie and Theresa, and my son, Luke, did not have as much access to me as they wished sometimes. But their patience and understanding made it possible to produce a better narrative, if not a better husband and father.

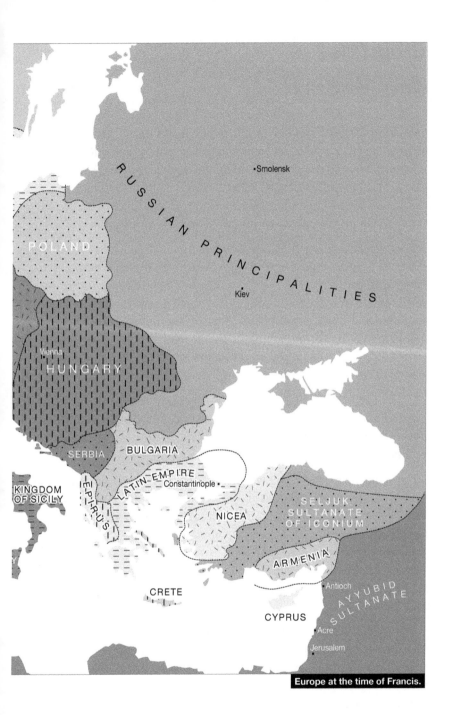

Europe at the time of Francis.

CHAPTER 9

THE KNIGHT

It was a brisk November day in 1202 when Assisi's militia marched through the city's streets. Citizens cheered as troops filed out of the city gates, down to the expansive plain that spread out below the city. Meanwhile, the militia of rival Perugia across the plain was also on the march, and by mid-morning the two armies studied each other tensely from less than a kilometre away.

Then Perugia charged. Suddenly the plain was filled with the thunder of hooves and the shouts of men intoxicated with fear and hate and the sheer joy of battle. For the next few hours, the fighting raged over the plain, spilling into the woods and private castles. Sweat and blood poured from man and beast, as merchants, farmers and nobility – called upon to defend their rights and to uphold their town's honour – swore and slashed at one another and then ran, some in pursuit, others for their lives. One contemporary historian noted, 'The final defeat came very late, but the slaughter was very severe.'

Assisi's army was defeated and then slaughtered. Those who tried to hide in the thick woods or in caves were hunted down like animals. Some were taken prisoner; others were mercilessly killed.

One chronicler, in overblown rhetoric that nonetheless captures the victors' pride, said that one river was so swollen by the blood of the dead that its banks overflowed. An Assisian partisan wrote, 'Oh, how disfigured are the bodies on the field of battle, and how mutilated and broken are their members! The hand is not to be found with the foot, nor the entrails joined to the chest; on the forehead horrible windows open out instead of eyes . . . Oh, you of Assisi, what a sad day and what a dark hour was this!'

It was an especially dark hour for Assisi's elite company, Compagnia dei Cavaliera, and particularly for one 21-year-old member of that company, a wealthy merchant's son. Like all young men of his day, he had spent much of his youth memorizing the songs of the troubadours – ballads of knights and ladies, and the glory of battle. Now he found himself bound in chains, dragged off as a prisoner across a battlefield littered with the bodies of childhood friends, through Perugia's streets, which were lined with taunting onlookers. Though the young man remained remarkably upbeat during the first few weeks of his imprisonment, he had already begun saying goodbye to the happy and heroic dreams of his youth.

New politics

The prisoner's Christian name, given by his mother at his baptism in autumn 1181, was John. The name did not please his father, Peter Bernadone. He had been away, again, on business to France when his wife, Pica, gave birth. When he returned, he insisted on calling the boy Francis. The name stuck.

Peter Bernadone was the type of husband and father who was used to having his own way at home. Increasingly, he was the type of citizen who also had his own way in his home town. This was partly due to his ambition, and partly due to changes in the social and political climate.

When Peter first started out in business, he and his fellow merchants complained much about their lack of voice in civil government. They complained about the crushing by taxes and forced labour imposed on them by the *majores* – the noblemen, knights and lords who gained their ranks and property by accident of birth. In fact, for as long as he or anyone could remember, in Assisi (and, for that matter, in all of Italy, France, Germany and Britain), *minores* such as Peter had been subject to the *majores*. To be sure, with the accident of birth came the responsibility to protect those lower on the social scale from robbery, rape, pillaging by foreign armies and so on. But the price the *minores* (made up of serfs and villeins) paid for this protection became increasingly oppressive. The serfs had essentially become slaves, belonging to the lord's land like so much livestock, enjoying no independence. Villeins – farm labourers, craftsmen and merchants such as Peter – were free in theory and had the right to own property. But between the taxes and forced labour, their freedom was difficult to enjoy.

However, things had begun to change in Peter's grandfather's day. Even Peter's father would have recalled that, in his day, the only

You are where you live

Writers enjoy waxing eloquent when describing the region in which Francis lived, for the area is believed not only to have inspired Francis's love of nature, but also to have had something to do with shaping his paradoxical character. A typical example comes from the pen of historian Omer Englebert:

Umbria, where St Francis's life was spent, is situated in Central Italy, between the March of Ancona and Tuscany. This region, full of contrasts and beauty, affords to man's spirit a variety of scenery which is truly captivating: solitary peaks and charming valleys, streams lazily meandering along the plain, torrents cascading down ravines, fields of wheat and unproductive volcanic soils, forests of ilex and fir, silver-leaved olive trees, engarlanded vines running along the mulberry trees, and clumps of black cypress mounting guard at wayside chapels. The winter is rugged, the summer scorching, autumn and springtime marvellously mild.

markets available to craftsmen and labourers were the local castle, monastery or town. But the Crusades opened up new trade routes. It was not long before ships crammed Mediterranean harbours, and caravans travelled along rebuilt Roman highways (destroyed centuries earlier by invading barbarian armies). Raw materials and manufactured goods found their way from one end of Europe to the other. The upshot was that many artisans and merchants reaped fortunes. Among these fortunate merchants was Peter Bernadone, who made his money in cloth.

By the time Francis was born, visitors to Assisi had told how in some towns, the authorities – both the nobility and the church – were granting economic privileges to wealthier merchants. They were even admitting them to their councils. Merchants in many Italian towns helped choose public officials, made and administered law, and meted out justice. These new political arrangements were called 'communes', and the commune's 'citizens' (those who owned a home and earned sufficient income) were now bound to a new 'lord' – the community – obliged by a feudal oath to, among other duties, place themselves as troops in the commune's service.

Francis, boy romantic

The rising Peter made sure that Francis and his only brother, Angelo, got at least a minimal education. He sent them to the school at San Giorgio Church in Assisi. But Francis was never much of a student; he barely learned to read and write, and always preferred to be read to. He wrote even less. As an adult, he was considered 'a man without learning', meaning that he never undertook advanced studies in theology or law.

It was not the life of the mind that captured the boy's imagination, but the cult of chivalry, then all the rage. In his youth, Francis sat rapt at the tales of travelling French troubadours. They sang at civic gatherings and tournaments, extolling the legends of Charlemagne and the Knights of the Round Table, celebrating love and women. He heard stories of love purified by sacrifice and loyalty; of devout knights who, 'without fear and without reproach', served in the holy crusades; of repentant warriors who, in atonement for their sins, built churches to the glory of God.

In addition to his impatience with learning and his romantic imagination, Francis was barely supervised by his parents. They pretty much let the boy do as he pleased. Bonaventure, a later biographer, put it discreetly in his *Major Legend of St Francis* (1260–63), saying that Francis 'lived among foolish mortals and was brought up in foolish ways'.

In short, Francis was spoiled. He was allowed to shirk his studies and pursue a carefree life. He was especially fond of whiling away the hours with friends: 'He was so accustomed to setting his heart on joining his companions when they called him,' writes the author of *The Legend of the Three Companions*, an early biography, 'he would leave the [family] table even if he had eaten only a little.'

Like many middle-class boys, Francis and his friends mingled with the sons of nobles (this mixing of social classes was another sign of the changing times). They partied together. They danced through the streets, serenaded young ladies late into the night (sometimes being rewarded for their singing by the more willing ladies). They also committed their share of juvenile vandalism and thievery.

Francis, it seems, was born for this lifestyle: 'He was an object of admiration to all, and he endeavoured to surpass others in flamboyant display of vain accomplishments,' writes Thomas of Celano in *The Life of St Francis* (1228–29). He was known for his 'wit, curiosity, practical jokes and foolish talk, songs, and soft and flowing garments'.

He was a natural leader, and many young men were anxious to be in Francis's presence, especially if it meant flirting with the law and social custom. 'Thus with his crowded procession of misfits, he used to strut about impressively and in high spirits', making his way through the streets of Assisi at all hours of the day and night, as Celano records. It felt especially cruel, then, when the witty, amiable, carefree Francis found himself languishing in a Perugia prison for a year.

Assisi becomes a commune

That this happy son of Assisi found himself imprisoned was due to both parochial rivalry and international politics. The news was full of war and rumours of war. If some powerful lord blocked a road and demanded a toll, or if a rival commune claimed rights to a coveted forest, the threatened city sent in troops to settle the issue. This sometimes meant besieging a castle, razing a town, burning crops or taking and torturing prisoners.

> 'That man, whom today we venerate as a saint . . . miserably wasted and squandered his time almost up to his 25th year of his life.'
>
> **Thomas of Celano, *The Life of St Francis*, 1228–29**

Pope Innocent III (who reigned in 1198–1216), hardly a paragon of virtue in such matters, nonetheless was alarmed at those who 'continue to lay waste cities, destroy castles, burn villages, oppress the poor, persecute churches, and reduce men to serfdom. Murder, violence, and rapine are rife, with quarrelling and wars'.

It was not just local flare-ups that were problematic. All through Francis's childhood, Assisi had been in a state of near constant civil war with the Holy Roman Emperor. Assisi merchants had rebelled against imperial control less than a decade before Francis's birth, in 1174, only to be crushed within three years by Emperor Frederick Barbarossa. Frederick installed a trusted lieutenant, Conrad, Duke of Spoleto, in

> 'In the time of St Francis, the people laughed at the agonies of enemies who were tortured and killed . . . They shed blood now in arrogant wholesale slaughter, now with delicacy. Revenge – the vendetta – became a fixed idea.'
>
> **Arnaldo Fortini, *Francis of Assisi*, 1992**

The medieval meal

As in our day, most medieval people wanted meat with every major meal. However, most people had to settle for it only on special occasions. Francis's family, wealthier than most, probably could afford meat more often. Beef, pork, chicken, squirrel, porpoise, magpie and peacock were all typical. A variety of spices and sauces were used to flavour food. One English recipe for broth instructed the cook to boil diced rabbit with almond milk, cypress root, ginger, rice flour and sugar.

Poorer families ate peas and beans, but the wealthy often tried to avoid vegetables, except for onions. Fresh fruit would have been available, certainly in Italy, and the most common were apples and cherries. Wine was the choice of the rich, and ale the choice of the poor. The poorest of all had to be satisfied with water.

Most families had to cook for themselves, but it is likely that Francis's family had a cook to bake bread (again, the rich would be more likely to have an oven), prepare meals and set the table.

La Rocca castle overlooking Assisi, and this kept the town in check – at least until 1197.

That was the year in which the next emperor, Henry IV, died. With no clear successor in view, German politics was thrown into chaos. It was a signal for a general uprising throughout Italy. Communes drove out imperial representatives and occupied imperial fortresses. The newly elected (in 1198) Pope Innocent III, seeing an opportunity to enlarge the church's power, supported the rebellious cities. He ordered Duke Conrad to hand over Assisi, and the duke, judging his situation hopeless, capitulated. He left La Rocca castle in the care of a German garrison, and headed for Narni to do homage to papal legates.

As soon as Conrad was out of sight, Assisi's militia besieged the castle. Assisi resented imperial control, to be sure, but they were in no mood to merely switch masters. Papal legates pleaded with them to back down. Assisi refused. They then threatened Assisi with excommunication – again, to no avail. The Assisi militia, of which Francis was likely a part, took the citadel by storm and dismantled it, stone by stone.

This was the occasion when Assisi organized itself as a commune. The first order of business was to provide the city with a secure perimeter. The men of the city, probably including Francis, threw together a rampart, using stones from the dismantled fortress as material.

Then the commune began the reprisals. Many outlying castles still pledged themselves to the emperor, and continued to levy road and bridge tolls. A resentful Assisi militia attacked and destroyed castle after castle. They also ransacked the Assisi homes where the nobility lived for part of the year. Some of the elite of Assisi's aristocracy, including the family of six-year-old Clare di Favarone (the future St Clare of Assisi), fled to Perugia, and pledged themselves and their lands to their new protector. Perugia, naturally, was only too happy to welcome them.

While Assisi was busy destroying castles, Perugia launched a series of raids across the Tiber (Tevere), the river which split the plain between the two cities, and began harassing Assisian landowners. Matters escalated when Perugia made an alliance with Foligno, 19 kilometres from Assisi. Assisi, in turn, made treaties with Gubbio, Fabriano, Nocera, Spello and Narni – all towns which had scores to settle with Perugia.

When, in November 1202, Assisi launched a pre-emptive attack, Perugia was amply prepared. The only Assisians not slaughtered were those whom Perugia thought could bring a decent ransom, such as the son of the merchant Peter Bernadone.

The dungeon into which Francis was thrown was lit by only a few torches, which still left it dark and did nothing for the dampness that hung heavy in the air. The place smelled of men's sweat, rotting hay and human waste.

But while most prisoners sat dejected, moaning about their state, Francis went about trying to cheer everyone up. He poked fun of his chains and laughed often. When one noble had become so bitter and unbearable that all the prisoners shunned him, Francis befriended him, and orchestrated reconciliation between him and the other prisoners.

> 'He [the young Francis] was naturally courteous in manner and speech and, following his heart's intent, never uttered a rude or offensive word to anyone.'
>
> **The Legend of the Three Companions**, 1241–47

Still, the relentless conditions took their toll and sabotaged even Francis's naturally buoyant spirit, and by the time negotiations for his release were arranged (it took a year, with his father paying a hefty ransom), Francis had become desperately ill. He spent many weeks in bed. When he finally could stand on his own, he was forced to use a cane for weeks.

Knightly ambitions

Francis's illness threw him into an uncharacteristic depression. But soon enough, military ambitions again clouded his mind, and he began planning another expedition. He had heard that an Assisi count named Gentile was preparing to leave for Apulia to engage in another

Becoming a knight

Before a man could enter knighthood, he had to prove himself worthy in battle and outfit himself in knight's armour. It was the latter requirement that limited knighthood to the nobility and wealthy.

A knight's outfit was enormously expensive. There was the hauberk (a long tunic made of chain mail), the cuisse (plate armour that covered the thighs), the *jambeaux* (armour for below the knees), the *sollerets* (steel shoes) and the helmet. Of course, the potential knight needed a sword, a hilt, a lance (with his pennant on top) and a shield with his coat of arms. On top of all this went the surcoat, a robe which covered the entire man. In addition, the candidate had to own a horse – no small expense – and outfit it with armour, which amounted to chain mail to protect the flanks, and the *chamfron*, armour which covered the front of the head.

To assist him, the knight also had to have a squire, who had to be similarly outfitted.

Once accepted by a sponsor, the candidate for knighthood passed the night in prayer before an altar on which his armour lay. In the morning, he participated in the Mass. On his knees, he took an oath to use his sword to serve God and the oppressed.

After this, his sponsor gave him the accolade, a symbolic blow with the fist on the back of the neck. Finally, the sponsor embraced him, saying, 'In the name of God, of St Michael and of St George, I dub you knight. Be brave, courageous, and loyal.'

battle between church and empire. Francis convinced the count to let him join him.

He feverishly began making preparations. Though not yet a knight, Francis insisted on looking like one – which cost his father a small fortune – sporting a coat of mail, a helmet, a sword, a lance with its pennant and a flowing robe.

(His father, it turned out, ended up paying for more than his son's outfit. As Francis was making ready for the expedition, he ran across a bedraggled knight with a threadbare outfit. Francis, in a characteristic gesture of generosity, invited the man to dinner and, before the evening was out, had given him a whole new knightly outfit.)

In the midst of his preparations, Francis had a dream. He found himself in his father's house, which had been transformed into a palace filled with arms. Instead of bales of cloths, he saw saddles, shields and lances. In one room, a beautiful bride waited for her bridegroom. Francis heard a voice saying that all this was for Francis and his knights.

When Francis awoke, he was ecstatic. He saw the dream as a portent of the expedition's success and the glory that was eventually to be his. As he bounced around his father's shop the next day, a customer asked him what he was so happy about. 'I know that I will become a great prince!' he replied.

The day to depart arrived, and the 25-year-old Francis, joined by a companion and squire, set off to join Count Gentile. The threesome got as far as Spoleto on the first day.

It turned out to be the last day of their adventure. That night, Francis had another dream, this one deeply troubling. In it, an unknown voice asked him where he wanted to go. When Francis explained his plans, the voice asked, 'Who can do more good for you? The lord or the servant?'

'The lord,' Francis replied.

'Then why,' said the voice, 'are you abandoning the lord for the servant, the patron for the client?'

A puzzled Francis asked, 'Lord, what do you want me to do?'

'Go back to your land, and what you are to do will be told to you.'

The next morning, Francis told his companions that he was abandoning the expedition. The dazed trio returned to Assisi immediately.

This mysterious dream, coming on the heels of a humiliating defeat and a year's imprisonment, got Francis's attention. To be sure, the youthful passions were almost impossible to shake off and, for the rest of his life, Francis would be haunted by knightly ambitions. But never again would he don military dress or take up the sword.

CHAPTER 10

THE HEDONIST

Francis's re-evaluation of his life had begun in fits and starts, and earlier than his aborted mission to Apulia. As a young man, Francis had been enchanted by the Assisi countryside. His father owned a considerable amount of land outside of town, and Francis would often visit these properties to allow the fields and woods to invigorate him. As his illness from the Perugia imprisonment had abated, he was anxious to take a stroll in the fields below the town. But, to his surprise, the outing proved disappointing. As Thomas of Celano put it, 'But this time, neither the beauty of the fields and the smiling vineyards, nor anything pleasant to the sight was able to charm him.'

Francis was astonished. He began to wonder why he had become so attached to things of this world and, 'profoundly disillusioned,' says Thomas, 'he sadly returned home.'

Risky business

Medieval merchants traded a variety of goods all over Europe and the Middle East. But the most financially rewarding product was cloth. Northern Italian towns produced silk, velvet and brocade and, sometimes woven into the fabric, threads of gold and silver.

Most international trade occurred at large markets, or fairs, held in large towns. The fairs held in Champagne, in eastern France, were the most well known. They were so important to the local economy that the king of France promised safety to merchants who had to cross France to get there. Highway robbery, though, remained a threat.

Because of this, few merchants carried large sums of money, but instead used bills of exchange – a kind of cheque which was recognized in all countries. The first banks arose to help to make such transactions possible.

Despite these precautions, such business still entailed risks. To share the risks, many merchants formed partnerships; one man would put up the money, the other would undertake the dangerous journey to the fair.

But he was still very much taken with things of the world. It would take more than a momentary depression or even one startling dream to completely wake him from his material stupor.

Wealth and business

Francis' father was not as greedy as some early biographers of Francis make him out to be. Still, Peter Bernadone was fond of money, sought public admiration and, like many merchants of Assisi, longed to rise in the social order. He wished nothing less for his son and, for a long time, the wish was coming true.

Peter's business was cloth and, in central Italy, the cloth trade flourished – thanks to peace brought about by Emperor Frederick Barbarossa, which helped this and other industries to grow. But, wanting to deal in more than coarse Italian wools, Peter often travelled to Provence and Champagne, to fairs where merchants from Europe, Asia and Africa exchanged the finest material then known. Peter did well for himself and his family; he was able to acquire extensive holdings around Assisi, and was a major benefactor to the commune of Assisi.

Naturally, Peter Bernadone's sons, Francis and Angelo, were taught the family business. Growing up, Francis waited on customers, and went on horseback to conduct business in Spoleto and Foligno. He travelled with his father to the fairs in France (which is where he also picked up French). In short, according to biographer Thomas of Celano, Francis too became 'most prudent in business'.

At the same time, he became most profligate in spending. 'He spent so much money on himself and others', says *The Legend of the Three Companions*, 'that he seemed to be the son of some great prince.'

His fondness for parties has already been mentioned, but clothes were another weakness. *The Legend of the Three Companions* notes, 'He was most lavish in spending, so much so that all he could possess and earn was squandered on feasting and other pursuits . . . spending more money on expensive clothes than his social position warranted.' Sometimes, just to show how much he could afford to squander his resources, he would combine the cheapest cloth with the most expensive materials in the same piece of clothing.

A change of heart

If Francis spent lavishly on himself, he was not hesitant to share his wealth – or, at least, his father's wealth. His outfitting of the bedraggled knight is one example. Another came earlier. Francis was minding his father's shop when a beggar came in and asked for alms, 'for the love of God'. Francis was preoccupied with his work and ignored the man. When the man would not go away, Francis became impatient and brusquely told him to leave.

As soon as the beggar stepped into the street, Francis regretted his rudeness. 'If that poor man had asked something from you for a great count or baron, you would certainly have granted him his request,' he scolded himself. 'How much more should you have done this for the King of Kings and Lord of Lords.' He rushed out of his shop and gave the man some money. He resolved never again to refuse anyone who begged in the name of God.

This sympathy for the poor may have been learned from his mother, Pica. Legend has it that she came from a distinguished family in France, and most early biographies paint her, in contrast to her husband, as a devout Catholic and 'a friend of all complete integrity'. She is said to have instilled into Francis as many Christian virtues as the young, wild man could absorb. It was not until after his aborted knightly errand to Apulia that some of those virtues began to blossom in Francis, albeit ever so slowly. Still, a change was evident to his friends.

One evening, they arrived at his house, handed him a mock sceptre and announced that they had made him 'king of youth'. What they really wanted was for him to foot the bill for another wild night on the town. Francis obliged, as usual. After a gluttonous banquet, the group spilled out into the Assisi streets, singing drunken refrains late into the night. Francis, sceptre in hand, dragged behind the rest, preoccupied. He found himself strangely bored with the very activity that had formerly given him such pleasure.

Suddenly, while considering the vanity of his life, Francis was filled with an inexplicable sensation. 'He was unable to speak or move,' says *The Legend of the Three Companions*. 'He could only feel and hear this marvellous tenderness', which he attributed to God.

'Kids today!'

The sorry state of children and youth was a constant refrain among many medieval writers. For example, Francis's biographer, Thomas of Celano, in *The Life of St Francis*, complained, 'A most wicked custom has been so thoroughly ingrained among those regarded as Christians . . . as a result, they are eager to bring up their children from the very cradle too indulgently and carelessly . . . Compelled by the anxiety of youth, they are not bold enough to conduct themselves honourably, since in doing so they would be subject to harsh discipline . . . But when they begin to enter the gates of adolescence, what sort of individuals do your imagine they become? . . . Since they are permitted to fulfil every desire, they surrender themselves with all their energy to the service of outrageous conduct.'

Such wholesale condemnations were usually written by men who had voluntarily submitted to the disciplines of the monastic life. In spite of their bias and hyperbole, however, many thirteenth-century people would have agreed with this description – as would have Francis looking back on his wild youth.

His friends had blithely gone on ahead. When they noticed his absence, they turned around to find him. They found him transfixed, and they began teasing him, asking if he was daydreaming about a woman he might marry. Francis came back in kind: 'You are right! I was thinking about taking a wife more noble, wealthier, and more beautiful than you have ever seen.'

Everyone laughed at Francis's characteristic bravado. But a few thought they had detected a change in him. What they did not understand, and what Francis himself still did not fully grasp for years, was that he was speaking of his future marriage to 'Lady Poverty'. Though he still had no idea what all this meant, this much was clear: 'He began to consider himself of little value,' says *The Legend of the Three Companions*, 'and to despise those things which he had previously held in love.'

To work out what was going on inside him, Francis began spending more time with one friend, whom the biographers never name. Together, they would walk outside the city to a certain cave (probably on one of

The medieval town street

The streets of a medieval town were not charming, as we might imagine today. In the daytime, towns were noisy and crowded places. Town criers shouted news of fairs, marriages and opportunities to buy property. Beggars pleaded for handouts. Merchants hawked their wares. Church bells rang throughout the day, announcing services, council meetings and the start and end of the working day.

Day and night, the streets were a mess. People sometimes threw rubbish and excrement into the street. Few towns could keep up with cleaning the streets. Lincoln, in northern England, smelled so bad that foreign merchants once boycotted the town.

At night, thieves often plied their trade in unlit streets. Some towns hired locals to police the streets, and most towns closed the city gates at night to keep out strangers. Most law-abiding citizens shut their windows and stayed inside for the night.

All of this suggests that Francis and his companions, in going about town at all hours, were not just young men out looking for a good time. They were pushing the edge of what was considered respectable and, perhaps, legal.

Peter Bernadone's properties), into which Francis would enter to pray, sometimes for hours at a time. He implored God to show him God's will. He trembled as he recalled his sins, and repeatedly repented of them. He worried that he would be unable to resist future temptations.

He suffered such torment inside the cave that, as Thomas of Celano puts it, 'When he came back out, he was so exhausted from his struggle that one person seemed to have entered, and another to have come out.' Francis endured these agonies of conscience for weeks.

And then one day they ended. After he pleaded once more with God, says Thomas, 'The Lord showed him what he must do.' But he still hesitated to speak plainly about what exactly that was. Perhaps he still did not fully know. With friends, he spoke of his 'hidden treasure'. He said that, although he refused to go to Apulia

> 'Many times . . . having sat down at table, he had barely begun to eat when he would stop eating and drinking, absorbed in meditation on heavenly things.'
>
> **Description of Francis's spiritual state after the vision at San Damiano, in *The Legend of the Three Companions*, 1241–47**

on a knight's errand, he would do great deeds at home. And when people wondered when he was going to take a bride, he spoke again of a mysterious lady who had captured his heart.

A change in behaviour

Slowly, Francis's actions began to make sense of his words. He gave more and more alms to the poor. If he had no money, he offered them his hat, belt or sometimes the shirt off his back. He purchased communion chalices for local priests. He saved leftovers from dinner for beggars. He also went on a pilgrimage.

It may have been at the suggestion of his friend or a priestly confessor (perhaps the local bishop). Perhaps it was a spontaneous idea. In any event, Francis walked to Rome with some companions (who, again, remain unnamed) to pray at the plethora of sacred sites there. The experience both scandalized him and changed him even more.

When he visited St Peter's Tomb, he was shocked at the stinginess of pilgrims, most of whom gave but paltry offerings. After watching this for a while, a disgusted Francis pulled a handful of coins from his pocket and threw them at the offering box, hoping that the clanging coins bouncing on the stone floor would shock people into giving more.

At another point, he was so intrigued by the hundreds of beggars who milled about pilgrimage sites that he decided to see what it would feel like to be one of them. He stripped himself of his middle-class attire and donned the rags of a beggar, shared in their meagre meals and walked about with them, begging for alms. His travelling companions soon put a stop to this. But the experience of begging so moved Francis that he began to ponder ever more deeply what was required of him, and what it meant to live a life of poverty.

When he returned to Assisi, he now spent even more time alone. When he did come out in public, he performed even more acts of charity for the poor and with lepers, in what the townspeople increasingly saw as Francis's strange obsession.

The Assisi countryside, like much of Europe, was dotted with chapels, churches and abbeys, each dedicated to one saint or another. Some were well endowed, others neglected, and most had a priest who depended on the generosity of locals to sustain him and the church.

San Damiano, just over a kilometre below Assisi, was such a church. It was guarded by olive trees and had a sweeping view of the wheat fields on the plain below. The church itself was in general disrepair; the walls crumbled all about it, and the priest only eked out an existence. He did not even have enough money to buy oil, let alone a lamp, to burn continually on the altar.

On one of his country walks, Francis decided to step into the chapel. In scattered light, he made his way to the altar, knelt before a painted Byzantine crucifix and began to pray.

How long he prayed and what exactly he said is unclear. But sometime in the middle of his prayer, as Francis gazed at the crucifix, he heard Christ speak from it: 'Francis, go and repair my house, which you can see is all being destroyed.'

Up to this point in his life, Francis had had dreams in which he believed God had spoken to him. He had also felt a sense of God's leading from time to time. But he had never experienced such a direct spiritual communication. He was 'more than a little stunned', as Thomas of Celano notes in *The Remembrance of the Desire of a Soul*, 'trembling and stuttering like a man out of his senses'. He pulled himself up from prayer and then pulled himself together. He vowed to carry out the command as quickly and as literally as he knew how.

The restoration of San Damiano

If Francis had abandoned his quest for knighthood, he did not abandon all knight-like behaviour. In that day, it was not uncommon for a knight to build or restore a chapel, especially if he was anxious to atone for his sins. In a like spirit, Francis began planning the restoration of San Damiano.

First, he needed money, and he knew exactly where to get some. He hurried to his father's shop, gathered up a variety of cloths, especially scarlet (which would fetch a good price). He mounted the family horse and set off for the market in Foligno, about 16 kilometres south. After he had sold all the cloth, he entertained offers for the horse, and then sold it as well. He walked back to San Damiano, found the priest, kissed his hands and presented him with the day's receipts.

The priest, aware of Francis's playful reputation, thought it a prank. And even if it was not, he was not about to take so much money from the son of Peter Bernadone, the powerful and ill-tempered city father. So the priest declined the offer.

Francis would not be so easily refused, partly because he had decided that he was not going to be weighed down with riches. So he tossed the bag of coins indifferently onto a window sill in the corner of the chapel. If the priest would not accept his money, he asked, would he at least accept the offering of himself? Could he begin living at the chapel and set about repairing it? To this, the priest relented.

A mystified Peter Bernadone, after making inquiries about town, finally worked out what happened to his inventory, his horse and his son. He was furious. He set out for San Damiano immediately to seize Francis and bring him home.

When Francis heard that his father was approaching, he was terrified. He knew that his father would not comprehend his new calling. Francis also knew himself. He knew that he was likely to crumble under his father's wrath and meekly return home. He did not think he could face his father just yet, so he ran. He found refuge in a nearby cave and huddled there for a month, asking God for courage and wisdom.

Facing his father

Francis's cowardice finally abated, and he decided that God had given him no choice but to get back to repairing San Damiano. And that meant first a return to Assisi to beg for more supplies, no matter the consequences, which he knew would be swift and harsh.

His ragged, soiled clothes hung more loosely than ever on his thin frame, and his face was drawn as he made his way through the Assisi streets, boldly asking for alms and supplies. His appearance

'[Francis's] progression towards a new vocation was slow and halting, subject to certain doubts which persisted throughout his life.'

Michael Robson, St Francis of Assisi: The Legend and the Life, 1997

created quite a stir. Was this not Francis, Peter Bernadone's son? The rascal about town turned thief? His friends were scandalized. Many thought that he had gone mad from starving himself. They mocked him – 'Lunatic!' And when he asked for stones to rebuild the walls of San Damiano, they obliged by throwing them at him, along with handfuls of mud.

Word soon got to Peter Bernadone, who was more horrified than ever. He had spent years building both his business and his reputation; he was finally a respected citizen of the commune. Francis was bringing shame to the Bernadone name, sabotaging all he had worked for these many years. Peter rushed about, desperately searching for his son, and finally found him just as the gossip mill had described him, wretched and a complete embarrassment. In a rage, he grabbed Francis and dragged him home. He beat him, then chained him in the basement. He cursed him, lectured him, and then cursed and lectured him again: Francis was going to stay chained up until he came to his senses, he shouted.

> '[Francis] went about by himself collecting stones. He begged all the people he met to give him stones. In fact he became a new sort of beggar, reversing the parable: a beggar who asks not for bread but a stone.'
>
> G.K. Chesterton, *St Francis of Assisi*, 1924

Business commitments soon called Peter away, and it was not long before Francis's mother, more pious than her husband and more sympathetic to Francis's religious awakening, unbound him. Francis headed immediately for San Damiano.

When Peter returned from his business trip and found out what happened, he flew into another rage. Again he stormed off to San Damiano. He bullied and threatened Francis, but this time Francis neither ran nor submitted. Peter rushed back to Assisi and filed a lawsuit against his son, demanding restitution and that his son be banished from the city.

Communal consuls rode down to San Damiano and told Francis he was going to have to appear in court, but again Francis refused. He reminded them that since he was living with a priest at a church, he was under the jurisdiction of the church; secular authorities had no power over him. Not wanting to turn a family matter into a contest of church and state, the consuls told Peter that their hands were tied.

Peter was unrelenting. Surely, he reasoned, the church would not condone thievery, even if done in the name of Christ, and off he went

Family prisons

Though Peter Bernadone's behaviour is considered abusive today, in medieval Italy, his treatment of his son was legally protected. At the request of just two relatives, any 'dissipater' could be thrown into the commune's prison. If a son, even as an adult, squandered family assets, a father was empowered to have the son imprisoned in the communal jail. Even without proof of charges, communal magistrates had to carry out a father's will in this regard. If a father preferred, he could take care of the matter himself, bind his son in chains and imprison him at home. The records of Assisi suggest that many families had private prisons.

to see the bishop. Bishop Guido was not unsympathetic to Peter. He had earned a reputation as one of the most acquisitive prelates in Italy. He owned even more land in and around Assisi than did Peter. He understood the value of money and the foolishness of squandering resources, no matter what the cause was. So he sent a messenger to San Damiano and told Francis to appear before him.

To this, Francis readily agreed. He knew that, despite the bishop's well-deserved reputation in temporal matters, he was also a man sensitive to things spiritual. Francis had been seeking the bishop's spiritual counsel during the past few months. Francis's reverence for the church, and for its priests and bishops, no doubt deepened through these encounters. As Francis put it, he gladly went because the bishop 'is the father and lord of souls'.

The day for the hearing arrived. Both Francis and his father, as well as a handful of spectators, gathered in the piazza of St Mary Major, in front of the bishop's palace. After official preliminaries, Peter rehearsed his complaints: the stolen cloth, selling the family horse and so on.

The matter seemed simple enough to Bishop Guido. 'Your father is infuriated and extremely scandalized,' he said to Francis. 'If you wish to serve God, return the money you have, because God does not want you to spend money unjustly acquired for the work of the church.' He also encouraged him to trust in God: 'He will be your help and will abundantly provide you with whatever is necessary for the work of his church.'

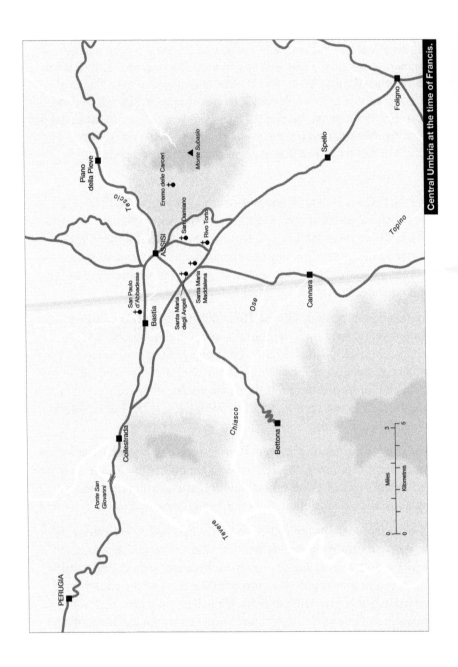

Central Umbria at the time of Francis.

Francis, already showing saintly forbearance, did not even hint at how hypocritical this advice sounded coming from one of Italy's most greedy bishops. He did not chide Guido, nor argue with his father. What he did – and it appears that he had given this next move some forethought – was to use his characteristic flair for the dramatic to make a point which neither his spiritual father nor his natural father would soon forget. 'Lord,' he replied to the bishop, 'I will gladly give back not only the money I acquired from his things.'

He then stepped briefly into the bishop's palace, disrobed and folded his clothes into a neat pile. He stepped back into the piazza, naked. He walked up to his father and presented him with the pile of clothes with a bag of money on top. The shocked observers took in his words: 'Listen to me, all of you, and understand: Until now, I have called Peter Bernadone my father. But, because I have proposed to serve God, I return the money . . . and all the clothing that is his, wanting to say from now on, "My father who is in heaven," and not "My father, Peter Bernadone."'

While the onlookers watched in stunned silence, Peter fumed. He grabbed the clothes and money, and stormed home. Francis's act of complete devotion could not be read in any other way than a deep insult to Peter. If father and son were ever reconciled, the biographers never recorded it.

The bishop, for his part, was deeply moved by Francis's gesture. Perhaps he understood it as a gentle, but well-deserved rebuke. In any case, he was not put off. Instead, he embraced Francis, took off his velvet mantel and wrapped it around Francis.

Francis, probably both frightened and delighted at the finality of this break, made his way through the streets of Assisi, out of the city gates and down the slope to San Damiano. He had the mantle returned to the bishop and then outfitted himself in the clothes of a hermit – a tunic tied with a leather belt at the waist, sandals and a walking staff. The break with his past was nearly complete.

CHAPTER 11

THE REFORMER

Church tradition says that Assisi was first evangelized just two decades after Jesus' death and resurrection, by one Crispoldo, said to be a disciple of the apostle Peter. But Assisians usually insist that it was Rufino's heroism two centuries later that converted the town. Francis, like all the children of Assisi, heard gruesome and heroic accounts of saints such as Felicianus, Victorinus and Savinus – third-century Assisi bishops killed for their faith. But no story told was more central to Assisi's identity than that of Rufino.

According to legend, Rufino arrived in Assisi and began preaching the message of Christ. The Roman proconsul Aspasio, hearing that another sovereignty was being proclaimed in his district, ordered the troublemaker to appear before him and told him to cease preaching – or else he would be forced to apply the usual punishments. Rufino, unfazed, replied, 'I fear neither you nor your emperors.'

So the proconsul ordered that a lead-tipped whip be applied to Rufino's back, and when that did not change Rufino's mind, he ordered that Rufino be stoned, and told the assailants to aim for his mouth. Still he refused to abandon his call.

Then the story has it that he was thrown into a flaming furnace as the proconsul taunted, 'Let us see if your god knows how to liberate you from my hands' – at which point an angel appeared and guided Rufino out of the flames. The hardened proconsul would not be defeated, and finally ordered, 'Tie a great rock about his neck and throw him into water so deep that the Christians cannot retrieve him.'

Rufino was drowned in the Chiascio River but, despite the proconsul's wish, Christians recovered his body and buried it, oddly enough, in a nearby temple dedicated to Diana. But Rufino's witness had proven effective, impressing enough people to mean that, slowly, the Christian faith took root in the region. By 412, as the Roman Empire was converting to Christianity, Rufino's memory was so revered that his body was exhumed and carried into the city in solemn assembly.

Such examples of unwavering devotion – courageous faith which resulted in the conversion of entire regions – were rehearsed in story and pageant on saints' days, and gave everyone in town pause for thought. This was especially true of Francis after he began re-evaluating his life. His conversion, he slowly realized, was not just about his own soul's salvation but also about the renewal of the entire church.

> *'Francis had set out to win his spurs but had relinquished his buckler and sword, had come of age but abandoned his birthright, and his "richest and most beautiful bride" had turned out to be Lady Poverty.'*
>
> **Adrian House, *Francis of Assisi: A Revolutionary Life*, 2000**

Self-examination

For a long time, Francis wrestled with his own soul, keeping the pressure on himself to convert more and more of his life. He soon concluded that it was not just ambition and pleasure that he had to give up. God wanted his very self, given with abandon. Nothing revealed this to him more than his neurotic fears.

He went through a period, for example, when he was obsessed with an old Assisi woman who carried a grotesque hump on her back, whose looks scared everyone. Francis got it into his mind – a suggestion of the devil, he later concluded – that if he did not abandon his spiritual quest, he would end up like this woman. The idea filled him with dread, pestering him throughout the day, forcing him to his knees in prayer. He finally found relief one day when he sensed God telling him, 'If you want to know me, despise yourself. For when the order is reversed, the things I say will taste sweet to you even though they seem the opposite.'

However, a bigger fear still blocked Francis's spiritual progress. As he put it years later in *The Testament*, shortly before his death, as a young man, 'It seemed too bitter for me to see lepers.'

On his frequent trips through the countryside, Francis had had many opportunities to run into lepers, and he did everything in his power to avoid them. 'The sight of lepers was so bitter to him that he refused not only to look at them, but even to approach their dwelling,' says *The Legend of the Three Companions*. If he felt moved to give alms, he would only do so through an intermediary and, even then, 'He always turned away his face and held his nose.'

Leprosy

Leprosy was still a not uncommon disease in medieval Europe, and once a person was afflicted with the disease – characterized by decaying flesh, ulcers and loss of feeling – he or she was socially isolated. Below Assisi, there were at least six lazar houses (so named after the biblical Lazarus, who in Jesus' parable was covered with sores – Luke 16:19–31). At San Lazzaro d'Arce, lepers were formally admitted by a priest. The leper stood in the cemetery while the priest pronounced him dead to the world, adding that this life's sufferings would lead him to the kingdom of heaven.

After sprinkling graveyard dust on the leper's head, the priest reminded him of the rules governing lepers. They could not leave the house unless they wore their distinctive grey cloak and sounded their wooden clapper to warn off other travellers. They were forbidden from attending fairs, markets, mills and farms, and from entering Assisi. They could beg for food only if they wore gloves and used a bowl to receive the offerings. They were forbidden from drinking directly from springs, rivers and wells (they could drink only from their own flasks). If they spoke with healthy individuals, they had to stand downwind from them.

While praying during the early months of his conversion, he believed that he heard this response: 'Francis, everything you loved carnally and desired to have, you must despise and hate if you wish to know my will. Because once you begin doing this, what before seemed delightful and sweet will be unbearable and bitter, and what before made you shudder will offer you great sweetness and enormous delight.'

A little while later, Francis was riding his horse near Assisi (apparently this took place before the rift with his father) when he saw ahead of him a leper standing in the road. He determined immediately to do something sweeping, something dramatic to change his attitude. He dismounted, walked up to the man and personally handed him a coin. But this still was not enough to a man of Francis's resolve. So he bent over, drew his lips near the man's decaying hand and kissed it. The man replied by giving Francis a kiss of peace; Francis did not recoil. Then Francis remounted his horse and went on his way.

Francis, though, went further still. To continue to purge his revulsion of lepers, he moved in among them for a time, distributing alms and kissing the hand of each until 'what before had been bitter . . . was turned into sweetness'.

This was how Francis slowly conquered his fears, which he saw stood in the way of complete abandonment to God. Such experiences showed him that divine revelations and extraordinary dreams were not enough. Spiritual experiences actually changed Francis little, except to give him a broad sense of direction in which to take his life. It was his stubborn determination – energized by God's grace, he would say – to do God's bidding, no matter the cost, that completed his conversion.

Begging

After Francis heard Christ say to him, 'Francis, go and repair my house, which you can see, is all being destroyed,' Francis began going about Assisi and the vicinity, begging for donations for the repair of San Damiano. 'Whoever gives me a stone will receive a reward from the Lord!' he shouted. 'Whoever gives me three will receive three rewards!'

Francis was completely taken with his new project, as much as he had been when he had partied late into the night with friends. While begging for, or working on, San Damiano, he would sometimes break out in song in praise of God. From the scaffold he had constructed around the church, he would joyously assault passers-by, inviting them to help.

> '[Medieval] hospitals . . . cathedrals and monasteries were often the "remorse in stone" by means of which great sinners attempted to atone for their crimes and violence.'
>
> **Omer Englebert, St Francis of Assisi: A Biography, 1965**

The San Damiano priest – the same one who rejected Francis's first monetary offering – soon warmed up to his crazy benefactor and, as poor as he was, began preparing meals for Francis. But Francis, after accepting the first few offerings graciously, felt uncomfortable. 'This is not the life of someone professing poverty!' he scolded himself. 'Get up, stop being lazy, and beg scraps from door to door.'

So Francis went through town, collecting leftovers into a large bowl. After collecting what amounted to so much garbage, he sat down to eat it, as he had vowed he would. But when he looked at the scraps before him, he immediately became nauseous. He paused, took a deep breath, forced the refuse into his mouth and swallowed hard. He later said that, to his surprise, it tasted better than the fine food he had enjoyed in his home. After that, he never let the priest cook for him again.

Outwardly, Francis appeared to accept the humility that begging demanded. But he admitted later that, during this time, he continued to wrestle with his pride. Once, as he went about begging for oil for the San Damiano chapel lamp, he approached a celebration in progress. He noticed that among the merrymakers were some old friends and, before they saw him, he ducked into an alley and started to slink back to San Damiano. But his pride was soon checked by his stubborn piety. He turned around and boldly stepped into their midst. He not only asked them for oil, but he also told them what he had just done and accused himself of cowardice before them.

Throughout his life, in fact, this ironic and very human pattern continued. Francis would deal a blow to one form of pride – in this case, shame before friends at doing what he felt God had called him to do – but he would feel compelled to point out his flaw publicly, thus drawing attention to his new-found humility! What he never seemed to realize was that this was a new form of pride, perhaps even more spiritually dangerous. Francis was indeed a saint, but a saint with ongoing character flaws.

A larger mission

When he had completed the repairs at San Damiano, Francis started work upon another local dilapidated chapel, St Peter's, and then another still, St Mary of the Angels (Santa Maria degli Angeli). It was only slowly, as he worked on these churches and as disciples started to attach themselves to him, that he began to realize his larger mission.

That the medieval church was in need of repair went without saying, though many, including the pope, were not reluctant to say it. At the Fourth Lateran Council, Pope Innocent III noted and condemned a variety of abuses prevalent throughout Europe:

Many priests have lived luxuriously. They have passed the time in drunken revels, neglecting religious rites. When they have been at Mass, they have chatted about commercial affairs. They have left churches and tabernacles in an indecent state, sold posts and sacraments, promoted ignorant and unworthy people to the clerical state, thought they had others better suited for it. Many bishops have appropriated the income of a parish for themselves, leaving the parish indigent. They have gone to the enormous abuse of forcing parishioners to make special payments so as to have still more income. They have extorted money from the faithful on every pretext. They have made a scandalous commerce of relics. They have allowed the illegitimate children of a canon to succeed the father in the benefice.

Assisi knew of such abuses first-hand, especially in the administration of its highest ranking cleric, Bishop Guido. The region under his jurisdiction was characterized by litigation and libel, pronouncements and sentences, as he sought land, goods and services 'for the diocese'. In 1216, he quarrelled long and viciously with the Benedictine monks of Monte Subiaso, claiming jurisdiction over some of their churches. In another dispute, Guido went down to the piazza and came to blows with an antagonist. On several occasions, the pope had to step in and reprimand Guido for his greed.

> 'Woe to all nations for the world has become darkness! The Lord's vineyard has perished; the Head of the Church is sick, and his members are dead. Do you sleep, shepherds of the flock?'
>
> **Elizabeth of Schönau** (1126–64), *Liber Viarum Dei*

Consequently, not even Guido's closest colleagues, the prior and canons of the cathedral, trusted him, let alone respected him. One part of the compromise reached after a dispute between Guido and his canons hints at how fractured the relationship had become: 'The prior and canons shall promise the bishop obedience and shall observe the reverence due him.' It goes on to mention that they had been quarrelling over the power of appointments, the right to certain offerings and so on. There is no indication that this compromise permanently healed the rift.

Corruption infected all levels of the church's life. Priors and canons regularly went to court to argue about fields and olive groves. Small monasteries rebelled against the rule of larger monasteries, sometimes each hiring mercenaries to insist, militarily, on their own way. In short, the litany of priestly abuses outlined by Innocent III could all be found in Assisi.

Though the abuses were transparent, the solution was not. Innocent III thought it 'would take fire and sword to cure it'. A number of ideas had been and were being tried by sundry prophets and reformers.

Reforming groups

In general, medieval reformers fell into one heresy or another, but one who seemed to start out solidly orthodox was Peter Valdes (1140–1218), who founded the 'Poor Men of Lyons'. Valdes (sometimes written as Waldo) was a wealthy merchant who sold his possessions and lived in voluntary poverty, preaching the gospel. His Bible-based preaching soon won him adherents, who together vowed to live in poverty, penance and perfect equality.

The church viewed all this with only mild suspicion until the group began lashing out at the failings of the clergy. The Archbishop of Lyon then excommunicated them. The group appealed to Pope Alexander III (who reigned in 1159–81) to hear their case. In the end, he praised their poverty and authorized them to preach morals to the people – only if the local bishop permitted, and only if they did not try to interpret scripture or teach theology.

Alexander's admonishes fell on deaf ears. The group went out and, acting according to conscience, did as they had always done. Finally, Pope Lucius III (who reigned in 1181–85) condemned them in 1184, when Francis was one year old. One thing led to another, and the greater part of the Waldensians (as they came to be called) began placing the authority of the Bible above the church, and rejected purgatory, indulgences and the veneration of saints. But a minority submitted to the pope, taking on the name 'Poor Catholics' (one historian called them 'pre-Franciscans'). They stopped disparaging priests, lived in poverty, tried to convert heretics, kept two Lents a year and prayed the 'Our Father' and 'Hail Mary' seven times a day.

The *Humiliati* was another reform-minded group of the era. They, too, were looked upon with suspicion by church authorities, but Pope Innocent III approved them in 1201. They took their name from the ash-grey habit they wore. They were composed of three orders: one of brothers, one of sisters and one of 'seculars'. The latter order comprised people who lived in the world with their families, while dressing modestly, serving the poor, fasting twice a week and saying seven 'Our Fathers' a day. Those in the other two orders ('the religious') lived in convents, performed manual labour, chanted the divine office and, if needed, went out begging to supply their needs. They arose in Lombardy, and within 15 years of their papal approval they already had 150 communities within the Milan diocese alone.

One reform group had the most notorious reputation in Francis's time. They were called the Patarini in Italy, the Albigensians in France and the Bogomiles in Eastern Europe. Mostly they are known as the Cathari.

They believed that two eternal principles competed for pre-eminence. One – God – was the author of all good and of all spiritual souls. The other – Satan or Jehovah – was the author of evil, suffering and all material things, including the human body. Human beings, composed of both soul and flesh, were the product of both principles. Christ came to liberate the spirit from the flesh. He took on human form merely to convince enslaved human beings to rebel against Satan and his church – the Church of Rome – and to bring people to the true church, the church of the Cathari – 'the pure' (from the Greek *katharos*).

This church developed rival priests (or the 'perfect'), a liturgy, parishes, schools and even a few convents. The Cathari had an

End-times prophet

The most widely influential prophet/reformer of the Middle Ages was a Cistercian monk called Joachim of Fiore (1145–1202). His mathematical analysis of the Bible led him to conclude that history was divided into three periods, represented by the Father, Son and Holy Spirit. The first was an era of law (obedience and fear) and the second was an era of grace (obedience in faith). The third would inaugurate an era of liberty and love.

This cosmology would have been dismissed as the ravings of a religious lunatic if Joachim did not live such an exemplary life. He was gentle and morally pure, and he exhibited a fiery passion for Christ. He basked in the wonders of the created order. He ministered to the dying by letting them spend their last moments lying against his breast. He lived in complete poverty – a marked departure from so many clerics and monks of the day. His teachings inspired thousands, not only to anticipate the millennium but also to shape their lives after his radical example.

evangelistic fervour: some became merchants so that they could preach at fairs; others became teachers to influence youth; and others still became doctors to minister to the sick and dying. Their preachers lashed out at the immorality of Catholic clergy, denied the efficacy of the sacraments and taught that the laying on of hands was enough to save a soul – assuming that one remained pure afterwards (which is why most Cathari delayed the ceremony until on their death beds). They denounced marriage and seemed indifferent about sexual morals (for the flesh meant nothing if the spirit was holy).

They could be found in many Italian cities, including Rome, and even dominated some towns. They were finally subdued only when church and state joined hands in a crusade against them. After the bloody Albigensian War of 1209, in which thousands of Cathari were ruthlessly slaughtered in southern France, it was just too risky to become a Cathar, and the sect slowly died out. But the lessons for the reform-minded such as Francis were obvious: if you wished to make a difference, you must stay within the bounds of church teaching and clerical authority.

An epiphany

Larger church reform, then, was in the air that Francis breathed, but such a large scheme did not inspire him until he experienced what he believed was another divine revelation.

It happened at the third church which Francis restored. It was legally owned by the Benedictine Abbey of Monte Subiaso, but except for the occasional Mass said there by a visiting priest, the chapel was neglected and in serious disrepair. Francis fell in love with the chapel almost immediately. It was secluded, located in the midst of a quiet forest. The chapel, though nicknamed the Portiuncula (the 'Little Portion') was officially dedicated to St Mary of the Angels, and thus, because of Francis's devotion to Mary, became a much-favoured place.

During a Mass held in honour of St Matthias at the end of February 1208, something extraordinary happened. As the priest read from chapter 10 of the Gospel of Matthew, in which Jesus instructs his disciples to go out and preach, the verses seemed to leap out at Francis: 'You received without payment: give without payment. Take no gold, or silver or copper in your belts, no bag for your journey, or two tunics, or sandals or a staff.'

Francis was mesmerized. After Mass, he rushed up to the priest and begged him to explain. The priest went over the passage line by line, adding parallel readings from the Gospels of Mark and Luke. He explained that Christ's disciples were not to possess gold or silver, nor any money at all for that matter, nor carry a wallet or a sack, nor bread, nor a staff, nor to have shoes and no more than one tunic, so that they could preach the kingdom of God and penance.

An overwhelmed Francis blurted out, 'This is what I want! This is what I seek, this is what I desire with all my heart!' Francis was flooded with joy. He immediately went about changing his ways even more. He exchanged his traditional hermit's garb for something even simpler. He took off his sandals, cast aside his staff and replaced his tunic with something much coarser ('so that in it he might crucify the flesh, with its vices and sins', notes Thomas of Celano in *The Life of St Francis*). Then he put on it the sign of cross ('so that in it, he would drive off every fantasy of the demons', records Thomas) and, instead of a leather belt, he girded himself with a simple rope.

He committed these passages of scripture to memory and, as Thomas notes, 'was careful to carry it out to the letter'. Francis had discovered not only what he was to do with his personal life, but he now also had a concrete method for rebuilding the church.

CHAPTER 12

LITTLE BROTHERS

Up to this point, Francis's conversion had been mostly a private affair, watched with dismay or amusement by those who knew him. So far, nothing that Francis had done or said inspired anyone but himself. As he became increasingly captivated by the idea of rebuilding the medieval church, that would soon change.

He began by preaching, first in the Church of San Giorgio, in which he had gone to school as a child, and later in the cathedral of San Rufino. He usually preached on Sundays, spending Saturday evenings devoted to prayer and meditation, reflecting on what he would say to the people the next day.

Francis also travelled the area with his message, sometimes preaching in up to five villages a day. He often preached outdoors, since many priests refused him permission to preach in their churches. In the countryside, Francis often spoke from a bale of straw or from a granary doorway. In the towns, he climbed on a box or up steps in front of a public building. He preached to serfs and their families as well as to the landholders, to merchants, women, clerks and priests – to any who gathered to hear him.

He began each sermon with a salutation, 'May the Lord give you peace.' In an era when war was chivalrous and blood vendettas common, when legal mutilations and murder were a part of everyday life, this greeting would have startled listeners.

They were also startled that he was preaching in Italian. Most famous preachers, such as Bernard of Clairvaux, had preached in Latin to win the respect of the educated elite. When preachers did use the local language, they often obscured their message with theological abstractions. Francis co-opted the techniques of the troubadours, making full use of poetic language and images that would drive a message home. When he described the nativity, listeners felt as if Mary was giving birth before their eyes. In rehearsing the crucifixion, the crowd, as well as Francis himself, would shed tears.

'His words were neither hollow nor ridiculous, but filled with the power of the Holy Spirit, penetrating the marrow of the heart, so that listeners were turned to great amazement.'

The Legend of the Three Companions, 1241–47

Medieval meeting-houses

Like the New England meeting-houses of the seventeenth century, the medieval church was more than a place where believers gathered for worship. It also served as community centre. In medieval society, no line separated religious and public life. Before the altar, communal assemblies gathered, heated public debates raged and important ceremonies were performed. Troops came together and prayed here before and after battle. Here, officials conducted legal transactions – deeds and contracts were signed, and the sentences of judges and consuls were announced. In short, it was the ideal place for an aspiring reformer to begin preaching his message.

From his mouth flowed both kindness and severity. One moment, he was friendly and cheerful; he would sometimes prance about as if he were playing a fiddle on a stick, or break out in song in praise to God and his creation. In another moment, he would turn fiery: 'He denounced evil whenever he found it,' wrote one early biographer, 'and made no effort to palliate it; from him a life of sin met with outspoken rebuke, not support. He spoke with equal candour to great and small.'

All in all, listeners felt as if something radically anew was afoot – the beginning of a religious awakening. Though all of society believed in God, when Francis spoke, it was as if God was real for the first time. As a result, 'Some men began to be moved to do penance by his example,' says *The Legend of the Three Companions*, 'and leaving all things, they joined him in life and habit.'

The first followers

Francis's first disciple was a man who followed only for a time before he returned to his previous life. The second follower, and the first to stay the course, was Bernard of Assisi. A rich and powerful lord, Bernard was so taken with Francis's words and conduct that he wondered if he should abandon his well-heeled life. He invited Francis to spend the night in his home to discuss the matter. They prayed together and talked long into the night.

At one point, Bernard asked, 'If, for many years, someone holds on to the possessions, many or few, he has acquired from his lord, and no longer wishes to keep them, what is the better thing for him to do?'

Francis said that he must give them all back to the lord from whom he received them.

Bernard replied, 'Then, brother, I want to give away all my worldly goods for the love of my Lord who gave them to me, as it seems best to you.'

'We will go to the church early in the morning,' Francis said, 'and through the book of the Gospels, we will learn how the Lord instructed his disciples.'

In the morning, they found another man, Peter Cantanii, who had also shown interest in Francis's way of life. Together, they went to the Church of San Nicolò next to the piazza. They immediately found the missal to look up the passage about renunciation. Francis, with dramatic flare, decided to drive home his vision to his potential disciples. He paused for prayer before he opened the book, and then, seemingly at random, his eyes fell on a saying of Jesus: 'If you wish to be perfect, go, sell everything you possess and give to the poor, and you will have treasure in heaven.'

Francis then opened to another passage, and then another. Each time a saying of Jesus came immediately into focus. One began, 'Take nothing for your journey . . .' and another, 'If any want to become my followers, let them deny themselves . . .'

Francis was already familiar with such passages and had been seeking to carry them out, literally. The triple gesture, which early biographers credited to miracle, seems instead to be Francis's dramatic way of impressing these two men with a theme that had captivated him. Francis concluded, 'Brothers, this is our life and rule, and that of all who will want to join our company. Go, therefore, and fulfil what you have heard.'

Both Bernard and Peter were smitten. Francis's vision seemed to strike at the heart of so much that was wrong with the church and the world. They each sold their possessions, gave the money to the poor and began living with Francis at the Portiuncula.

Downward mobility

The exaltation of poverty was not a new idea by the time of Francis. It began with Jesus, whom Francis liked to quote on the matter: 'None of you can become my disciple if you do not give up all your possessions' (Luke 14:33). Acquiring and caring for material possessions (which Jesus called 'mammon') distracts one from complete devotion to God. Hence Jesus' famous saying, 'You cannot serve God and mammon.'

This emphasis on poverty was muted, however, until the third and fourth centuries, when thousands of hermits, such as Antony of Egypt, sold their possessions and lived on bare essentials in order to give themselves fully to God. The monastic movements inspired by these early hermits – those of Basil in the East and Benedict in the West, among others – included poverty as one of their principal vows.

The fascination with poverty ebbed and flowed, but in the 11th and 12th centuries, a new wave of reformers began to yearn for the 'perfect life' of 'evangelical poverty'. They meant the life of poverty as practised by Christ and the early apostles.

This was partly a reaction to growing materialism. Towns flourished; a new class of merchants (such as Francis's father) were growing wealthy, and the gap between the wealthy and the poor was widening. Reforming monks and itinerant preachers spoke against greed and exploitation, especially against the rising practice of lending money out at interest – the sin of usury. Evangelical poverty was an act of penitence for such sins, as well as an attempt to imitate the life of Christ.

One day, while Bernard distributed the proceeds of the sale of some of his goods, a priest named Sylvester approached Francis. Francis had purchased stones from Sylvester, on credit, to repair San Damiano.

'You did not completely pay me for the stones which you bought from me!' Sylvester complained.

Francis immediately reached into Bernard's pocket and drew out a fistful of coins and handed them to Sylvester. 'Do you now have full payment, Lord Priest?'

An overjoyed Sylvester replied, 'I have it completely, brother,' and hurried home.

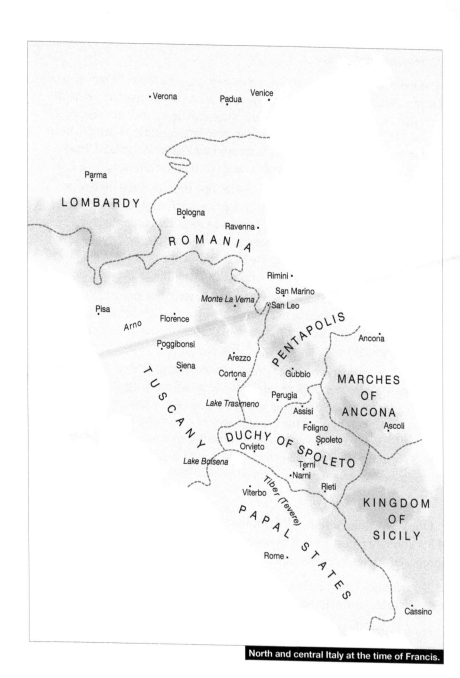

North and central Italy at the time of Francis.

But, over the next few days, Sylvester found that he could not live with himself. 'Am I not a miserable man?' he said to himself. 'Old as I am, don't I still covet and desire things of this world? And this young man despises and scorns them all for the love of God!'

He would continue to wrestle with himself like this for months before finally joining Francis.

Meanwhile, Francis, Bernard and Peter set up quarters in the dilapidated St Mary of the Angels, three kilometres below Assisi. This was where Francis had been mesmerized by the Gospel reading about poverty. The Benedictines who owned the grounds were happy to have guests to take care of the place. So the three built a little hut – a primitive affair of branches, sticks, reeds and clay – to live in while they worked on the chapel. A week later, a young farmer named Giles joined this new community. By late April in 1208, four small seeds of new life for the church had been sown.

> 'Throughout his life from now on Francis emanated an almost radioactive energy which seemed to derive from his sense of continuous proximity to God.'
>
> **Adrian House, *Francis of Assisi: A Revolutionary Life*, 2000**

Spreading out

Sometime during the next few weeks, Francis divided the group into two. He sent Bernard and Peter in one direction, while he and Giles set off for the Marches of Acona. Francis's ambition to do something glorious with his life was still very much part of him, but he was channelling that ambition to more noble ends. He told Giles, 'Our religion [meaning their way of life] will be like a fisherman who casts his nets into the water catching a great number of fish, and, leaving the small ones in the water, he puts the large ones into his basket.'

As they walked, Francis played the joyful troubadour of the Lord. He went about singing, as *The Legend of the Three Companions* records, 'with a loud and clear voice, in French, the praises of the Lord, blessing and glorifying the goodness of the most high'.

He encouraged listeners to fear and love God, and to do penance for their sins. Some hearers thought of Giles and Francis as fools or drunkards. Others reasoned, 'Either they cling to the Lord for the sake of the highest perfection, or they are demented for sure, because their life seems reckless. They use little food, walk barefoot, and wear wretched clothes.' Young women, startled by the brothers' seeming madness, ran when they saw them coming.

But when all four returned to the Portiuncula, four more men asked to join the band. With that, the people of Assisi become concerned. To have Francis and one or two men live an eccentric life at the edge of town was one thing. To be the centre of a growing movement, one that often came into town begging – well, that was another. They ignored the brothers when they begged for food and building supplies. They mocked them for ridding themselves of their possessions and living off others. Even their families called them senseless and stupid.

Bishop Guido, to whom Francis often went for advice, decided to intervene. His first response was to try to convince Francis to moderate his lifestyle. He should take on a few possessions so that his brothers would not have to beg so much. 'It seems to me that your life is very rough and hard,' the bishop explained, 'especially in not possessing anything in this world.'

'Lord, if we had possessions, we would need arms for our protection,' he replied. 'For disputes and lawsuits usually arise out of them, and, because of this, love of God and neighbour are greatly impeded. Therefore, we do not want to possess anything in this world.'

That Francis actually got away with this is surprising. It is a testimony to his winsomeness. He was making a jab at the bishop's lifestyle, but the bishop did not seem to mind.

Penance and forgiveness

During this period, Francis was stricken with another bout of conscience. He was assaulted by memories of the sins of his youth, his years of vanity and greed. He was filled with guilt and dread for his soul. He kept repeating the phrase, 'Lord, be merciful to me, a sinner.' But darkness and fear continued to engulf him.

One day, as he repeated the prayer, though, an 'indescribable joy and tremendous sweetness began to well up in his heart', writes Thomas of

Celano in *The Life of St Francis*. 'He began to lose himself. His feelings were pressed together, and that darkness disappeared.'

Suddenly, a new certainty about the forgiveness of his sins poured into him. He felt himself engulfed in light, and he saw much more clearly the future that lay before him. Thomas writes, 'He now seemed to be changed into another man.'

It was now autumn 1208, just a few months after Bernard and Peter had joined Francis. Francis was now emboldened to send the brothers out two by two to even more distant reaches. He told them to consider their mutual calling: 'To go throughout the world, encouraging everyone, more by deed than by word, to do penance for their sins and to recall the commandments of God.'

Despite the modern temptation to sentimentalize Francis and his mission, he did not send his brothers out, on this occasion or ever, to proclaim a saccharine message about God's love and the wonder of creation. In an early guide written during this period, Francis instructs his brothers to tell their listeners, 'Do penance, performing worthy fruits of penance, because we shall soon die . . . Blessed are those who die in penance for they shall be in the kingdom of heaven. Woe to those who do not die in penance, for they shall be children of the devil whose works they do and they shall go into everlasting fire.'

Francis warned his brothers about the hostility they were likely to meet, but told them that they were not to be afraid. It would not be long before 'many learned and noble men will come to us, and will be with us preaching to kings and rulers and great crowds'. Many would be converted, he concluded, adding confidently that God would 'multiply and increase his family throughout the entire world'.

He then blessed them and sent them out. He added one other point of instruction. Whenever they happened upon a cross or church, they were to pray, 'We adore you, Christ, and we bless you in all your churches throughout the whole world, because by your holy cross, you have redeemed the world.'

Again, the reception for the brothers was mixed. Their dress and way of life amazed people. They 'seemed almost like wild men', says *The Legend of the Three Companions*. Some received their message, and others mocked them. Others still asked where they came from, and which order they belonged to. They replied that they were penitents from Assisi and that, no, they were not an official order of the church.

At the end of each day, they sought lodging, but few people trusted them into their homes. They were forced to sleep in porticos in churches and homes. Since this mission was conducted in the autumn and winter, this meant some cold, sleepless nights.

One memorable exception was Bernard's and Giles's experience in Florence (on their way to St James of Compostela). At the end of a long day of preaching and begging, they came across a portico that had an oven. They received permission from woman of the house to sleep by the oven. When her husband found these strangers in the portico, he scolded his wife and called the men 'scoundrels and thieves'. Still, she managed to convince him that they could do no harm where they lay.

The next morning, Bernard and Giles went to church, as was their custom, and the wife secretly followed them. She watched them as they prayed with evident devotion, and then as a man offered, and they refused, alms. 'While it is true that we are poor, poverty is not burdensome for us,' said Bernard. 'For by the grace of God we have willingly made ourselves poor.' Now thoroughly convinced of their sincerity, the women rushed up and invited them to stay in her home – again to the dismay of her husband.

Still, more times than not, people abused them. Sometimes, angry crowds would strip the tunics off their backs. Since they had vowed, according to Jesus' command, to give to anyone who asked and to ask for nothing in return, and to go about with only one tunic, they were sometimes left semi-naked in the street. On top of that, and according to another command of Jesus, they prayed for their persecutors.

Slowly, people came to respect their gracious steadfastness in the face of abuse, their refusal to handle money, the patience with which they bore suffering (one story tells of how they left footprints of blood in the snow as they journeyed barefoot). And people could not get over the joy with which they carried themselves and preached their message. Some actually came up to them and asked forgiveness for mistreating them. Others came up and asked to join them.

Penance

Francis was not alone in highlighting penance. Many reform movements of the era, such as the *Humiliati* of Italy, were known as penitents, as were Francis and his followers.

Francis wanted his followers to practise both the sacrament and virtue of penance. In the sacrament (still practised today in Roman Catholicism), the penitent confessed his sins to a priest, received absolution and performed acts which satisfied the holy demands of the Law. This delivered the sinner from the temporal punishments due to sin (eternal punishments being remitted at absolution).

The virtue of penance was a heartfelt sorrow for sin, even the hating of one's sin, a necessary condition for the expiation of sin. But, in either case, it entailed concrete acts: prayers, fasting and sometimes self-flagellation. But it also meant such things as giving alms to the poor and reconciling oneself with one's enemies.

As the Middle Ages progressed, the practice of penance slipped into an exacting and oppressive legalism. But early on, most people thought of it as liberating. Theologically, every medieval Christian knew the utter holiness of God and the utter depravity of humankind. Human sin could hardly be atoned for by mere contrition and acts of satisfaction. The offence to God's perfection was too great. Yet God's mercy made forgiveness possible again. Because of Christ's sacrificial death on the cross, God commissioned the church to forgive sins through the sacrament of penance.

At times, Francis seemed caught between the two. Sometimes he saw penance as liberating; at other times, he seemed to use it as a legalist stick to keep his friars in order. It was a tension that neither he nor the Middle Ages ever resolved.

When they returned to the Portiuncula in early 1209, another four joined the band, bringing the total to a biblical 12. They felt that they were the Lord's disciples for a new era. Their enthusiasm for their way of life seemed to know no bounds.

One day as two of them walked along the road, a man began throwing stones at one of them. The other immediately put himself in the path of the stones to spare his brother.

If one happened to utter an annoying word to another, his conscience so troubled him that he could not rest until he admitted the fault. He would lay prostrate on the floor, asking the offended brother to place his foot over his mouth. If they saw a beggar and had nothing to give him, they would often tear off a portion of their own tunics and give them to the man.

They sought complete devotion to God, which meant in their minds a complete break with their families. They even avoided visiting areas where relatives lived, so that they could observe the prophetic psalm, 'I have become a stranger to my kindred, an alien to my mother's children' (Psalm 69:8).

Such acts were not the morbid gestures of the seriously self-righteous. They would never have attracted the numbers they eventually did. All this piety was imbued with a sense of joy at feeling that they had given themselves completely to a gracious and loving Lord.

As *The Legend of the Three Companions* puts it, 'They constantly rejoiced in the Lord, not having within themselves nor among themselves anything that could make them sad. For the more they were separated from the world, the more they were united to God. As they advanced on the way of the cross and the paths of justice, they cleared all hindrances from the narrow path of penance and of the observance of the gospel.'

CHAPTER 13

THE ORDER'S FOUNDING

Francis knew that if he was going to attract 'many learned and noble men' to preach to 'kings and rulers and great crowds', then he and his men would have to become more than a local affair – a new order would need to be founded. If his Lord was going to 'multiply and increase his family throughout the entire world', he would need the approval of the church – more particularly, of the pope, Innocent III.

> *'Beware of pride and vainglory. Let us guard ourselves from the wisdom of this world and the prudence of the flesh.'*
>
> **Francis, The Earlier Rule, 1209/10–21**

The mere thought of getting an audience with Pope Innocent III was ridiculous. Francis had sacrificed everything that would have made a positive impression on a man as sophisticated as Innocent, who, in a series of deft political and military moves, had become the most powerful man in Europe.

Innocent III had thwarted the Germans when they tried to wrest control of papal lands near Rome. The kings of Portugal, Aragon, Leon, Norway, Bohemia, Hungary and Bulgaria trembled at the political and moral pronouncements he directed at them. He subjected England to one of his interdicts, in which he denied the country the church's services and sacraments – and threatened King John with excommunication.

Then there was the oddity of the Fourth Crusade. Though sent off to recover Jerusalem, the Crusaders ended up sacking and pillaging the capital of Eastern Christendom, Constantinople. Innocent was appalled by the turn of events, but he ended up in control of the eastern half of the old Roman empire and the Eastern Orthodox Church.

Francis, the buoyant optimist, thought nothing impossible with God, and so he set off to Rome with his 11 companions. Francis insisted, as became his custom, that someone else lead the band for the journey, and Bernard was picked. The band stopped to pray frequently, and all along their journey they found people willing to give them food and shelter in the evenings.

Arrival in Rome

When they arrived in Rome, they went immediately to the piazza in front of the Lateran, the epicentre of Europe's spiritual power. They passed the equestrian statue of the one whom everyone thought was the first great friend of the church, Emperor Constantine (later historians concluded that it was actually of Marcus Aurelius, one of the church's earliest persecutors). To the left was the pope's palace, next to it was the city's first basilica, and on the right was an eight-sided baptistry. The brothers headed straight for the basilica, with its paintings, mosaics (notably that of Christ the redeemer) and the altar that everyone said contained relics of a table on which St Peter had said Mass.

Church versus state

The rule of Innocent III shows how the church fought morally and politically to control medieval society. Innocent was born Lotario di Segni, and ascended the throne of St Peter in 1198, at the age of 37. He immediately began extending the church's control over both secular and ecclesiastical spheres. First, Innocent gained power in Italy, wresting control from German princes, such as Count Conrad in Assisi. When the German emperor Henry IV died, and two aspirants (Otto IV and Philip of Swabia) vied for the throne, Innocent threw his weight first behind one and then behind the other, all the while asserting that although 'the German princes have the right to elect their king, who is afterwards to become emperor . . . The right to investigate and decide a king thus elected is worthy of imperial dignity belongs to the pope.'

Innocent strove to end hostilities between Christian princes and placed interdicts against any, such as Philip Augustus of France and Richard of England, who refused to put down their arms. He declared the Magna Carta null and void, mainly because it had been obtained by violence. He annulled royal marriages in Portugal, settled succession disputes in Norway and Hungary and prepared crusades against Moors in Spain and heretics in France. Power for Innocent III and most medieval popes, then, was mostly a means of asserting what they felt was Christ's rightful sovereignty over the whole world.

They then walked to the *logia* of the palace, past ancient bronze statues (among them, that of the founders of ancient Rome, Romulus and Remus, sucking from a she-wolf). Then providence or God smiled upon them again. They ran into Bishop Guido of Assisi.

The bishop was just as surprised as the brothers, but also perplexed. God forbid that Francis and his band were leaving Assisi. The bishop thought of them as spiritual assets to his diocese. He was relieved when he heard the reason for their visit. He then introduced them to a good friend, the cardinal bishop of Sabina, Lord John of St Paul. It was more than a fortunate contact.

The cardinal, a Roman aristocrat by birth, had risen in the Curia on the strength of his learning, spirituality and wisdom. He was not only Innocent's confessor; his special expertise was knowing the difference between theological idiosyncrasy and heresy.

The cardinal was immediately sympathetic to Francis. He himself had financed a hospital near the Vatican. Though he was responsible for maintaining tight control of public spending in Rome, he gave generously to the poor. After several days of questioning Francis, he agreed to represent him to the pope.

'I have found a most perfect man, who wishes to live according to the form of the holy gospel, and to observe evangelical perfection in all things,' he told Innocent and a group of cardinals. 'I believe that the Lord wills, through him, to reform the faith of the holy church throughout the world.'

This was no easy speech to make to this audience. Most of the cardinals did not appreciate Francis's implicit challenge to their luxurious lifestyle.

Church government

The Roman Catholic Church of the Middle Ages had become, in effect, another state on the European scene. The pope as head oversaw the Curia, a cabinet of cardinals, made up of archbishops, bishops, priests and deacons. The three main 'cabinet departments' were responsible for liturgy, correspondence and finances. Other cardinals oversaw matters of canon law, other still acted as the pope's legates on diplomatic missions. The pope even hired armies to wage war against sovereigns, such as Frederick II, who threatened papal lands.

A few of them had suffered the outrages of heretics, such as the Cathari, and they were in no mood to entertain a 'new teaching'. Nonetheless, Innocent asked to see Francis the next day.

Audience with the pope

Francis and his companions were escorted through the Lateran Palace, past the elegant dining hall, through the immense conference chamber and into the Hall of Mirrors. The 12 simple men in brown tunics found themselves facing the pope, judges and cardinals in caps or mitres, and robes of white, crimson or gold.

The contrast was in one way deceptive. Francis and Innocent III had a great deal in common. Both were musically inclined, had attractive voices and were capable of eloquence. They both had a sense of humour, as well. Innocent once joked that he regretted that his bishops were not always able to preach 'due to the surplus of their burdens, not to mention the deficit of their learning'.

Innocent was passionate about church reform and haunted by the possible demise of the church. Before Francis arrived, he had dreamed that the papal palace was on the verge of collapse, only held up by a small and shabbily dressed monk. This may have been a recurring dream; some said he had a similar dream during a visit of Dominic, the other great medieval reformer, years later.

> 'Francis's filial love for the Church of Rome remains one of the most striking aspects of his character. From his youth to the day he died, his fidelity to it never wavered.'
>
> **Julian Green, God's Fool, 1985**

As Francis pleaded his case for his new order, Innocent warmed to him. But he still had his doubts.

'My dear young sons, your life seems to us exceptionally hard and severe,' he finally replied. 'While we believe there can be no question about your living it because of your great zeal, we must take into consideration those who will come after you, lest this way of life seem too burdensome.'

Cardinal John of St Paul reminded the pope and the cardinals, 'If we refuse the request of this poor man as novel or too difficult, when all he

What did Francis look like?

Several thirteenth-century painters drew portraits of Francis, and many historians think that the portrait by Cimabue in the lower church of the Basilica San Francesco (Church of St Francis) in Assisi is likely to be the most faithful. He painted it sometime about 1265, just a few decades after Francis's death. Many who knew Francis would have still been alive to confirm the likeness. It also corresponds to the description given by Thomas of Celano, one of Francis's earliest biographers, in *The Life of St Francis*:

He was of medium height, closer to short [his skeletal remains confirm that he would have stood 160 centimetres tall]; his head was of medium size and round. His face was somewhat long and drawn, his forehead small and smooth, with medium eyes black and clear. His hair was dark; his eyebrows straight, and his nose even and thin; his ears small and upright, and his temples smooth . . . His teeth were white [a feature that those who exhumed his remains briefly in 1978 especially noted], well set and even, his lips were small and thin; his beard black and sparse; his neck was slender, his shoulders straight; his arms were short, his hands slight, his fingers long and his nails tapered. He had thin legs, small feet, fine skin and little flesh.

asks is to be allowed to lead the gospel life, we must be on our guard lest we commit an offence against Christ's gospel.'

He noted ironically that if anyone in the room was to argue that Francis's ideas were irrational or impossible, he would be saying that Christ's teaching on poverty were the same and would thus be 'guilty of blasphemy against Christ'.

But Innocent remained sceptical: 'My son, pray to Christ that through you he may show us his will, so that once we know it with more certainty, we may confidently approve your holy desire.'

So Francis and his companions took the next few days to pray. They attended Mass each day at one of the four principal basilicas in the city: St John Lateran, St Peter's, St Paul's (outside the walls) and Santa Maria Maggiore, dedicated to Christ's mother. While in prayer, or asleep one night, Francis had another of his visions. He described it to Innocent the next time they met:

There was a little, poor and beautiful woman in the desert, whose beauty fasci-
nated a great king. He wanted to take her as his wife, because he thought that
from her, he would have handsome sons. After the marriage was celebrated
and consummated, there were many sons born and raised.

Their mother spoke to them in this way: 'My sons, do not be ashamed, for
you are sons of the king. Therefore, go to his court and he will provide for all
your needs.'

When they went to see the king, he was struck by their good looks, and no-
ticing a resemblance to himself in them, he asked them, 'Whose sons are you?'

When they answered they were the sons of the little poor woman living in
the desert, the king embraced them with great joy. 'Do not be afraid,' he said,
'for you are my sons. If strangers are fed at my table, how much more will you,
who are my lawful sons.'

He then ordered the woman to send to his court all the children she had
borne to be fed.

Francis then explained to the pope, 'My lord, I am that little woman whom the loving Lord, in his mercy, has adorned, and through whom he has been pleased to give birth to legitimate sons. The King of kings had told me he will nourish all the sons born to me, because, if he feeds strangers, he must provide for his own.'

To this appeal, Francis added a number of assurances. In contrast to the reform movements that gave the Curia headaches, he would not teach new doctrine nor denigrate the church's sacraments. He would also respect clergy and bishops. The pope still hesitated, but he did give informal approval for Francis to live his life and 'preach penance to everyone'. He did not wish to commit too much to the enterprise – nothing, for example, was put down in writing – but he did invite Francis to return in a few years: 'When almighty God increases you in number and grace, come back to us; we will grant you more and entrust you with greater charge.'

The pope also required Francis to be ordained a deacon, entitling him to read the Gospels in church (though not to administer the sacraments). In addition, the pope required that Francis and his companions, like all religious, be tonsured, meaning that the crown of the head would be shaved at least once a month.

With that, Francis's new order headed back to Assisi, intent on changing the world. As they journeyed back, Francis came to understand another mysterious dream he had had during the trip. In it, a strong, thick tree towered above him. As he marvelled at its height and beauty, suddenly he himself grew immense, to the very height of the tree. When he touched it, the tree bent easily to the ground. Francis, with a mixture of satisfaction and pride, noted that the great and towering tree of the papacy had indeed bent to his wishes. He had become more powerful than any knight.

When the party returned, they made Rivo Torto ('crooked stream') their new home, about one and a half kilometres from the Portiuncula. They passed the autumn and winter of 1209 in an abandoned hut, barely large enough to hold them all. Francis had to write their names on the beams to mark each brother's place to pray and sleep.

Life was not easy. 'The place was so cramped that they could barely sit or rest,' says *The Legend of the Three Companions*. Sometimes their only meal was composed of the turnips they had begged for.

Yet, in *The Life of St Francis*, Thomas of Celano says that 'they . . . hardly ever stopped praying or praising God'. When they started to doze in prayer, they would prop themselves up with a stick to keep themselves awake. Some anchored themselves to the floor with ropes, so they would not toss and turn at night and disturb their neighbour who might be praying.

They were hardly perfect, however. Sometimes they ate or drank more than they believed was right. Sometimes fatigue tempted them away from their disciplines. Then remorse would set in, and they would punish their bodies to obey their highest desires.

They kept a holy silence most of the day, hardly speaking to one another; they did not want to be accused of idle chatter. They kept their gazes fixed to the ground so they would not be distracted from prayer by those around them.

Francis spoke with each of them daily about their spiritual state and, says Thomas, 'drove from their hearts any negligence'. He also examined himself, 'watchful of his guard at every hour'. And if any temptation struck him, Francis immediately plunged himself into a ditch filled

> 'Francis, above all, seemed [at Rivo Torto] to be filled with a new ardour, and, like a valiant knight, he burned to throw himself into the thick of the fray.'
>
> **Paul Sabatier, *Life of St Francis of Assisi*, 1905**

with ice water, remaining in it until 'every seduction of the flesh went away'.

Then one day a peasant barged into the hut, pushing his donkey ahead of him, saying, 'Go in, go in, because we will do well in this place.' An annoyed Francis turned to his brothers and said, 'I know, brothers, that God did not call us to prepare a lodging for a donkey, nor to have dealings with men.' With that, Francis and his brothers left. They stayed a short time with some lepers before getting permission from the Benedictines to use the Portiuncula as their home.

CHAPTER 14

THE EARLIER RULE

Over the next dozen years, Francis's order exploded in both numbers and geography. Twelve brothers living together outside of Assisi became an order, commonly called the Franciscans, whose thousands of members could be found from England to Africa, from Portugal to Hungary. This rapid growth left none of the brothers time to chronicle events in these years. Because of this, many incidents in the early biographies pile one on top of the other, eluding historians' ability to pin them down as to date or even sequence.

Even the Rule informally approved by the pope was under constant revision during these years. It was an informal guide when they left the pope's presence in 1209, but a formal document by Pentecost in 1221, when it took the official form we now call the Earlier Rule.

In spite of some historical riddles, a close look at the Earlier Rule (or the Rule, for the remainder of this chapter) reveals the essence of Francis's vision. It also hints at what it was that inspired men, and soon women, all across Europe to cast in their lots with his seemingly strange regimen.

Obedience

The Rule says, 'The rule and life of these brothers is this: namely to live in obedience, in chastity, and without anything of their own, and to follow teaching and footprints of our Lord Jesus Christ.' Though Francis would become famous as a champion of poverty, the vow of obedience came first for him.

Obedience was first for the brothers as well as for Francis himself, as the Rule says: 'Brother Francis – and whoever is head of this religion [that is, religious order] – promises obedience and reverence to the Lord Pope Innocent and his successors.' But it applied to all: 'Let all the brothers be bound to obey Brother Francis and his successors.' So important was obedience that the Franciscan life itself is sometimes summed up in this one word, for example, when the Rule speaks of new members being 'received into obedience'.

This was not a mindless obedience: 'If any one of the ministers [a brother in authority] commands one of the brothers something contrary to our life or his soul, he is not bound to obey him because obedience is not something in which a fault or sin is committed.' But other than that exception, Francis expected prompt obedience on all occasions: 'Carry out an order at once,' he told the brothers, 'and don't wait for it to be repeated. Don't plead or object that anything in a command is impossible.'

On this point, Francis often became exasperated with his brothers. One day he blurted out, 'There is hardly a single religious in the whole world who obeys his superior well!'

The brothers with him were alarmed, and they asked, 'Tell us, Father, what is the perfect and best form of obedience?'

'Take up a dead body', he replied, 'and lay it where you will. You will see that it does not resist being moved, or complain . . . or ask to be left alone!'

Obedience for Francis was the foundation of humility, the cardinal virtue of a Franciscan brother. Thus, whenever Francis embarked on a trip, he always appointed another brother to be in charge so that he, Francis, could practise obedience as well. Francis abolished the title of 'prior' and settled on 'minister' or even 'servant' for those in authority in the order. And the brothers, no matter their title, were to wash one another's feet, and if a brother hurt or provoked another, he must kiss the foot of the offended brother in apology.

Obedience was not passive or something a superior could demand autocratically, but something the brothers offered one another as a gift: 'Let no brother do or say anything evil to another; on the contrary, through the charity of the Spirit, let them serve and obey one another voluntarily. This is the true and holy obedience of our Lord Jesus Christ.'

Along with submission came another duty: the brothers held each other and their superiors accountable. They were to admonish them 'if they see any of them walking according to the flesh and not according to the Spirit in keeping with the integrity of our life'.

Watching out for each other's sins, Francis recognized, could easily tempt the brothers to self-righteousness. Thus, the Rule added that both ministers and brothers should 'be careful not to be disturbed or angered at another's sin or evil, because the devil wishes to destroy many because of another's fault'. Monitoring another's spiritual life was to be an act of concern so that all would grow in spiritual maturity. It was not to be a game of 'Gotcha!'

Furthermore, Francis encouraged his brothers to go to one another for help and guidance: 'Let each one confidently make known his need to another that the other might discover what is needed and minister to him.' This rule may have arisen because the early brothers were striving heroically, but often silently, about their spiritual struggles. But, as Francis reminded the brothers, they should be able to count on one another's compassion: 'Let each one love and care for his brother as a mother loves and cares for her son in those matters in which God has given him grace.'

Francis illustrated this early on, while the brothers were still at Rivo Torto. They were in the middle of a particularly severe fast when, one night around midnight, one of the brothers cried out, 'I'm dying! I'm dying!' The other brothers woke up, startled and frightened.

'Brothers, get up and light a lamp,' ordered Francis. When the lamp was lit, he asked, 'Who was it who said, "I'm dying"?'

After the brother, probably sheepishly, identified himself, Francis asked, 'What's the matter, brother? Why are you dying?'

'I'm dying of hunger,' he said.

Francis immediately ordered that the table be set, and they all ate a meal together with the brother. When they were done eating, Francis said, 'My brothers, I say that each of you must consider his own constitution, because, although one of you may be sustained with less food than another, I still do not want one who needs more food to try imitating him in this . . . Just as we must beware of overindulgence in eating, which harms body and soul, so we must beware of excessive abstinence even more, because the Lord desires mercy not sacrifice.'

Francis tempered his demand for obedience, then, with mercy.

Worship and work

In popular imagination, Francis and his brothers were carefree nature lovers who wandered the countryside picking flowers, singing with the birds and composing poems extolling the wonders of nature. The brothers actually had little time for such frivolities, as they would call them. Rather than selfishly basking in a sunny meadow, they went about giving themselves completely to God and to others.

They conceived of their main work as prayer, and not a spontaneous, carefree prayer, but the regular prayers prescribed by the church: 'Let all the brothers, whether clerical or lay, recite the Divine Office, the praises and prayers, as is required of them,' says the Rule. This liturgy, also called the Daily Office, consisted of seven services of prayer each day (known as the Hours), called Matins, Prime, Terce, Sext, None, Vespers and Compline. In addition to the church's requirements for these services, Francis added his own: 'Let the lay brothers say the [Apostles'] Creed and 24 Our Fathers with the Glory to the Father for Matins . . . for Prime, the Creed and seven Our Fathers with the Glory to the Father . . .' and so on for each service. In addition, the brothers read Bible passages in each service, so that all 150 Psalms were said each week and the entire Bible was read every 12 months.

Francis composed prayers of his own for each of the services, in a cycle sometimes called *The Office of the Passion*. He had the brothers not only read, but also memorize these.

These formal prayers did not result in a merely formal relationship with the divine. The brothers experienced many moments of mystical rapture. One night, while Francis was away praying in the Assisi cathedral, one of the brothers, who himself was praying alone late into the night, suddenly saw a chariot sweeping back and forth around the rafters of their small hut. He watched in amazement, and then woke the brothers, who said they also saw it. They all interpreted it to be the soul of Francis at prayer.

Another time, Bishop Guido made a call on Francis while Francis prayed in his cell. When Bishop Guido tried to open the cell door and stick his head inside, he was met by an inexplicable force: 'All of a sudden,' says *The Assisi Compilation*, an early collection of stories about

Dominic's new order

Francis was not the only visionary who was trying to change the world by founding a new order. Another was Dominic (1170–1221).

When he was Bishop Domingo de Guzman, Dominic took a mission through southern France to convert the Cathari in Languedoc. On this trip, the bishop was shocked to meet members of the Cistercian Order who, in also trying to convert the ascetic Cathari, were trying to impress them with their horses, regalia, fancy robes and fine food. 'The heretics are to be converted by an example of humility . . . far more readily than by any external display or verbal battles,' he said. 'So let us arm ourselves with devout prayers and set off showing signs of genuine humility and barefooted to combat Goliath.'

This was the germ idea from which the Dominican Order eventually emerged. Besides embracing poverty, the Blackfriars (as they came to be known, from the colour of their cloaks) specialized in preaching and teaching to refute heretical arguments. With papal approval in 1215, their official name became the Order of Preachers.

This twofold approach of humility and persuasiveness convinced many a heretic to convert – but not enough, apparently. The Dominicans eventually agreed with the papacy that the church could defeat heresy only if it also applied political and social pressure as well, so they became key players in the Inquisition in the coming centuries.

After Dominic's death and subsequent canonization (1234), the order continued to grow rapidly, counting 12,000 followers within a century. They attracted not only the great souls of the era, such as the mystic Catherine of Siena, but also the greatest minds, such as that of Thomas Aquinas. Together with the Franciscans, says historian Adrian House in *Francis of Assisi: A Revolutionary Life*, they were 'the most distinctive and original force for good in medieval Europe'.

Francis, 'by the will of the Lord . . . he was forcefully pushed outside, willy-nilly, stumbling backwards.' The brothers chalked it up to be the spiritual force of Francis's prayer life.

It is hard to know how to take such stories, since they border on the mythical. In any event, they are not central to Franciscan spirituality. Francis never told his brothers to seek mystical moments and, as much as he exalted prayer, he wanted more than prayer from the brothers: 'Let all the brothers always strive to exert themselves in doing good works, for it is written, "Always do something good that the devil may find you occupied."' And again, '"Idleness is an enemy of the soul." Servants of God, therefore, must always apply themselves to prayer or some good work.' Thus, we find the brothers, when not in prayer or worship, visiting lepers, planting, threshing, nursing families with smallpox or dysentery and so on.

> 'Let them [the brothers] be careful not to appear outwardly as sad and gloomy hypocrites but show themselves joyful, cheerful, and consistently gracious in the Lord.'
>
> **Francis, The Earlier Rule, 1209/10–21**

Poverty

The incident when the man and donkey burst into the brothers' hut at Rivo Torto may have been the occasion for Francis's penning of another key sentence in his Rule: 'Wherever the brothers may be, either in hermitages or other places, let them be careful not to make any place their own or contend with anyone for it. Whoever comes to them, friend or foe, thief or robber, let him be received with kindness.'

> 'Francis was not a systematic theologian articulating an explicit, developed doctrine of poverty. He preferred acting out the truth to stating it in bald words.'
>
> **William S. Stafford, Virginia Theological Seminary, Christian History Magazine, 1994**

Francis is famous for embracing poverty at any cost, and rightly so. It went hand in hand with the humility that Francis wanted to instil in himself and his brothers. It was also a way of transforming a world that seemed to know only the rule of acquisition at any cost.

In a hermitage north of Borgo San Sepulcro, some thieves would regularly come and ask the brothers for bread. The brothers knew very well who these men were because their reputation for highway robbery was widespread. Soon, the brothers began to question their generosity: 'It's wrong to give them alms,' they reasoned, 'for they are robbers who inflict all sorts of evil on people.' When Francis made one of his regular visits to them, they asked him what they should do.

Francis, as usual, turned the tables on them. He told them not to wait for the thieves to come to them, but to prepare a meal, then go to find the robbers and invite them to eat: 'Spread out a tablecloth on the ground, put the bread and wine on it, and serve them with humility and good humour.' Once the robbers were in a good mood, they were to ask them one favour: 'Make them promise you not to strike any man and not to harm anyone.'

After that, Francis told them to prepare another meal, and then another and so on. At each meal, the brothers were to ask the robbers to give up one more piece of their trade. The story goes that the robbers slowly gave up their ways and converted to Francis's order.

Such generosity arose from their complete freedom from possessions. Not only did the brothers relinquish all rights to individual ownership of any item, the Rule forbade the order itself from owning land or buildings. Wherever they lived or stayed, they depended on the invitation and hospitality – and whims – of others. If it was not hard enough to conceive of sustaining a growing order with this restriction, Francis added one more: 'Let none of the brothers . . . wherever he may be or go, carry, receive, or have received in any way coin or money, whether for clothing, books, or payment for work.'

If a brother was sick, or a leper needed immediate medical attention, Francis permitted begging for money to pay for a doctor or medicine. But other than that, the brothers were never to touch money. They were not even to be seen with a beggar who asked for money.

Francis saved some of his strongest language for offenders of this rule: 'If by chance, God forbid, it happens that some brother is collecting or holding coin or money . . . let all the brothers consider him a deceptive brother, an apostate, a thief, a robber.'

He also saved some of his harshest disciplines for those who broke this rule. According to The Assisi Compilation, one day a layman happened to enter St Mary of the Portiuncula to pray and, as an offering, he laid some money near the cross. After he left, a brother unthinkingly picked the money up and placed it on a window ledge. When the brother heard that Francis had learned of the incident, he immediately rushed to Francis and implored his forgiveness. He even offered his body, saying Francis should whip him for penance. Francis, however, was not so easily placated; he had a better idea. After rebuking the brother sternly, he ordered him to go to the window sill, pick up the money with his mouth and carry it

On loan from on high

Something of Francis's reasoning about possessions comes through in one story told by Thomas of Celano. Francis was returning from Siena with a companion when a poor man, barely clothed, approached them. 'Brother,' Francis said to his companion, 'we must give back to this poor man the mantle that is his. We accepted it on loan until we should happen to find someone poorer than we are.'

The companion vehemently disagreed, saying that Francis should not expose himself to the elements to help this poor man. But Francis would have none of it, and ended up giving away his mantle. Francis thought that everything he possessed was merely on loan from God and, as such, he needed to give it away if another had more need of it than he did.

outside. Then, again with his mouth, he was to deposit it on a heap of ass's dung. The brother obeyed gladly.

Francis believed that money was like a drug, as addictive and destructive to the soul as we today believe heroin or cocaine is to the body. For Francis, money was not something one could use moderately or 'recreationally' without it eventually enslaving the soul. He took literally Jesus' statement that one cannot serve God and mammon, as well as the command to give away one's coat if asked for it.

Stories of Francis giving things away, especially his mantel, abound in the early biographies. One winter's day, an old woman approached Francis and his companion while they were staying at the bishop's palace in Celano. She asked for alms, but Francis merely took the cloth that was wrapped around his neck to keep him warm and gave it to her, saying, 'Go and make yourself a tunic; you really need it.' The old woman thought it was a joke and laughed. But when Francis just stood there extending the wrap to her, she suddenly grabbed it and ran off. As she was cutting it up to make it into a tunic, she soon realized that she would be short of cloth. So she returned to Francis and told him of her problem. Francis then turned to his companion and said, 'Brother, do you hear what this old woman is saying? For the love of God, let us bear with the cold!' With that, Francis and the brother gave the woman their cloaks, and both of them were left standing in their underwear.

Chastity

Chastity was, of course, another cardinal feature of the brothers' life, as it had been of all the orders of the Roman Catholic Church for 1,000 years. But Francis was after more than formal chastity. Again, the ultimate goal was freedom – in this case, freedom from a passion that, as much as any other, has the ability to consume and distract people from more virtuous pursuits.

So the brothers worked at this long before they ever put themselves in a position to physically break their vows: 'Wherever they may be or may go, let all the brothers avoid evil glances and associations with women. No one may counsel them, travel alone with them or eat out of the same dish with them.' This was not because women were evil but because,

Francis's temptations

Francis readily admitted that he was tempted by the very things he warned his brothers about.

As his notoriety increased, Francis tried to keep his humility and wits about him. When people tried to touch his garments in veneration, he told them not to canonize him too soon, adding that a 'saint' such as him might still fall into temptation, and 'bring sons and daughters into this world'.

In spite of his spiritual advancements – and maybe because of them – he still found himself battling against what Thomas of Celano, in *The Remembrance of the Desire of a Soul*, called 'a violent temptation to lust'. One winter's day, while he prayed at a hillside hermitage at Sarteano, he suffered an especially severe bout. So he took off all his clothes, and 'lashed himself furiously' with a whip; he addressed his body as 'Brother Ass' and scolded it for its lustful passions.

When that seemed to have no effect, he went out to the garden and threw himself naked onto the snow. He then made seven snowmen, and went on to lecture himself: 'Here, this large one is your wife, and those four over there are your two sons and your two daughters; the other two are your servant and your maid, who are needed to serve them. So hurry, get all of them some clothes, because they're freezing to death! But if complicated care of them is annoying, then take care to serve one Master!'

human nature being what it is, one thing leads to another. If one wants complete freedom in anything, it is best to begin at the source.

However, as the history of asceticism shows, this freedom is hard to win, and Francis's brothers found it no easier than have aspirants of any era. At Rivo Torto, for example, while the brothers experienced extraordinary moments of mystical elation, lust remained a frequent and disturbing temptation. Their regular antidote was to jump into a ditch of icy water in winter, or scourge themselves in summer – the medieval version of the cold shower.

Catholics through and through

'Let all the brothers live and speak as Catholics,' says the Rule. Faithfulness to things Catholic was the decisive test of loyalty for Francis: 'If someone has strayed in word or in deed from Catholic faith and life and has not amended his way, let him be expelled from our brotherhood.'

It was not just a matter of loyalty and respect, but of obedience to something larger than themselves: 'Let us consider all clerics and religious as our masters in all that pertains to the salvation of our soul and does not deviate from our religion.' This was not merely politic – a way of fending off charges of heresy or schism. More than anything, it was another means of instilling humility.

Francis was not blind. He did not fail to see the rank corruption that infected the church, high and low. He was, after all, on a mission to reform the church. He knew that the priests had concubines, that bishops greedily accumulated land, that archbishops lived lives of luxury and that popes loved power. Still, he told his brothers that when they met a priest, no matter his reputation, they were to bow and kiss his hand, and if he was mounted, they were also to kiss the hooves of his horse. For one, priests administered the eucharist, which brought Christ tangibly to the people. For another, any reasonable person could honour those who deserve honour. But only a humble person could do what Francis asked of his brothers.

'If they obstruct the salvation of the people,' he explained, 'vengeance belongs to God, and he will punish them in his own time . . . If you are sons of peace, you will win both clergy and people, and this will be more pleasing to God than if you were to win the people alone and alienate the clergy. Conceal their mistakes and make up for their many defects; and when you have done this, be even more humble than before.'

> 'Let everyone be struck with fear, let the whole world tremble, and let the heavens exult when Christ, the Son of the living God, is present on the altar in the hands of a priest!'
>
> **Francis, *A Letter to the Entire Order*, 1225–26**

From start to finish, then, the Rule nourished humility. But it was not humility for humility's sake. Humility was the highest virtue for Francis because, more than any other virtue, it prepared the soul to receive and praise God.

The Rule was a tool designed to quash any human affection that stood in the way of God. This is why Francis said, 'Let us hate our body with its vices and sins, because by living in the flesh, the devil wishes to take away from us the love of Jesus Christ and eternal life.' Talk of 'hating the body' was common in the Middle Ages, and it unfortunately encouraged a great deal of self-abuse: people whipping themselves, fasting excessively and so on. Even Francis was guilty of this, and his own bodily abuse led to his relatively early death at the age of 46. But what the medieval world grasped rightly in all this was the truth that the body, with its ravenous desires for food, sleep, leisure and sex, often undermines complete devotion to God.

To be fair, Francis and most medieval spiritual counsellors were not dualists. The body needed discipline, yes, but it was not itself the source of evil. Quoting freely from Jesus, Francis wrote in the Rule, 'From the heart proceed and come evil thoughts, adultery, fornication, murder, theft, greed, malice, deceit, licentiousness, envy, false witness, blasphemy, foolishness.' He concluded, 'All these evils come from within a person's heart, and these are what defile a person.'

Obedience, poverty, chastity, prayer, loyalty and all the rest were means by which his brothers could atone for their defilement, conquer temptation and give themselves completely to God. At the end of the Rule, Francis appended an extended, poetic exhortation that sums up what every line of the Rule is about:

Therefore,
*   let us desire nothing else,*
*   let us want nothing else,*

let nothing else please us and cause us delight except our
Creator, Redeemer, and Saviour,
the only true God,
Who is the fullness of good,
All good, every good, the true and supreme good,
Who alone is good,
Merciful, gentle, delightful, and sweet,
Who alone is holy,
Just, true, holy, and upright,
Who alone is kind, innocent, clean,
From whom, through whom, and in whom
Is all pardon, all grace, all glory
Of all penitents and just ones,
Of all the blessed rejoicing together in heaven.

CHAPTER 15

CLARE

Once people began to believe that Francis had a special relationship with God, the order began to grow. It was not so unusual any more for men of some standing to seek Francis out. Young men such as Masseo di Massignano, who came from one of the better families in the area, was one example. He was proverbially tall, dark and handsome, and a dynamic public speaker as well. He also had the necessary arrogance found in every successful politician, which is why everyone said that his political future looked bright. Instead, he decided that success meant a life of humility and poverty in obedience to Francis.

A second convert, Rufino di Scipione came from one of Assisi's most powerful and controversial families. He had joined the order after watching a violent quarrel between two Franciscan brothers. (This is evidence that Francis's brothers were, in spite of their discipline and piety, still very human.) Just as the two were about to come to blows, Brother Barbaro, who had been the more aggressive, suddenly bent down, grabbed some dung lying on the ground and shoved it into his mouth. This symbolized what he thought of the harsh words that had spewed from his own mouth. He then apologized to his companion. This act of humility won over Rufino immediately.

A third key recruit at this time was Leo, a priest from Assisi. He soon became Francis's confessor, secretary and almost constant companion. (Later, Leo joined Rufino and Angelo [Francis's 12th recruit] in writing two documents – *The Assisi Compilation* and *The Legend of the Three Companions* – which give us valuable information about Francis.) But it was not just men who were drawn to Francis during these exciting years.

A female follower

Given the station that she had been born into, Clare di Favarone should have lived a peaceful and sheltered life. As it turned out, the best known of Francis's female disciples grew up knowing violence and terror. As a child, she lived with her parents and sisters in a *palazzo* they shared

The Third Order

Not everyone taken with Francis could abandon family and vocation to follow him. So Francis, recognizing their situation, outlined in his document *A Letter to the Faithful* how they might live. This became the basis for the Rule of the Third Order, which Cardinal Ugolino approved in 1221.

Tertiaries, as they were called, were to dress modestly, and to avoid banquets and dances. They were to eat but two meals a day and to fast every Friday (and some Wednesdays). They were each to give away 10 per cent of their income, pay off their debts and make restitution for any goods they had unjustly gained. They were to observe all the hours of the daily office and, if they could not, they were to say 54 'Our Fathers' and 'Glory Be to the Fathers'. They were supposed to examine their consciences every night, confess their sins and receive the eucharist three times a year. Once a month, they were to meet with other tertiaries to worship together.

Three features, in particular, made the Third Order a potent force for social change. First, tertiaries were to will their estate to the poor or to the church. This created a significant social welfare system. Second, they were forbidden from carrying arms. This cut down on the incessant violence of the era. Third, they were only permitted to makes oaths to God or to the pope. This freed the tertiary from many feudal obligations, for since he had given his allegiance to the pope, he was now subject not to secular courts, but to church courts. The popes used this allegiance to thwart the aggression of the Holy Roman Empire; instead of serving the emperor in battle, the tertiaries could serve the Church. Overall, this vow helped to bring more peace to an era characterized by incessant 'gang warfare'.

We do not know the numbers of men and women who committed themselves to the Third Order, but the order has had among its ranks some of history's most influential people, including many popes, King Louis IX (St Louis), Michelangelo and Christopher Columbus.

with the rest of their extended family on the San Rufino Piazza. She was four years old when angry Assisians destroyed Duke Conrad's castle and then, one by one, began attacking the homes of Assisi's wealthy and powerful people. Her family escaped to rival Perugia until things settled down.

Clare's father, Favarone di Offreduccio, was a knight. Her aristocratic mother, Ortolana, was a woman with a deep religious devotion. She made many pilgrimages to Rome, one to Mount Gargano on the Apulia coast (where Michael the Archangel was said to have visited) and one to Jerusalem – a journey considered dangerous even for a man. After she felt she had sufficiently atoned for her sins, she settled down with her husband and bore him Clare (in 1193 or 1194), then Catherine (in 1197) and finally Beatrice (in 1205).

Clare adopted her mother's piety early on. Clare's spiritual hero was the Roman martyr St Agnes, whose refusals to give up her virginity, no matter the cost, proved her devotion to Christ. The traditional story goes that Agnes' parents became so angry at her refusal to entertain suitors that they sent her to a brothel. But God protected Agnes's sexual modesty, growing her hair miraculously long so that her body could not be seen, and protecting her from the flames when she was put to the stake. It took a beheading to kill her, the legend says.

Clare said more than her share of prayers, dressed modestly, and saved food from her meals and gave them to her friend, Bona, to distribute to the needy. From time to time, she also asked Bona to take food to the Portiuncula, where her childhood friends Angelo and Rufino were members of the order that Francis Bernadone had started.

Most Assisians thought Francis a fanatic and, perhaps for that very reason, the 16-year-old Clare was curious. One Sunday, she went to hear him preach at the cathedral, and she was henceforth smitten with his devotion and passion. She wanted to know more, but she knew that her parents would forbid her from talking with the outcast. So, one evening, she sneaked off with her six-year-old sister Beatrice and Bona to meet secretly with Francis, then aged 29, and one of his friends. Soon enough, she felt a call to do something with her life that she knew her family would not approve of.

At about this time, Clare came into some money. Her father had died and left her dowry to her. The pressure on her to marry intensified – she was, after all, a good catch: well-educated (at home, anyway) and well-connected – a marriage that would bring many tangible benefits to the Offreduccios. But Clare managed to stall the suitors with whom her family set her up. When she turned 18, she announced that she was going to give away her money to the poor.

Her uncle Monaldo, the head of the family, was stunned. He pleaded with her to change her mind. So did a neighbour, Ranieri di Bernardo, who even proposed to her. Clare would have none of it.

Then, on the night of Palm Sunday in 1212, as her mother, uncles and cousins slept, Clare slipped silently down the stairs of the *palazzo*, turned away from the main door guarded by a man-at-arms, and quietly removed the pile of rocks and the heavy beams that blocked a back door. She forced it open and slipped away via a back lane. She met up with Pacifica, one of her mother's lifelong companions, and her cousin Rufino, who guided them to the Portiuncula.

> 'Never was there a closer and more harmonious union than that existing between St Clare and St Francis. Never were two souls in more perfect accord in their way of looking at things of earth and heaven.'
>
> **Omar Englebert, St Francis of Assisi: A Biography, 1965**

Francis and a few companions were waiting with torches when Clare arrived. They escorted her into the church, where she made her confession and received absolution from Sylvester, a priest who now followed Francis. She took off the beautiful dress she had been wearing since morning services, and put on a simple habit. Then she made her vows ('I promised him obedience,' she wrote years later in her *Testament*). To seal the vows, Francis cut her pale, almost gold hair in the form of a tonsure.

Francis, Clare and all present rejoiced, but only for the moment. They were still in danger, so Clare was hurried off to nearby St Paul's (San Paulo), a Benedictine convent protected personally by the pope. Francis felt that she would be safe there from any legal or physical assaults of her family. It turned out that Clare needed more than ecclesiastical protection.

Monaldo led seven Offreduccios by horseback to St Paul's and forced their way inside the convent. Monaldo demanded that Clare return home. She refused. This scenario was repeated several times over the next few days, with Monaldo alternating threats with bribes, all to no avail. One day, Monaldo and his party cornered Clare in a chapel and lunged at her. She grasped the altar as they tried to pull her away. Clare's head-covering fell to the floor, and they all gasped. The aggressors saw that she had been tonsured, that she had already taken the crucial symbolic step of a cloistered life. They abandoned their quest and went on their way.

A little later, Catherine, Clare's now 16-year-old sister, fled home and joined Clare, and Monaldo led a party of 11 men to rescue her. Again, he pleaded and threatened and, again, lost his patience. One of the knights rushed up to Catherine, and tried to slap and kick her into submission. He grabbed her hair while others tried to grab her flailing arms to carry her.

She was dragged down a hill and over a muddy path. Bushes tore at her clothes, and her hair came out in tufts as she fought. The story goes that, at just this moment, a helpless Clare, who had been witnessing the horrid scene, dropped to her knees in prayer. Suddenly, the armed guard – perhaps exhausted from the struggle, perhaps ashamed of having abused Catherine into near-unconsciousness, perhaps merely prompted by divine command – abandoned her.

In the early days, it was not easy becoming a Franciscan! At any rate, eventually the family left Clare and Catherine alone. In fact, Pacifica, the 40-year-old friend of Clare's mother, joined the girls and, later, so did Clare's sister Beatrice. Catherine eventually changed her name to Agnes, who was her hero as well. Francis arranged it so these women could stay permanently at San Damiano, and he gave them his official blessing and support in a brief letter to Clare: 'Since by divine inspiration you have made yourselves daughters and servants of the most high King, the heavenly Father, and have taken the Holy Spirit as your spouse, choosing to live according to the perfection of the holy gospel, I resolve and promise for myself and for my brothers always to have that same loving care and special solicitude for you as [I have] for them.'

The Poor Ladies

In this way, a new order was born. They called themselves the Poor Ladies (today they are known as the Poor Clares). Within a few years, Clare had 50 sisters at San Damiano, many of the women having come from the better families in the region.

Francis's brothers begged food for them, supplied them with firewood and built them extra rooms when their numbers expanded. The women dressed simply, worked with their hands (for example, producing altar linens for local churches) and prayed and fasted like the Franciscan brothers. Clare, like Francis, fasted so severely that she often became ill. When Francis heard of one bout of illness brought on by fasting, he ordered that, from then on, she was not to go for 24 hours without at least a little food.

Like the brothers, the sisters prayed together several times a day in the chapel, and gave regular confessions to Leo and Sylvester, who also celebrated Mass for them. Clare prayed even more hours, before the others had even risen for the day and after all had drifted off into sleep. The sister noted that she often cried as she meditated on the crucifixion of Christ. The slightest word could transport her into mystical ecstasy. One Sunday, she was so struck by one antiphon that she spent the rest of the day sprinkling her companions with holy water to remind them of the water that flowed from Jesus' side.

Clare insisted on calling the Poor Ladies sisters, rather than nuns, for she believed that they shared equally in the work and worship of the order. She was just 21 years old when church authorities insisted that she

Staving off an army

Many artists have depicted Clare's most legendary miracle, which many scholars conclude occurred on a Friday in September 1240. The imperial army, composed of mercenary Saracens that Frederick II had hired, had invaded central Italy, 'burning cities, cutting down trees, laying waste vineyards, and torturing women and children', according to the *Legend of St Clare* (1255). And they showed no restraint when they fought the pope's armies, and displayed even less respect for any nuns who fell into their hands.

Assisi found itself in the middle of this war and, on this Friday, some imperial soldiers began scaling the walls of San Damiano, intent on entering the cloister. In desperation, Clare grabbed the sacrament and marched towards the invaders, praying, 'Lord Jesus, do not permit these defenceless virgins to fall into the hands of these heathen. Protect them. For I, who have nourished them with your love, can do nothing for them.' She prayed like this for the city of Assisi as well.

'Immediately,' says the *Legend of St Clare*, 'the boldness of those dogs was changed into fear and they quickly clambered over the walls they had scaled.' This was one of the miracles described to authorities during Clare's canonization hearings.

accept the role of abbess in the community. She agreed reluctantly, but she never used the title during her 40 years of service.

Clare was as ascetically heroic as her mentor. To discipline her flesh, she slept on boards and, when she was not fasting, she refused to eat cooked food. (As she got older, she realized the need to temper such asceticism, as she wrote to her sister Agnes in 1229: 'Our flesh is not of bronze, nor is our strength that of stone. So I urge you to be less strenuous in your fasting, so as to render reasonable worship to the Lord.') Clare also fetched water for sisters who were too ill to get out of bed, and washed the mattresses of the sick ('not running away from their filth nor shrinking from their stench', says one account). She even washed and kissed the feet of her sisters as a sign of her respect.

> '*Place your mind before the mirror of eternity! Place your soul in the brilliance of glory! Place your heart in the figure of divine substance! And transform your whole being into the image of the Godhead itself through contemplation.*'
>
> **Clare of Assisi, third letter to Agnes of Prague, 1238**

As Clare's reputation for sanctity spread, so did the belief in her ability to perform cures and other miracles. Francis, for example, sent brother Stephen to her when he thought that Stephen was suffering from some form of madness. Clare made the sign of the cross over Stephen (as she did to everyone who came to her), and then told him to go to sleep in the place where she normally prayed. The story goes that the next morning, when he arose, he was in his right mind, and he returned to Francis immediately.

In spite of her good works and efficacious prayers, Clare could not get official recognition of her order. The sticking point for each papal administration was her wish that her order should not own property, but simply rent or live off the goodwill of those who did own property. For Clare, this went to the very heart of what she and Francis were about. The forsaking of possessions was required not only of individuals, but of the whole order.

Clare, like Francis, sought to emulate Jesus. In her *Testament*, written at the end of her life, she exhorted her sisters to always observe poverty: 'out of love of the God who was placed poor in the crib, lived poor in the world, and remained naked on the cross'. Physical poverty, however, was merely a means of attaining poverty of spirit, which was necessary to make room for Jesus within.

In this, she saw the Virgin Mary as the prime model. As she told Agnes, 'As the glorious Virgin of virgins carried him materially, so you, too, by following her footprints, especially those of poverty and humility, can without any doubt, always carry him spiritually in your chaste and virginal body, holding him by whom all things are held together.'

> 'O God-centred poverty, whom the Lord Jesus Christ, who ruled and now rules heaven and earth . . . condescended to embrace before all else.'
>
> **Clare of Assisi, first letter to Agnes of Prague, 1234**

Papal officials who, in this case, seemed to understand human nature better than Clare, insisted that severe poverty and relinquishing ownership was unrealistic and would eventually sabotage the order. In 1218, when papal legate Cardinal Ugolino approved a rule for the Poor Sisters, it lacked the provision about forsaking ownership. Clare protested, but Ugolino would not budge. This tug of war over poverty continued for the rest of Clare's life. But on her deathbed, in August 1253, a messenger told her that the pope had approved her rule, which included the provision she had long fought for – the first approved rule written by a woman.

Clare and Francis

Clare's own achievements were many, and her relationship with Francis was one of the most spiritually intimate between a man and a woman. *The Little Flowers of St Francis*, a collection of stories about Francis edited some 100 years after his death, contains a story that best characterizes their relationship. Many stories in the book have the aura of legend about them and tend to overstress the miraculous. Yet they often are able to throw unexpected light on Francis. One story tells of a remarkable meal enjoyed by Francis and Clare.

> 'What a great laudable exchange: to leave the things of time for those of eternity, to choose the things of heaven for the goods of earth, to receive the hundredfold in place of one, and to possess a blessed and eternal life.'
>
> **Clare of Assisi, first letter to Agnes of Prague, 1234**

Francis had often visited Clare at San Damiano to give her spiritual counsel but, for years, Clare had wanted to visit the Portiuncula, the home of her spiritual father, a place that, to her, was holy. After Francis had rejected her numerous requests (probably to keep female contact with his brothers to a minimum), she asked intermediaries to intercede for her.

Transcendent friendship

Clare's uncompromising commitment to poverty and to Christ so impressed Francis that Clare soon became one of his most trusted confidants. Though he was Clare's religious superior, Francis deferred to Clare's judgment often when it came to making decisions for her community.

In his later years, he depended more and more on her care (when he fell ill) and advice. For one period, Francis debated about whether he should give up his life as an itinerant preacher and instead become a hermit, devoting his life completely to prayer. As he wrestled with this decision, he asked for prayer from only two people: his former confessor, Sylvester, and Clare. (Both advised him to remain an evangelist.) At the end of Francis's life, it was Clare who nursed him at San Damiano for weeks.

Some modern biographers find it impossible to believe that Clare and Francis did not share some sort of romantic attraction, but this is to read a modern sensibility back into the medieval world, which had a larger imagination that does our own age. Even if their relationship was charged by subliminal sexual attraction, that energy was clearly channelled into something transcendent – a common commitment to incarnate the humility and poverty of Christ in their world.

'Father, we do not think this rigidity is in keeping with divine love,' they began. They reminded Francis that Clare's request for a simple meal was a small favour, especially considering how 'holy and beloved' Clare was. Do not forget, they added, 'it was through your preaching that she abandoned the world and her riches'.

After going back and forth, Francis finally relented. 'If it seems good to you, it seems good to me.' He concluded that Clare, who indeed had been cloistered for many years at San Damiano, should 'see again the place where her hair was cut and where she became a bride of Christ'.

The day arrived, and Clare, escorted by one of her sisters and some Franciscan brothers, arrived. She reverently greeted the statue of the Virgin, where she had received the veil, and then was given a tour of the place.

Meanwhile, Francis had prepared a meal and spread it on the bare ground, as was his custom. Clare, some sisters, Francis and a few brothers sat down. Francis began speaking about spiritual matters and, the account continues, he did so with such eloquence that all 'were rapt in God by the overabundance of divine grace that descended upon them'.

While they sat in mystical rapture, citizens in Assisi thought that they saw something like an immense fire burning near St Mary of the Angels. They rushed down to help put it out but, when they arrived, they only saw Francis, Clare and their companions sitting in an ecstatic trance. They concluded that 'it had been a heavenly and not a material fire that God had miraculously shown them to symbolize the divine love which was burning in the souls of those holy friars and nuns'.

Later, 'after a long while', Francis, Clare and their companions 'came back to themselves'. They felt so refreshed by spiritual food, the account concludes, that they had no need to eat the meal set before them.

CHAPTER 16

BEYOND THE ALPS

In these early years, Francis confined his missions to nearby regions such as Umbria and Tuscany. Still, these short forays attracted many men to his order. In the city of Ascoli Piceno, in the Marches of Ancona, for example, he recruited 30 individuals in one visit.

But Francis's word was spreading, especially as he and the brothers travelled outside Italy. Before the close of 1215, Franciscans could be found not only in north and central Italy, but also in southern France and Spain. Furthermore, people were warming up to the 'Little Poor Man', as people were calling him. Upon his arrival in some towns, church bells rang and people greeted him, shouting, *'Ecco il santo!'* ('The saint is here!')

Gifts started pouring in, as well. Giovanni di Velita, lord of Greccio, gave the brothers part of his farm above the Reiti Valley as a hermitage. After hearing Francis preach, Count Roland, lord of Chuisi-in-Casentino, gave Francis a tract of land on top of Mount La Verna to use for prayer and contemplation.

> 'He used to view the largest crowd of people as if it were a single person, and he would preach fervently to a single person as if to a large crowd.'
>
> **Thomas of Celano on Francis's Preaching, *The Life of St Francis*, 1228–29**

Even nature itself seemed to warm to Francis. Once, when travelling through the Spoleto valley, says Thomas of Celano, Francis saw a large number of birds – doves, crows and magpies – gathered. He rushed up to greet them, as he usually did. But this time, the birds did not fly away, as they always had in the past. So he preached to them: 'My brother birds, you should gently praise your Creator, and love him always.'

Another time, Francis was trying to preach in the village of Alviano, when a flock of swallows started shrieking and chirping. They were so loud that Francis could not be heard. So he turned to the birds and said, 'My sister swallows, now it is time for me also to speak, since you have said enough. Listen to the word of the Lord, and stay quiet until the word of the Lord is completed.'

'Immediately,' says Thomas of Celano, 'those birds fell silent – to the amazement and surprise of all present – and did not move from that place until the sermon was over.'

Council of the pope

In November 1215, Pope Innocent III opened the Fourth Lateran Council. He addressed 400 bishops and archbishops, 800 abbots and prelates, and ambassadors from all over Europe. After deploring the Muslim Saracens for profaning sacred sites in the Holy Land, Innocent turned his sights on the church. He castigated bishops and priests for their greed, sloth and lust. He recalled Ezekiel's famous vision in which God, his patience exhausted, tells his messenger, 'Go through the city, through Jerusalem, and put a mark [literally, a "Tau"] on the foreheads of those who sigh and groan over the abominations that are committed within it' (Ezekiel 9:4).

His words inspired many a resolution: against the heretical Cathari; for the establishment of more theological schools; commands to the faithful to confess and receive the eucharist at least once a year. And delegates passed a host of rules to check the greed and ambition of prelates.

Innocent was also concerned about the explosion of new orders and spiritual movements. Some were clearly heretical, such as the Cathari, but some were clearly not, such as the Franciscans and Dominicans (another reform order similar to that of Francis). Many of these groups were unknowns, and it was difficult to keep track of, much less give adequate guidance to, such enthusiasts. Yet, without oversight, such groups easily fell into heresy. Some abused their followers by insisting they practise severe austerities; others fleeced locals to support their religious work. More fearful of potential dangers than possible good, Innocent announced a moratorium: his office would approve no more new orders. And in the future, aspirants could only enter orders that had steady and secure sources of income.

This put Francis's growing, but still unofficial, order in a bind. Francis still insisted that begging was to be the only source of income for the order. Yet he was also anxious for papal approval. The impasse was temporarily solved by Bishop Guido who, through his connections, made sure that papal authorities still gave unofficial support to Francis.

Priests and bishops largely ignored the council's sweeping resolutions demanding reform. But the climate of reform created by Innocent greatly encouraged the rising mendicant orders such as that of Francis and Dominic. In fact, from this time on, Francis adopted the Tau (the Hebrew letter that is shaped like a uppercase 'T') as his personal emblem, to signal his devotion to Innocent's reforms. He used it as a signature, painted it on his door and placed it in his writings. Some of his followers had visions of Francis with the Tau marked on his forehead.

> '[Francis] admonished the brothers not to judge anyone, not to look down upon those who live with refinement and dress extravagantly or fashionably. For, he would say, their God is ours.'
>
> **The Legend of the Three Companions**, 1241–47

Missionary outlook

Just as King Arthur gathered his Knights of the Round Table annually at Pentecost, so Francis assembled his brothers at the Portiuncula. In the early years, he held these 'general chapters' twice a year – in spring, at Pentecost, and in September, at the Feast of St Michael. As the order grew and spread geographically, the brothers could gather only once every three years. On these occasions, Francis renewed friendships with companions who had been travelling, updated the Rule and gave fatherly advice to the brothers.

The general chapters of 1217 and 1219 discussed expansion. The order had continued to grow numerically (it was probably as large as 3,000 by 1219) and spread geographically. As a result, the brothers felt that they needed more structure. They divided themselves into 12 provinces, and a minister provincial was appointed for each. Later, provinces were subdivided into custodies, presided over by *custos*, and below them came residences, hermitages and friaries, under the jurisdiction of 'guardians'. Francis was not enthusiastic about these administrative layers; he knew the temptations that would come with offices of authority. So he insisted that provincials and guardians think of themselves as servants, or as mothers, to those under their care.

At the chapter of 1217, the order decided to make its first concerted effort to reach out beyond Italy. Unfortunately, enthusiasm to spread the gospel outpaced the brother's preparations for foreign missions.

Most of the brothers, usually sent out in pairs, were ignorant of the language and customs of the countries to which they were sent. They went forth, as Francis demanded, without money and without permission to receive it. They had no letters of recommendation from pope, bishop, count or lord. Though the brothers went forth enthusiastically, Bishop Ugolino, a realist, only rebuked Francis: 'Why have you sent your friars to such distant places to die of hunger and undergo other hardships?' Undergo hardships they did.

The missionaries to Hungary thought they had received a stroke of providence when they ran into a Hungarian bishop on their way to his homeland. But once they arrived, he deserted the mission and, left on their own, they were treated cruelly. People thought that they were charlatans who had come to exploit them. Citizens drove them from their cities; farmers set their dogs on them; shepherds poked them with sticks.

The 60 or so friars who made it to Germany fared no better. Not one of them spoke the local language – except for the word *'ja'* ('yes'). They used the word with great success one night when they were hungry. When asked a question, they replied, *'Ja'*, and they received an ample meal. So the next day, when they were asked a question, they replied, *'Ja'*, but this time people backed away. They later discovered that they had been asked if they were the heretics who had been corrupting Lombardy and were now going to corrupt Germany. The rumour spread that they were the dreaded Cathari, and they found themselves inexplicably arrested, bound naked to the pillory and whipped until they bled. Once freed, they fled the country.

There were exceptions. The friars who preached in Portugal were treated suspiciously at first. But Queen Urraca saw what they were about, and the royal family soon granted them protection. But, overall, these missions were a failure. The brothers returned to Italy miserable and discouraged.

Through trial and error, the brothers slowly learned the keys to foreign missionary work. The next time that Franciscans ventured into

A missionary sermon

The essence of a typical Franciscan evangelistic sermon can be found in the Earlier Rule, in which Francis says that friars should preach following message:

Fear and honour, praise and bless, give thanks and adore the Lord God Almighty in Trinity and Unity, Father, Son, and Holy Spirit, the Creator of all.

Do penance, performing worthy fruits of penance because we shall soon die. Give and it will be given to you. Forgive and you shall be forgiven. If you do not forgive people their sins, the Lord will not forgive you yours. Confess all your sins.

Blessed are those who die in penance, for they shall be in the kingdom of heaven. Woe to those who do not die in penance, for they shall be children of the devil whose works they do, and they shall go into everlasting fire. Beware and abstain from every evil and persevere in good till the end.

Germany (in 1221), for example, they went in small groups so that they would not look like an invading army. They were more patient, attempting only slowly to win people over, to make recruits and to found friaries. In a few years, Franciscans had established themselves not only in Germany, but even farther afield, in Bohemia, Poland, Romania and Norway.

England was the scene of another successful mission. In September 1224, nine brothers landed in Dover. Some settled in Canterbury, others in London and others still in Oxford. Many Oxford students and professors immediately joined the order. When they began building a friary together, bystanders were amazed to see a former high prelate carrying stones and mortar like a mason's apprentice. Some Franciscan university students refused to wear shoes even in winter, trudging through snow to classes. Of the three friars who took up residence at the friary, one was so lame that the others had to carry him to prayers. But the group was so overcome with joy at this new life that their prayers were sometimes punctuated with gales of holy laughter.

The first English novice recruited was Brother Solomon. The young man had a reputation for enjoying the finer things of life, but he now happily went begging with bowl in hand, as the Rule required. Once, he knocked on his sister's door. She handed him some bread but turned her face away and exclaimed, 'Cursed be the hour I ever saw you thus!' For Brother Solomon, this was a defining moment. He took the bread with joy and noted that he was being treated by his family as Francis had been treated by his.

'As you announce peace with your mouth, make sure that greater peace is in your hearts.'

Francis, to his brothers before sending them out to preach

The English order gained a reputation for humility and apostolic poverty. They were more commonly known as the Brethren of the Order of the Apostles. Within ten years of their arrival in England, Franciscans counted some of the country's leading men in their ranks and, 20 years after that, they had 49 friaries in the region.

Preaching to non-Christians

At the chapter of 1219, Francis raised the stakes and enlisted the order in a more challenging mission still: the evangelization of pagan lands. Since the end of 1212, Francis had tried unsuccessfully to take his message to non-Christian lands. On the way to Syria, winds prevented his ship from completing the voyage. On the way to Morocco two years later, illness thwarted his plans and forced a return home. After 1219, though, Franciscans in general had better success at getting to pagan lands, although they still had no success at winning converts.

Brother Giles, for example, headed for Muslim Tunis. But when the few Christians already there heard about his arrival, they forced him to board a ship and head home. They thought that his zeal would not only get him into trouble with the authorities, but that he would get them into trouble, as well. They were probably right: Giles did not hide his desire – a desire shared by many of the early brothers, including Francis – for martyrdom, the ultimate sacrifice for Christ.

The five brothers who went to Morocco got their wish, but less because of innocent devotion to Christ and more because of their offensive behaviour. When they arrived in Seville, still under the power of the Moors, they entered a mosque and began preaching against the Qur'an. This was as much an offence then as it is today. The worshippers immediately threw them out and beat them. Unfazed, the brothers next went to the royal palace and, when the prince discovered what their mission was, he had them arrested and taken in chains to a tower. From there, the brothers shouted down to passers-by that Mohammed was an imposter and, when they were moved to other quarters, they attempted to convert their jailers and other prisoners.

When they appeared before the local magistrate, he gave them the choice of returning to Italy or being exiled in Morocco. They choose the latter and, shortly after they arrived, they were arrested again. This time, they were whipped and tortured, but they refused to recant, and they foolishly persisted in despising the Qur'an. The local prince, Miramolin, threatened them with death, but they reportedly replied, 'Our bodies are in your power, but our souls are in the power of God!' With that, Miramolin had them beheaded. They were the first Franciscan martyrs, but they do not seem to have represented what was best in the order.

Francis, meanwhile, had appointed two brothers – Matthew of Narni and Gregory of Naples – as vicars to lead the order while he was away. He then headed to the port of Ancona, with a large group of brothers accompanying him. He intended to catch a ship conveying crusaders to the East. He wanted to make his way to the Muslim sultan in Egypt to preach to him and convert him.

Francis found his ship, but it did not have room for all the brothers. So Francis called to a young boy playing on the wharf and told him to pick 12 friars at random. These, Francis said, were the ones whom God wished to accompany him. They set sail in June 1219. (Francis often resorted to such arbitrary methods to determine the will of God. Once, when he and Brother Masseo came to a fork in the road, Francis spun Masseo around and around until he dizzily dropped to the ground. The direction in which Masseo ended up, Francis determined, was the direction God wanted them to go. Francis is often praised for such childlike trust in God's providence. But, as the order grew, this method of determining God's direction for the order only threw it into deep confusion.)

After arriving in Acre, Francis took Illuminato, one of the brothers, with him and sailed next for the crusader camp at Damietta, at the tip of the Nile Delta. They arrived there in late July. The crusaders had been

Crusades update

The Crusades had been going on for a little more than a century. They began with Pope Urban II's 1095 call for Christians to regain control of Jerusalem from the Saracens. 'A horrible tale has gone forth,' he exhorted his listeners at a church council. 'An accursed race utterly alienated from God . . . has invaded the lands of the Christians and depopulated them by the sword, plundering, and fire.' He wanted to return Jerusalem to its rightful Lord – Jesus – and, while he was at it, to humiliate the infidels: 'Tear that land from the wicked race and subject it.' The listeners were so taken with the speech that they began shouting, *'Deus vult! Deus vult!'* ('God wills it!'). This, in fact, became the battle cry of the crusaders.

There were eight major crusades in all, between 1096 and 1291, and dozens of minor crusading expeditions. In the First Crusade, the Christians recaptured Jerusalem, but it was only a few decades before this was again lost, and the rest of crusade history was concerned with getting it back.

By the time of the Fifth Crusade, the one which Francis joined, the Saracen Ayyubid dynasty controlled nearly the entire Levantine coast, from Byzantium to Egypt. The only exception were pockets in the Holy Land where Europeans maintained some sovereignty. The sultan at that time, al-Adil, had denied the crusaders access to Palestine, so the crusaders had switched their objective. They planned to attack the Saracen's main port and power base in Egypt, Damietta.

besieging the city (population 80,000) for a year with little success. For several months, Francis and Illuminato remained with the troops, who were some 40,000 strong (not counting another 20,000 nurses, cooks, pilgrims, sightseers, beggars and other civilians). By their preaching and charm, they won the admiration of many, some of whom, in fact, joined the order then and there.

The two brothers also helped to tend the sick. In the summer heat, epidemics of disease and dysentery swept through the crusader camp, and septicaemia and gangrene inflicted the wounded. November brought torrential rains and a strong north wind, which drove the sea inland, flooding the camp. Corpses of fish, donkeys, horses, and even of men and women, floated about. In the winter months, an outbreak of scurvy killed 10,000 people. Francis and Illuminato were kept very busy.

At the end of the summer of 1219, Francis finally convinced the papal legate to let him cross enemy lines to go to preach to the sultan. The convincing took some doing because, according to the *Chronicle of Ernoul* (whose author, Ernoul, was a shield-bearer for a feudal lord in the Holy Land), the cardinal 'would never want to give them permission to go to a place where they would only be killed'.

Francis and his companion had replied that the cardinal would not be blamed, because he and Illuminato were not asking to be ordered there.

They only wanted permission to go. They begged the cardinal insistently until he finally relented.

So Francis and Illuminato headed for the Saracen camp, probably in September 1219, during a truce between the armies. When Saracen sentinels spotted them, of course, they seized them and dragged them before the sultan. The sultan asked them if they had come with a message from the Christian army. Or perhaps they had come to convert to Islam. (Both Muslims and Christians crossed lines to join the faith of their enemies.)

Francis and Illuminato replied that they had come as messengers of the Lord God. They said that they were hoping that the sultan might convert to Christianity. According to the *Chronicle of Ernoul* they said, 'If you wish to believe us, we will hand over your soul to God, because we are telling you in all truth that if you die in the law which you now profess, you will be lost and God will not possess your soul.' They then laid down a challenge: if the sultan would call in 'the most learned teachers of your realm', Francis and Illuminato would convince them that their religion was false.

Ernoul may be a little confused here. Dominicans would attempt to use reason to argue another out of his religion. But that was never the way with Francis. Most likely, he simply wanted to preach his standard message of penance. In his Rule, in fact, he expressly told his brothers 'not to engage in arguments or disputes' but instead to simply 'announce the Word of God . . . in order that [unbelievers] may believe in God, the Father, the Son, and the Holy Spirit'.

Whatever it was that Francis wanted to say, he never had a chance to say it. When the sultan assembled his 'highest nobles and wisest men' and explained the reason for the gathering, the Muslim teachers – conservatives, if not fundamentalists – balked.

'Lord, you are the sword of the law,' they reminded the sultan. 'You have the duty to maintain and defend it.' They went on: 'The law forbids giving a hearing to preachers [of another religion],' adding that anyone who spread a faith other than Islam should be killed.

'It is for this reason', they concluded, 'that we command you, in the name of God and the law, that you have their heads cut off immediately, as the law demands.' With that, they stormed out of the room.

After only what could have been an awkward silence, the sultan turned to Francis and Illuminato. He assured them that he was not going to behead them. He tried, in fact, to put the best face on things. 'That would be an evil reward for me to bestow on you,' he said, 'who conscientiously risked death in order to save my soul for God.' He then said that if they decided to remain in his care, he would give them 'vast lands and many possessions'. This may have been an exaggerated offer of Middle Eastern hospitality. It may have been a test of their sincerity.

The two brothers replied bluntly that they no longer wished to stay, since it was clear that the sultan had no intention of converting. They only asked to be allowed return safely to the Christian camp. The sultan then offered them presents of gold, silver and silk garments before they left but, again, they refused. A meal would be a sufficient gift to send them on their way. They were then escorted safely back to the Christian army.

Francis escaped his martyrdom only by luck or God's providence. Like the brothers in Morocco, he did nearly everything wrong. He began preaching his message without earning the right to be heard. He offended the religious leaders. He insulted the hospitality of his host. How he got away cleanly is nothing less than a miracle.

Francis, however, probably thought himself a failure. He failed to convert the sultan – and neither did he suffer martyrdom. Francis was, no doubt, further discouraged by the military turn of affairs. By January 1220, Damietta was on its last legs – a mere 3,000 emaciated men, women and children remained alive in the city. When the crusaders entered it, they beat and raped the remaining adults, and then sold them into slavery. They then spent three months arguing about who was going to control which part of the city.

On top of that, Francis's physical health had seriously deteriorated. Nursing, preaching and prayer, combined with the unsanitary conditions in the Nile region, had worn him down. He had contracted an eye disease, probably trachoma, an infection spread by flies, which chronically inflames the underside of the eyelids. This disease would plague him for the rest of his life.

Sometime in early 1220, he returned to Acre, and then wandered about the Holy Land for months. Where he went and what he did, we do not know. It is not unlikely that he went about in deep discouragement, trying to discern what God would have him do next.

One day during these wanderings, he ran into a brother who probably embraced him enthusiastically. Some people in Italy suggested that Francis's long stay away could only mean he had been killed, so the brother was overjoyed to see him. The brother then blurted out some astonishing news: the order had forsaken his ideals and was in complete disarray.

Francis now knew what he needed to do next. He made preparations to return to the Portiuncula immediately.

CHAPTER 17

FRANCIS IN CONFLICT, ORDER IN CONFLICT

By the general chapter of 1219, it was clear that the innocence and naivety of the early years were over for the Franciscan Order. A simple Rule for a dozen men, living together in humble dwellings, guided by a charismatic leader was one thing, but now there were thousands of people, from many parts of Europe. Some of them had had no contact with the founder. Many had never been nurtured and shaped by his ideals.

So why did they join? Some simply preferred the order's companionship to their families or to a solitary life. Others were taken with the humility and friendliness of the early friars. Others seemed to have simply misunderstood what the order was about. They imagined that, like other orders of the day, the rule would be moderate and that they would have opportunity for study. Some even thought that a stint in the order would bode well for their church careers.

With this mixture of motives and members, it was inevitable that some would begin to chafe at the Rule. Many brothers who had been appointed superiors or ministers had been outstanding or influential clerics before joining the order. They soon resented having to obey an uneducated man such as Francis. And age-old class distinctions were difficult to erase.

Thomas of Celano tells a story of Francis and Brother Leonardo as they returned from an overseas mission. They were both exhausted from their travels. Francis rode on their donkey while Leonardo led it by the reigns. Leonardo, whose family's standing in Assisi had been much higher than that of Francis's family, began to grumble to himself. 'His parents and mine did not socialize as equals, and here he is riding while I am on foot leading this donkey.' Francis, sensing Leonardo's resentment, said, 'Brother, it is not right that I should ride while you go on foot, for in the world you were more noble and influential than I.' Leonardo felt ashamed and begged forgiveness.

Francis's personal charm and humility could disarm such resentment but, as the order grew, he was not able to intervene every time that human nature threatened to disrupt things. At the chapter of 1219, a number of brothers made no effort to conceal their concerns about the order. They wanted the order to be more like the other religious orders of the day. This would allow them to study more, to adhere to a more moderate poverty and to take advantage of the influence of prelates (for example, getting letters of introduction so that they could more easily preach in new regions).

> 'Those who do not wish to taste how sweet the Lord is and who love the darkness more than the light, not wishing to fulfil God's commands, are cursed; it is said of them by the prophet, "Cursed are those who stray from your commands."'
>
> Francis, in an admonition to his brothers upon his return from Syria in 1220

External pressures

In addition to these internal tensions, there was pressure from outside. Since early in 1217, Pope Honorius had appointed Ugolino, bishop of Ostia, as his legate in northern Italy. Ugolino gained recruits for the next crusade, kept an eye on German incursions, enforced the decrees of the Fourth Lateran Council and supervised religious houses in his province.

Ugolino took this last responsibility especially seriously. He was described once as a man 'afire' with love for Francis. Thomas of Celano, in *The Life of St Francis*, wrote of him, 'When he saw that Francis despised all earthly things more than the rest, and that he was alight with the fire that Jesus had sent upon the earth, his soul was from that moment knit with the soul of Francis, and he devoutly asked his prayers and most graciously offered his protection to him in all things.' He sometimes donned the dress of Francis and walked about barefoot with Francis and his brothers. He wanted Francis's order, and that of Clare, who also deeply impressed him, to grow and remain strong.

But he differed with Francis about how to ensure that. In this regard, he was probably more realistic about human nature and church politics than was Francis. It is also fair to say that many of his decisions saved the order for future generations. The only problem was that, at the time, his decisions thwarted some elements of Francis's original vision.

He was not happy with the Rule's contempt of owning property, handling money, gaining papal favours and practising judicious planning. In *this* world, he reasoned, such things were necessary if the order was to survive. He was especially troubled about Clare and her sisters at San Damiano. He was anxious to take steps to maintain their orthodoxy, find regular means to support their house and protect their virginity in a cruel and capricious society.

Bishop Guido had for some time put pressure on Francis to avoid becoming an excessive burden on others, especially now that the order numbered more than 1,000. No more relying on the generosity of a lazaret, a priest or a citizen to house them; they were to construct their own shelters, he had said.

Francis felt caught. On the one hand, he had more than once preached and acted against such property ownership. The most dramatic example, told in *Mirror of Perfection*, came at one of the annual general chapters, probably the chapter of 1219 or 1221. Francis had been travelling as preparations were being made for the chapter, and the Commune of Assisi, knowing that the order had been growing dramatically, erected a large building of stone and mortar to house many of the brothers while they attended the chapter. When Francis arrived, he was astonished – he thought that the brothers had built a huge house for their own comfort. This was a far cry from the simple thatch huts that had characterized their lives.

He immediately climbed up on the roof of the house and ordered some brothers to join him. They began, one by one, to lift the tiles from the roof and toss them to the ground. Francis intended to dismantle the building completely. Some knights of Assisi, who helped with crowd control at these chapters (in these years, many sightseers would gather to watch the brothers), approached Francis. 'Brother, this house belongs to the Commune of Assisi,' they explained. 'And we are here to represent the Commune. We forbid you to destroy our house.' Francis stopped and looked at the knights. 'If the house is yours,' he said, 'I will not touch it.' And immediately he and the other friars descended.

On the other hand, Francis recognized the wisdom of Guido's advice. He did not want to be a burden to others, so he sought a middle ground. The brothers could build huts for themselves for private prayer, he said, but nothing elaborate. They could construct only 'poor houses of wood and plaster' (bricks, stones and tiles were forbidden). And the property was to be surrounded not by a high wall (typical of the day), but simply by a hedge. For corporate prayer, chapels could be erected, but not big churches.

Francis still did not want the brothers to own holy or service books, such as New Testaments or missals. He felt that owning things would eventually lead to indolence and pride. One story in *The Assisi Compilation* describes an incident when a brother was badgering Francis for a book of Psalms of his own. Francis replied, 'And when you have a Psalter, you will want a breviary, and when you have a breviary, you will install yourself in a chair like a great prelate, and you will order your brother, "Bring me my breviary!"'

On the other hand, he wanted his brothers to pray the offices and read the Psalms. So he compromised. The Dominican-style, large books used for study, were forbidden. But Franciscans could have tiny versions, no bigger than the palm of a hand, and which could easily be tucked in a sleeve.

Francis's departure

It is no accident that Francis chose this time to embark on his longest missionary journey – his trip to Syria after the chapter of 1219. He may have had more than Muslim evangelism on his mind. He may have longed to escape the headaches of administrating an order that required more and more compromises. It is clear, in retrospect, that leaving was a mistake. And his taking with him Peter Cantanii was another. If Peter had stayed behind and acted as one of the order's vicars, he might have prevented the confusion that set in under the leadership of vicars Gregory of Naples and Matthew of Narni (relative newcomers to the order).

It was not long before a wave of insecurity swept over the order. After a few months' absence, it was rumoured that Francis was dead. So Gregory and Matthew took it upon themselves

'Francis's decision to leave [Italy in 1219] must have . . . been instinctive, an act of impulse or faith, which changed both him and his family, for better or worse, irreversibly.'

Adrian House, *Francis of Assisi: A Revolutionary Life*, 2000

to bring a little more discipline to the order. They multiplied fasts and prescribed many privations that went beyond the spirit of the Rule. To speed up missionary work, the vicars solicited favours from the Roman Curia and letters of commendation.

On top of that, some friars moved into permanent buildings. In Bologna, for example, the provincial Peter Staccia became envious of the great educational facilities owned by the Dominicans. Peter had held a chair in jurisprudence before joining the order, and he had a high view of education. Francis had bent his rules to allow Peter to supervise a number of brothers who wanted to study the Bible and liturgy. But now Peter went too far; he had accepted, on behalf of the brothers (and with the approval of the vicars), a large building where they could live and study.

Bishop Ugolino, for his part, decided that it was time to enforce some of his ideas. He imposed on Clare's order, and on all the women's communities in his province, his own rule – the *Constitutions*. This rule said that each convent must have a Visitor, or informal inspector, connected with it. For Clare, who had enjoyed regular visits, but only from Francis's brothers, this must have been a hard obedience.

All this was too much for friars who had been with Francis since the early years. Many raised their voices in protest. Others refused to submit to the vicars' orders. Others still refused to live in community and just wandered about longing for their shepherd and guide.

Francis's return

As Francis returned from the Holy Land, he knew that things were out of control. He also realized that, alone, he would not be able to rein things in. Before he had left the Holy Land, he had asked two brothers – Elias, provincial minister of Syria, and Caesar, a diligent scribe – to join him. Francis had sized up the two men and recognized that their strong leadership was needed to help him.

But Francis knew that even this would not be enough. Sometime earlier he had had a dream, which turned out to be a premonition of things to come. In the dream, he saw a small, black hen, with feathered legs but with the feet of a dove. It had so many chicks that it was unable to gather them all under its wings, so they wandered about in circles. Francis came to understand the dream. As he later explained, 'I am that hen: short in stature, and dark by nature. I must be simple like a dove, flying up to heaven with the feathered strokes of virtue. The Lord in his mercy has given, and will give me, many sons whom I will be unable to protect with my own strength.'

As he was returning to the fractured order, he concluded, 'I must, therefore, commend them to the holy church who will protect and guide them under the shadow of her wings.'

So, before he returned to Assisi, Francis headed for Rome. He found Bishop Ugolino, and together they went before the pope. Francis knew

Elias: black sheep of the order

Elias was a man of remarkable gifts, possessing a character that was an ironic combination of faith and pride. He was a notary in the town of Bologna when he joined Francis, and he quickly became a trusted friend. Francis placed great confidence in him, perhaps because of Elias's organizing genius. Elias was appointed provincial of the friars in Syria and, in 1221, minister general of the entire order.

Elias was close to Francis in his last years. According to Thomas of Celano in *The Life of St Francis*, he received Francis's dying blessing: 'You are my son. I bless above all and throughout all.' At Francis's death, the grieving Elias gathered witnesses to verify Francis's stigmata and wrote the letter informing friars of their founder's passing.

But he seems to have misunderstood his mentor's message of poverty. After Francis's death, he completed the ornate lower church of the great basilica that today dominates Assisi. As minister general, he became an autocrat, appointing, transferring and dismissing provincials without hesitation. On the grounds of personal health, he insisted on having a personal cook, and he wanted his servants to wait upon him in proper attire.

Conservatives finally orchestrated a coup in 1239, and Elias was deposed. He joined the perpetual papal enemy, Frederick II, and was then excommunicated. But a small body of friars stuck with him and, for them, he erected a monastery at Cortona.

Ugolino: machiavellian reformer

It is not surprising that Francis, when he was looking for a papal representative to help bring order to the Franciscans, asked for Bishop Ugolino. Though Francis's biographers refer continually to Ugolino's humility, history mostly remembers him as a wily political animal. This did not become evident until he became Pope Gregory IX in 1227.

At the time, the West was in the middle of a crusade to the East. But Emperor Frederick II was having second thoughts, and had decided not to lead an offensive. When the freshly installed Gregory heard this, he excommunicated Frederick. The tactic worked, and Frederick relented and left for Palestine. Gregory then lifted the excommunication – but went on to have his papal armies attack Frederick's Italian lands. When Frederick hurried back to recover his territory, Gregory excommunicated him again for deserting the crusade!

Ugolino is also the pope with the dubious distinction of founding the Inquisition. He did so, giving special responsibility to the Dominicans, in order to combat heresy. But Gregory was a complex man and, all the while, he was fostering the growth of the Franciscans, the Poor Clares and the Dominicans. Indeed, helping these orders only enhanced his power as pope, since they were directly accountable to him. Yet he also knew that they could reform the church from the bottom up, just as he was trying to reform the church from the top down.

that Ugolino had enforced some decisions that were not in the spirit of the order. But he believed that Ugolino had the best interests of the order at heart. Francis saw that now that his order numbered in the thousands, Rome would be increasingly tempted to dictate policy, and that Francis's ideals of radical poverty and simplicity would be undermined. Rather than trust his order to the capricious nature of papal politics, he asked the pope to make Ugolino protector of his order. To this, the pope agreed.

Francis and Ugolino immediately sat down to talk. Francis explained why he objected to a number of Ugolino's decisions. Ugolino relented on a few matters, and Francis also compromised. The two friars, Gregory and Matthew, would be posted elsewhere. Their amendments to the Rule would be struck. Brothers who had branched out on their own (such as John of Capella, who had organized a sub-order composed solely of lepers) would be censured. And papal letters of introduction would be given to all missionary brothers, to ease their way into new territories.

Francis's resignation

In addition to these agreements, Francis said that he was going to step down as head of the order. He saw that he was not the man to lead the order through its next stage. He would turn matters over to Peter Catanii.

When he announced this at the next general chapter, in September 1220, many brothers wept openly. But Francis refused to change his mind, and he symbolically bowed before Peter to indicate his new authority. He also asked Peter to appoint him a companion, 'who will represent your authority to me and whom I shall obey as if I were obeying you'. He did this, he said, as a 'good example and for love of the virtue of obedience'.

The early biographers make Francis's relinquishing of leadership look easy. It must have been anything but that. His early ambitions for a large brotherhood that would redeem the world were being fulfilled. But he found himself incapable of negotiating the new situation, which demanded organization, financial accountability and the wise use of church politics. Such things, Francis knew all too well, were not his forte. Even worse – they were the very things he had stood against when he started his order a little over a decade earlier. He was simply mystified as to how he personally could retain his ideals while providing for a growing order. He decided that he could not, and he turned matters over to others whom he trusted.

But he would never, for the rest of his life, be able to keep his hands out of things. Though Francis promised to obey other minister generals who presided over the order, he always made his presence and ideals known. For example, he was forever telling his friars to distrust learning: 'A great cleric must in some way give up his learning when he comes to the order, that he may offer himself naked to the arms of the cross.' Another time, he said, 'My brothers who are being led by their curious passion for learning will find their hands empty on the day of retribution when books, no longer useful, will be thrown out of windows and into cubby holes.'

St Anthony: Hammer of the Heretics

Today, Anthony of Padua – the popular St Anthony – is widely invoked by Catholics for the return of lost property, for protection during travel and for health during pregnancy. In paintings, we see him with a Bible or a lily in his hand, representing his knowledge of scripture, or with a donkey, which supposedly knelt before the sacrament he once held aloft.

But history shows a more rugged side to Anthony. Born in 1195 in Lisbon to a noble family, he joined and began studying with members of the Augustinian Order at the age of 15. Ten years later, his life was revolutionized.

One day, some relics passed through town. They were the remains of the Franciscan friars who had recently been martyred in Morocco. Anthony was deeply moved and, like many spiritual athletes of the day, nothing excited him more than the thought of dying for Christ. He begged his order to release him from his vows so that he could join the Franciscans. He then convinced the Franciscans to make him a missionary to Morocco.

But on the way to Morocco, a storm forced his ship to Sicily and, from there, he made his way to Assisi. For some reason, he determined that this was where God wanted him to spend the rest of his days in quiet prayer and study.

When he preached at his own ordination, however, listeners were amazed at his eloquence and passion. He was soon given various administrative posts in the order – including being a teacher at Bologna. He also preached, sometimes attracting crowds of up to 30,000 people. His favourite themes were denouncing the elite for their unjust treatment of the poor and the heresies of the Cathari. He became known, in fact, as the 'Hammer of the Heretics'.

From 1230 onwards, he spent the remainder of his life at Padua, and he died at the premature age of 36. He was canonized within six months, an extraordinarily brief time. He was named a Doctor of the Church in 1946.

He worried that if the brothers spent too much time studying, they would neglect the higher work of prayer and service. Even if in the service of better preaching, there could be problems: 'When they have preached to a few men or to the people, and learn that certain ones were edified or converted to penance through their discourse, they are puffed up and pride themselves on the results.'

Still, Ugolino and Elias, minister general after Peter Catanii died, pushed for more learning. They realized that for all its spiritual temptations, learning was necessary for the long-term success of the order. Though an unschooled Francis could preach with wisdom beyond his education, most friars needed some training if they were to convince hearers of their message.

Francis eventually saw the wisdom of this, at least to some degree. When one particularly gifted brother, Anthony of Padua, was appointed by Elias as a teacher at Bologna, Francis confirmed the decision. He wrote a little note to Anthony: 'I am pleased that you teach sacred theology to the brothers,' adding, 'providing that, as is contained in the Rule, you "do not extinguish the Spirit of prayer and devotion" during study of this kind.'

> 'Francis depended far too much upon direct personal influence and upon the hour-to-hour guidance of the Holy Spirit. He could not plan ahead because he was never certain where God would lead him.'
>
> **John R. Moorman, *St Francis of Assisi*, 1950**

A new Rule

In 1222, Ugolino and Elias decided that, given the order's new situation, it was time to modify and formalize the Rule. Naturally, they asked Francis to begin to draw up the document. Francis asked brother Bonizzo of Bologna and his companion brother Leo, among others, to help him.

Some of the brothers panicked when they heard this. 'We are afraid that he will make it so difficult that we will not be able to observe it,' they blurted out to Elias. They told Elias to tell Francis they would refuse to obey such a rule: 'He may write it for himself, but not for us!'

Elias went with an escort of brothers to meet with Francis and his companions, who were living at a mountain retreat. When Elias explained what concerned the brothers, Francis lifted his eyes upward and said, 'Lord, did I not tell you that they would not have confidence in you?'

Then, according to *The Assisi Compilation*, a voice from above said, 'Francis, nothing in the Rule comes from you; everything comes from me. I wish this Rule to be observed to the letter, to the letter, to the letter, without gloss, without gloss, without gloss!'

Francis turned to the brothers and said, 'Did you hear? Do you want me to have it repeated?' The brothers, says the chronicler, 'withdrew totally ashamed and striking their breasts'.

The story seems to be a fabrication created by later followers, who were lobbying the order to retain a strict interpretation of the Rule. But it speaks poignantly of the changing nature of the brotherhood, and of the divisions within it. Even Francis could not stop these developments.

The new rule, now called the Later Rule, thus does not have the stamp of Francis's personality and vision, as did the Earlier Rule. It is a document that has gone through the layers of church bureaucracy. It is clear and practical, and is easily memorized, but the poetry and passion of Francis are gone. To be sure, much of the original vision remains. But it also shows evidence of compromise. The command to 'carry nothing for your journey' is absent. The command to return no violence to an offender has been omitted. And the brothers' right to admonish superiors for abuses of office is nowhere to be found.

The compromised version was presented at the next general chapter, in September 1223, and the brothers approved it. In November, Honorius III approved it as the official Rule of the order.

CHAPTER 18

IMITATION OF CHRIST

At one point in *The Life of St Francis*, Thomas of Celano sums up the meaning of Francis's life. 'His highest aim, foremost desire and greatest intention,' he wrote, 'was to pay heed to the holy gospel in all things and through all things, to follow the teaching of our Lord Jesus Christ and to retrace his footsteps completely with all vigilance and all zeal, all the desire of his soul and all the fervour of his heart.'

Francis insisted that he and his brothers *obey* the commands of their Lord as literally as possible. The habit began early. He read a passage from the Gospels – about Jesus' command that his disciples have only one tunic and no sandals – and Francis took it as a personal command to himself and, later, to his brothers. For Francis, *poverty* was a synonym for *obedience*. Furthermore, poverty meant not only physical poverty, but also a life of self-denial, humility and service to Christ.

> 'Inwardly cleansed, interiorly enlightened, and inflamed by the fire of the Holy Spirit, may we be able to follow in the footprints of your beloved Son, our Lord Jesus Christ.'
>
> **Francis, a prayer in *Letter to the Entire Order*, 1225–26**

Yet obedience was only part of Francis's method. Obedience alone, he recognized, would only lead to legalism and self-righteousness. The Christ-like life demanded something more.

Ardent love was one thing. Francis concluded his Earlier Rule with an extended doxology to his love for God. 'With our whole heart, our whole soul, our whole mind, and with our whole strength and fortitude, with our whole understanding, with all our powers, with every effort, every affection, every feeling, every desire and wish, let us love the Lord God.'

In fact, when he became caught up in this theme, he could hardly control himself:

Wherever we are, in every place, in every hour, at every time of the day, every day and continually, let us truly and humbly believe, hold in our heart and love, honour, adore, serve, praise, bless, glorify and exalt, magnify and give thanks to the Most High and Supreme Eternal God, Trinity and Unity, Father,

Son and Holy Spirit, Creator of all, Saviour of all who believe and hope in him, and love him.

This love for God was focused like a laser beam on the second member of the Trinity. It was Jesus who spoke to Francis from the San Damiano cross. Jesus' words shook Francis out of his materialistic stupor and drove him to take up the life of poverty. And so for Francis, nothing less than imitation of Christ – perfect God and perfect man – would do. The imitation of Christ was the highest aspiration of humankind.

An early passage in the Earlier Rule shows how important this was to Francis right from the beginning of his order: 'The rule and life of these brothers is this, namely: to live in obedience, chastity, and without anything of their own, and to follow in the teaching *and the footsteps* of our Lord Jesus Christ' [emphasis added].

Francis joined obedience to Christ with his love of Jesus; he expressed both by giving himself to a life of pure imitation of Christ. Thus Thomas of Celano notes, 'Francis used to recall with regular meditation the words of Christ and recollect his deeds with most attentive perception.' And as if the reader had not yet understood the point, Thomas adds, 'Indeed, so thoroughly did the humility of the Incarnation and the charity of the Passion occupy his memory that he scarcely wanted to think of anything else.'

The living nativity

When Francis turned over the administration of the order to others in 1220, he spent more time in prayer than ever. And he sought more than ever a perfect imitation of Christ. Two of the most memorable and remarkable incidents of his life occurred during these, his last, years. Each one, in its own way, is a culmination of his desire to imitate Christ in all things.

The first concerned the beginning of Jesus' life on earth. For Francis, few feasts of the church year compared to Christmas. The image of Jesus in his mother's arms made him stammer with emotion. Sometimes he wept when he pondered the poverty into which the Son of God was born. One day, when at a meal, a friar was talking about the humble

The good Catholic

Francis was not only enamoured with Christ, but with anything that 'carried' Christ to the rest of humankind – hence his devotion to Mary, Jesus' mother. Thomas of Celano sums it up like this: 'He embraced the Mother of Jesus with inexpressible love, since she made the Lord of Majesty a brother to us. He honoured her with his own praises, poured out prayers to her, and offered her his love in a way that no human tongue can express.'

One song of praise composed by Francis reads, 'Hail, O Lady, Holy Queen, Mary, Holy Mother of God . . . Hail his palace! Hail his tabernacle! Hail his dwelling!'

Likewise, Francis venerated the church and its priests because, as he believed, they carried Christ in the holy eucharist. Just before he died, Francis dictated a document which is now called *The Testament*, his last admonitions to his brothers. Towards the beginning, he explained once more his relationship to the church:

The Lord gave me, and gives me still such faith in priests who live according to the rite of the holy Roman Church because of their orders that, were they to persecute me, I would still want to have recourse to them . . . I act in this way because, in this world, I see nothing corporally of the most high Son of God except his most holy body and blood, which they receive and administer to others.

In an undated admonition to his brothers, he nearly equated the Incarnation with the sacrament of Communion: 'As he [Jesus] revealed himself to the holy apostles in true flesh, so he reveals himself to us now in sacred bread . . . And in this way the Lord is always with his faithful.'

circumstances of the birth of Jesus, Francis began shaking with sobs. He got up from the table and finished his meal on the dirt floor, in honour of the poverty of Christ's birth.

One time when Christmas fell on a Friday, Brother Morico asked him if they should be eating meat, since Friday was normally a fast day. An indignant Francis replied, 'You sin, brother, when you call Friday the day when "unto us a child is born". I want even the walls to eat meat on that day, and if they cannot, at least on the outside they be rubbed with grease!'

With such feeling he approached Christmas in 1223. Two weeks prior to the holy feast, he had arranged with his friend, and now disciple, John Velita, lord of Greccio, to allow him the use of a steep hill opposite the town. The slope was dotted with caves and small woods. There, Francis said, he wanted to 'enact the memory of that babe who was born in Bethlehem, to see as much as is possible with my own bodily eyes the discomfort of his infant needs, how he lay in a manger, and how, with an ox and an ass standing by, he rested on hay'. Francis publicized what he was about to do, so that on Christmas Eve both friars and people of the area joined him on his retreat.

> 'He [Francis] use to observe the nativity of the child Jesus with an immense eagerness above all other solemnities, affirming it was the feast of feasts, when God was made a little child and hung on human breasts.'
>
> **Thomas of Celano, The Life of St Francis, 1228–29**

Thomas of Celano describes the scene. People carried candles and torches as they wound their way up the mountain. They finally reached the spot where Francis had arranged for a living nativity to be placed, with an ox and a donkey, and hay in the manger, and a baby asleep within. A priest led the group in the Mass, at which Francis assisted in singing the liturgy. He also preached on 'the birth of the poor King and the poor city of Bethlehem'.

'At length,' Thomas concludes, 'the night's solemnities drew to a close and everyone went home with joy,' as 'simplicity is given place of honour, poverty is exalted and humility is commended'.

In this account, Thomas mostly uses the present tense. This suggests that the living nativity had become an annual event at Greccio. Indeed, the custom soon spread throughout Europe. Scholars argue as to whether this was the first living nativity but, at a minimum, it was a custom popularized by Francis – in imitation of Christ.

Stigmata

The second event, shrouded in some mystery, was Francis's imitation of the end of Christ's life. In September 1224, Francis went with some companions (including Leo and Angelo) on a 40-day retreat on Mount

La Verna, the lonely mountain in Tuscany that had been given for his use by Count Orlando 11 years earlier. Sometime about the Feast of the Exaltation of the Cross (on 14 September), Francis, deep in prayer, experienced a vision. He saw an angel with six wings above him, with its arms outstretched and fastened to a cross.

Bonaventure, in *The Major Legend of St Francis*, says that Francis 'rejoiced at the gracious way Christ looked upon him under the appearance of the Seraph, but the fact that he was fastened to a cross pierced his soul with a sword of compassionate sorrow'. Francis meditated on this vision. He eventually understood that he, Francis, was 'to be totally transformed into the likeness of Christ crucified'. It was not to be by the martyrdom he had longed for his whole life, 'but by the enkindling of his soul'.

> *'In all things he wished without hesitation to be conformed to Christ crucified, who hung on the cross poor, suffering, and naked.'*
>
> **Bonaventure, *The Major Legend of St Francis*, 1260–63**

When the vision departed, says Bonaventure, 'It left in his heart a marvellous fire and imprinted in his flesh a likeness of signs no less marvellous.' Immediately, wounds appeared on his body – one on each hand and each foot, and one on his side – all of which would bleed periodically for the rest of his life.

The marks came to be called *stigmata*, from the Greek word *stigma*, meaning 'brand mark' or 'scar'. The word is found in Paul's letter to the church at Galatia, where he says, 'I carry the marks (*stigmata*) of Jesus branded on my body' (Galatians 6:17). The same word was carried over into the Latin Vulgate translation, the common Bible version of Francis's day. Clearly, in the mind of Francis and his followers, the marks were the final evidence of Francis's imitation of Christ.

At first, Francis tried to hide the marks, even from his closest followers, but they could not but help notice his bleeding as they nursed him when he fell ill. When they pestered him for information about them, he eventually relented and told them what had happened. Nonetheless, he insisted that they keep it as secret as possible. 'Although he tried to hide the treasure found in the field,' remarks Bonaventure, 'he could not prevent some from seeing the stigmata in his hands and feet, although he always kept his hands covered and from that time on always wore shoes.'

Other stigmata

Francis was the first person in history to receive the stigmata – but he was not the last. Subsequent Christian history records many people who received the same marks. The most famous in the late Middle Ages were Catherine of Siena (1347–80) and Catherine of Genoa (1447–1510). In the nineteenth century, some 20 cases were known, including that of Marie de Moerl of Tyrol (1812–68). At the age of 20, she began experiencing spiritual ecstasies which reoccurred regularly for the rest of her life. Louise Lateau of Belgium (1850–83) began nursing victims of cholera at the age of 16, and experiencing ecstasies and the stigmata at the age of 18.

In the twentieth century, the most famous stigmatic was Padre Pio. He became a novice of the Capuchin Friars, a Franciscan order, at the age of 15, and became a priest in 1910. At the age of 31, in September 1918, the stigmata appeared on his body as he prayed before a crucifix. The marks remained on him for nearly the rest of his life. Thousands sought him out in Italy to make their confession and to seek his counsel. By the time of his death in 1968, though, the wounds were no longer visible. His beatification is still under consideration by the Vatican.

Over the centuries, some cases of stigmata have proven to be frauds and, in general, the Roman Catholic Church is very slow to recognize or highlight the miraculous nature of the phenomenon.

By the time of his death, however, some 50 brothers, along with Clare and a number of lay followers, had seen and touched the wounds.

There is no reason to doubt whether Francis had such wounds – the evidence is overwhelming that he did. Besides numerous witnesses, the wounds were described in vivid detail by Thomas of Celano, among others ('marks on the inside of the hands were round, but oblong from the outside, and small pieces of flesh were visible like the points of nails, bent and flattened').

How the wounds came to be is another matter. Some scholars, even Catholics such as the late Herbert Thurston, believe that they can be explained as a physical reaction to intense ecstatic and psychological experiences. Francis so desired to become fully like Christ that his mind convinced his body to produce the wounds of the crucifixion. Others, such as Sr Joanne Schatzlein, a nurse, and Dr Daniel Sulmasy, a physician, conjecture that the wounds may have manifested themselves as a result of Francis's having contracted leprosy and/or tuberculosis. Or perhaps Francis inflicted himself with the wounds, not as an effort to deceive, but as another of his dramatic demonstrations to become a living metaphor of the imitation of Christ.

In the end, it is beyond the ability of science or history to determine the ultimate cause of the stigmata. Francis and his followers certainly believed that the marks were a miracle. More importantly, for Bonaventure, among others, the stigmata completed a spiritual life that had begun with a revelation from a crucifix, and had been devoted to imitating Christ. As Bonaventure put it, 'For the cross of Christ, both offered and taken on by you at the beginning of your conversion and carried continuously from that moment throughout the course of your most proven life . . . shows with such clarity of certitude that you have finally reached the summit of gospel perfection.'

CHAPTER 19

BROTHER SUN

In the months following receiving the stigmata, Francis continued to travel, often by donkey because he no longer had the strength to walk, as was his custom. He visited Borgo, San Spolcro, Monte Casale and Citta' di Castello on his way back to the Portiuncula. Then he set out on a preaching tour of Umbria and the Marches. All the while his body deteriorated, especially his stomach, liver and spleen. His eye problems became worse. In spring 1225, he stayed with Clare and her sisters at San Damiano to receive their care.

After much badgering by Brother Elias, now head of the order, Francis agreed to undergo medical treatment. For the rest of his days, Francis would have to endure all sorts of treatments for his eyes. The most brutal consisted of cauterizing with a red-hot iron the flesh around the eyes, from ear to eyebrow. But no matter the method, Francis's eyes did not improve. He could not bear sunlight, and even firelight hurt his eyes. His eyes caused him so much pain sometimes that he could not sleep.

As he was wont to do, just when nature was failing him – his body falling apart, his eyes incapable of taking in the beauty of nature – Francis crafted one of the most exquisite poems ever. It was a fitting culmination of one theme that characterized his life and ministry.

> 'My brother birds, you should greatly praise your Creator, and love Him always. He gave you feathers to wear, wings to fly, and whatever you need.'
>
> **Francis's Sermon to the Birds,** in Thomas of Celano, *The Life of St Francis*, 1228–29

Love of nature

We have already noted two incidents in which Francis's presence calmed flocks of birds. These are but two stories that were told about him, starting in his lifetime. Some are quite fantastic, others borrow themes from Greek mythology. The historical authenticity of any one of the Francis nature stories can be debated, but they cannot all be dismissed as fairy tales. The overall picture that emerges from the earliest sources is that Francis had an extraordinary relationship with the created order.

Once, while staying near Greccio, reports Thomas of Celano, a brother brought to Francis a live rabbit caught in a trap. When Francis saw the rabbit, he was 'moved with tenderness'. He said, 'Brother rabbit, come to me. Why did you let yourself get caught?' The brother who had been holding the rabbit let it go, and the rabbit bounded over to Francis and jumped into his arms. Francis, 'caressing it with motherly affection', finally put it down to let it hop back into the woods. After a few hesitant hops, the rabbit turned and bounded back to Francis. This happened again and again until Francis ordered a brother to take the rabbit some distance away before releasing it. Thomas then noted that this also happened with another rabbit when Francis once visited the island on the Lake of Perugia (also known as Lake Trasimeno).

> 'From a reflection on the primary source of all things, filled with even more abundant piety, he would call all creatures, no matter how small, by the name of "brother" or "sister".'
>
> **Bonaventure, *The Major Legend of St Francis*, 1260–63**

Thomas reports a similar instance with a fish. Once, while he was sitting in a boat on the Lake of Reiti, a fisherman caught a tench (a type of carp) and offered it to Francis as a gift. Francis accepted it gladly, calling it 'brother' as he took it in his arms. Then he put it back in the water, blessing God as he did. 'For some time that fish did not leave the spot but stayed next to the boat,' wrote Thomas of Celano, 'playing in the water.' Only when Francis gave it permission to leave did it do so.

Francis seemed to have had a special fondness for sheep. Once, while travelling through the Marches of Ancona with a brother, he came across a man headed for market, carrying two little lambs on his shoulders. Thomas of Celano says that when Francis heard the bleating lambs, he was moved and 'he touched them as a mother does a crying child'.

'Why are you torturing my brother lambs,' Francis asked the man, 'binding and hanging them in this way?'

'I am carrying them to market to sell them, since I need the money,' the man replied.

'What will happen to them?' Francis continued.

The man responded, 'Those who buy them will kill them and eat them.'

'No!' Francis blurted out. 'This must not happen!' He ripped off the cloak, heavy and finely made, that he had borrowed because of the

The wolf of Gubbio

The most famous nature story about Francis seems clearly to be a fabrication, but nonetheless it is an example of the type of nature stories that grew up around Francis soon after his death.

A 'fearfully large and fierce wolf', says *The Little Flowers of St Francis*, had been plaguing the town of Gubbio. It was 'rabid with hunger', devouring both animals and man. The townspeople often went into the forest with weapons, 'as if they were going to war', but 'they were not able to escape the sharp teeth and raging hunger of the wolf when they were so unfortunate as to meet'.

When Francis visited the town, he had compassion on the people when they told him their story. He went out to meet the wolf with just one brother as a companion. Upon seeing Francis and his companion, the wolf charged with mouth agape, but Francis made the sign of the cross, and the wolf stopped dead in its tracks.

'Come to me, Brother Wolf,' said Francis, and the wolf obeyed. 'In the name of Christ,' he continued, 'I order you not to hurt me or anyone.' He then lectured the wolf for 'destroying God's creatures without any mercy'. He concluded, 'I want you to promise me that you will never hurt any animal or man.'

The wolf signalled his promise by nodding his head. Francis then took the wolf into town, preached a sermon to both people and wolf, and asked both parties not to hunt one another again. The people voiced their assent, and the wolf gave a visible pledge by raising his right paw. 'From that day,' the story concludes, 'the wolf and the people kept the pact which St Francis made.'

The story is a near-exact match of the Greek myth of Hercules' slaying of the lion. But Hercules' power could resolve the conflict between man and nature only by killing the lion. Francis managed to reconcile man and nature, by the power of Christ.

inclement weather. He shoved it towards the man. 'Here, take my cloak as payment and give me the lambs.'

The man, who thought he was getting the better out of the bargain, happily made the trade.

Francis now wondered what in the world he was going to do with the lambs! After getting advice from his companion, he gave the lambs back to the man, but not before making him promise that he would never sell or butcher them.

Even worms became an object of Francis's compassion. One day, he read a text about Jesus that quoted him as saying, 'I am a worm and not a man.' From then on, whenever he saw a worm on the road, he stooped over, picked it up and placed it safely to the side so that it would not be crushed by travellers.

This last story reveals the essence of Francis's ecological sensitivity. It was not an abstract love of nature, or Henry Thoreau's notion (in his essay 'Walking') that 'in wildness is the preservation of the world', that prompted his love of nature. For Francis, nature was a living metaphor for his relationship with God.

He took his cues from the Bible. In the medieval Bible (and Bibles with the Apocrypha today), there was a passage in the book of Daniel that Francis often read: 'The Song of the Three Young Men'. It is a prayer that extols the wonders of the created order – rain, dew, wind, fire, heat, frost, lightning, mountains, plants, birds and so on. Because 'the three young men . . . invited all the elements to praise and glorify the Creator of all things', says Thomas of Celano, Francis 'never stopped glorifying, praising and blessing the Creator and Ruler of all things in all elements and creatures'.

Francis delighted in the beauty of flowers because they sprang up from 'the root of Jesse', from the biblical passage that alludes to Christ. By a flower's fragrance, he would say, 'it raised up countless thousands from death'. So, whenever he came across a field of flowers, Thomas of Celano says, he would 'preach to them and invite them to praise the Lord'. He told one friar to save room in his garden for flowers, 'out of love of him who is called the Rose on the plain and the Lily on the mountain slopes'.

Sheep were dear to Francis because they reminded him of Jesus, the Lamb of God, by whose suffering and death salvation was brought into the world. He once spotted a sheep amid a flock of goats, and it immediately brought to Francis's mind an image of Jesus walking meekly and humbly among the Pharisees and chief priests. While

An excerpt from the Song of the Three Young Men

Bless the Lord, all the Lord's creation:
  praise and glorify him for ever! . . .

Bless the Lord, sun and moon,
  praise and glorify him for ever!
Bless the Lord, stars of heaven,
  praise and glorify him for ever!
Bless the Lord, all rain and dew,
  praise and glorify him for ever!
Bless the Lord, every wind,
  praise and glorify him for ever!
Bless the Lord, fire and heat,
  praise and glorify him for ever!
Bless the Lord, cold and warmth,
  praise and glorify him for ever!
Bless the Lord, dew and snowstorm,
  praise and glorify him for ever! . . .

Bless the Lord, mountains and hills,
  praise and glorify him for ever!
Bless the Lord, every plant that grows,
  praise and glorify him for ever!
Bless the Lord, springs of water,
  praise and glorify him for ever!
Bless the Lord, seas and rivers,
  praise and glorify him for ever!
Bless the Lord, whales, and everything that moves in the waters,
  praise and glorify him for ever!
Bless the Lord, every kind of bird,
  praise and glorify him for ever!
Bless the Lord, all animals wild and tame,
  praise and glorify him for ever!

Daniel 3:57, 62–68, 75–81

Francis was staying at the monastery of San Verecondo, he was told that one of the monastery's newborn lambs had been killed by a sow. 'Alas, brother lamb,' he said, 'innocent animal, always displaying Christ to people!'

'The Canticle of Brother Sun'

It is not surprising, then, that, as his natural body wasted away, Francis turned to the created order to give him perspective. One day, when he had been praying for strength to bear his illnesses, he felt that God spoke to him. 'Be glad and joyful in the midst of your infirmities and tribulations,' the voice said. 'As of now, live in peace, as if you already share in my kingdom.'

The next morning, he told a brother he was determined to 'be full of joy in my infirmities and tribulations'. He was going to 'seek my consolation in the Lord, to give thanks to God the Father, to his only Son our Lord Jesus Christ, and to the Holy Spirit'. He decided there was no better way to do that than to compose a song praising God for his creation. He said, 'Every day we fail to appreciate so great a blessing by not praising as we should the Creator and dispenser of all these gifts.'

The final version of the song, which today is called 'The Canticle of the Creatures' or 'The Canticle of Brother Sun', reads like this:

> *'Everyone says the great problem in Western society today is our collapse of values. For Francis, the supreme value, the value that gave value to everything else, was God.'*
>
> **Conrad Hawkins OFM, St Bonaventure University, New York, *Christian History* Magazine, 1994**

Most High, all-powerful, good Lord,
yours are the praises, the glory, the honour, and all blessing.
To you alone, Most High, do they belong,
and no man is worthy to mention your name.

Praised be you, my Lord, with all your creatures,
especially Sir Brother Sun,
who is the day and through whom
you give us light. And he is beautiful and radiant with great splendour;
and bears a likeness of you, Most High One.

Praised be you, my Lord, through Sister Moon and the stars;
in heaven you formed them clear and precious and beautiful.

Praised be you, my Lord, through Brother Wind,
and through the air, cloudy and serene, and every kind of weather,
through which you give sustenance to your creatures.

Praised be you, my Lord, through Sister Water,
which is very useful and humble and precious and chaste.

Praised be you, my Lord, through Brother Fire,
through whom you light the night,
and he is beautiful and playful and robust and strong.

Praised be you, my Lord, through our Sister Mother Earth,
who sustains and governs us,
and who produces varied fruits with coloured flowers and herbs.

Praised be you, my Lord, through those who give pardon for your love,
and bear infirmity and tribulation.
Blessed are those who endure in peace,
for by you, Most High, they shall be crowned.

Praised be you, my Lord, through our Sister Bodily Death,
from whom no living man can escape.
Woe to those who die in mortal sin.
Blessed are those whom death will find in your most holy will,
for the second death shall do them no harm.

Praise and bless my Lord and give Him thanks
and serve Him with great humility.

Francis used this song not just as a personal comfort, but as a means to further the order's mission. He asked Elias to send Brother Pacifico, who had once been the emperor's King of Verse, to take a band of friars around the country to sing it after they preached. They were to end by saying to their audiences, 'We are the Lord's minstrels, and you can repay us for our performance by leading a life of penance.'

A musical product of his age

Despite a lack of radios, CDs and MTV, people in the Middle Ages had plenty of access to music. It was heard and played in both church and street. In the great cathedrals, monks and priests chanted hymns in plainsong, or plainchant – singing with a single melodic line. Since few churches had organs, most singing was done *a cappella*.

Outside of church, kings and noblemen could hire musicians to play harps and lutes for their banquets. Ordinary people sang folk songs, and danced to flutes and drums on their feast days. By 1400, most towns had a civic band of professional musicians, which accompanied official processions and festivals.

Troubadours, travelling musicians and singers, were found all over France and Italy in Francis's day. The songs were often accompanied by a fiddle, which was larger than a modern violin and rested on the musician's lap. The songs were mostly about the glories of romantic love.

Francis loved music from his youth, though we have no indication that he ever learned an instrument. Using the troubadours as his model, as he travelled and preached, he often sang of love, in his case, the love of God. The culmination of a lifetime of his singing in this tradition was his 'Canticle of Brother Sun'.

When Francis heard that Assisi's podesta and bishop were angrily feuding, he ordered a friar to sing 'The Canticle of Brother Sun' in their midst, adding the stanza, 'Praised be You, my Lord, through those who give pardon for Your love and bear infirmity and tribulation. / Blessed are those who endure in peace.' When the rival parties heard the song, they were so moved that they repented of their mutual hatred, and reconciled.

This was a song, then, that not only reconciled Francis to his fate, but also reconciled people one to another and to their God.

CHAPTER 20

SISTER DEATH

Francis was at San Damiano when he composed 'The Canticle of Brother Sun'. Before he left, he composed another song for the Poor Ladies who had so faithfully cared for him. In the summer of 1225, he also wrote them a letter, encouraging them to continue 'to live and die' in their 'austere and poor' life. There was much weeping as he left for Reiti.

'Listen, poor ones called by the Lord, who have come together from many parts and provinces. Live always in truth, that you may die in obedience. Do not look at the life without, for that of the Spirit is better.'

Francis, 'Canticle of Exhortation to the Poor Ladies of San Damiano', 1225

Reiti was the papal courts' home away from Rome, and where some of Italy's best physicians were to be found. Francis, under a papal command, now made his way to their care, though dreading every step. He abhorred being fussed over by Elias and others, even if his health was suffering. Besides, travel was painful. The brothers had to wrap his face in cloth so that sunlight would not penetrate and sear his eyes. Still, his infected eyes wept continually.

Pope Honorius and Cardinal Ugolino warmly welcomed Francis, whose presence in the city created an immediate stir. Merchants broke off business engagements to ask his advice or hear him talk. The ill sought his prayers for healing. Many hangers-on simply wanted to bask in the presence of someone who was clearly headed for sainthood.

To escape such attention, Francis moved to a country church, five kilometres from Reiti. Still, parties of cardinals, bishops and their retainers, and other curious clergy, still sought out the holy celebrity. Finally, Francis retired to a hermitage in the woods of Fonte Colombo, where earlier he had completed his Rule. He underwent further eye treatments, but with no success.

Elias and Ugolino recommended a trip to Siena, where more doctors could be consulted. But one night, soon after he arrived, Francis began vomiting uncontrollably, and blood started coming up. Everyone thought that this was the end. Then he recovered. Then he suffered a relapse.

Medieval medicine

In addition to the illnesses which plague all ages, medieval people had to deal with scourges that are rarely known today: smallpox, leprosy, St Antony's fire and St Vitus's dance. Such illnesses were the product of overcrowding and unsanitary living conditions, as well as malnutrition.

Most medieval people believed that disease was the result of an imbalance in the four bodily fluids, or humours: choler, phlegm, black bile and blood. Restoring the balance was seen as the path to health. Cauterization, surgery, diet and herbal medicine were all used to restore that balance. But the most popular method was bloodletting – a specific vein was opened to treat a specific disease, and the blood was then analysed for its smell or greasiness.

Later medieval doctors were guided by elaborately illustrated charts, helping them to inspect the patient's urine (for colour, smell and sedimentation). They also used calendars and tables for applying astrological medicine, or manuals depicting herbs and their applications. By the end of the Middle Ages, cadavers were being experimented on to further medical science.

Only the wealthy or well-connected (such as Francis) were able to afford physicians, though some thirteenth-century Italian cities retained physicians for their citizens. Otherwise, peasants had to depend on local folk healers – and prayer.

It was clear that Francis's 46-year-old body was slipping away. Today, medical scholars believe that Francis suffered from osteoporosis, fatal malnutrition (probably from excessive fasting), possibly tuberculosis, a peptic or stomach ulcer and the side effects of malaria (contracted in North Africa). His stomach began to swell, as did his legs and feet, due to dropsy, and he could take in no food. Elias rushed him to Assisi, so that Francis could die in his hometown.

The last months

During these last months of his life, Francis became increasingly anxious about his order. He had formally resigned as its head six years earlier, and he had dutifully submitted to the new minister general, Elias (as of

1221). But he became increasingly nervous about the direction which the increasingly large order was taking. The larger the order, the more layers of administration it needed. And, with that, came a pastoral relaxation of the Rule to accommodate the weaknesses of those who had joined, but who had not been inspired by Francis's original vision. Perhaps he sensed how Elias would guide the order after Francis's death, with an authoritarian hand and a more luxurious lifestyle.

For all his symbolic acts of letting go, Francis understandably could not quite let go. In the last weeks and months of his life, he composed a document, a sermon to his brothers, calling them back to his pristine vision. It is called *The Testament*.

In the first part, Francis reminisces. He remembers how lepers were 'too bitter for me to see', and how, after showing them mercy, 'what had

Francis's relics at home

Elias made haste to get Francis to Assisi because he knew his world. It was important that Francis die and be buried in the town he was associated with, so that his hometown could house his relics.

Medieval piety was rooted in the veneration of saints and their *relicta* ('things left behind'). Christians, especially, believed that the barrier between this life and the next could be bridged. They also believed that saints were not dead, any more than was Jesus. Church teachers said that the prayers of saints could be sought from anywhere, but people came to believe that saints were especially present at the saints' shrines – Peter at Rome, James at Compostela, Thomas Becket at Canterbury. At shrines, the saints' bones, or items associated with the saint (such as a part of the sword that slew the martyr), were held in a reliquary. People flocked to such places to say their prayers. They often expected miracles, especially healing, at shrines. At a minimum, they expected to experience some sense of transcendence there, where they believed that a bit of heaven was touching earth.

To be sure, a popular shrine garnered income for local merchants and for the church, but it is too cynical to say this was the only reason for which Assisi officials would want Francis to be buried in his hometown. No doubt civic pride played some role, as well. But, more than anything, the town fathers wanted Francis close because they wanted to be close to heaven.

seemed bitter to me was turned into sweetness of soul and body'. He recalls the early prayer he adapted as he went about churches: 'We adore you, Lord Jesus Christ, in all your church throughout the whole world and we bless you because by your holy cross you have redeemed the world.'

Then comes an extensive paragraph on his loyalty to his church: 'The Lord gave me, and gives me still, such faith in priests who live according to the rite of the holy Roman Church because of their orders that, were they to persecute me, I would still want to have recourse to them.'

In fact, the order still experienced hostility in parts of Christendom, and it attracted people who were disgusted with the church and who sought a purer path to holiness. For these and other reasons, in less than a century, some later Franciscans found themselves seriously at odds with the hierarchy. Some were even excommunicated as heretics and burned to death. Francis, no doubt, sensed that the seeds of alienation had already been planted. He spends considerable words in *The Testament* to mandate faithfulness to things Catholic: 'We must honour all theologians and those who minister the most holy divine words and respect them as those who minister us spirit and life.'

> 'Who are these people? They have snatched out of my hands my religion and that of the brothers. If I go to the general chapter, I'll show them what is my will.'
>
> **Francis, after a severe illness later in life, *The Assisi Compilation*, 1244–60**

Then come a variety of reminiscences about the life of poverty, each of which seems to be an indirect admonition to the brothers. He notes that the early brothers 'were content with one tunic, patched inside and out, with a cord and short trousers'. Then Francis adds, 'We desired nothing more.' He remembers, 'I worked with my hands, and I still desire to work; and I earnestly desire all the brothers to give themselves to honest work.'

To be sure, he had given the brothers permission to do other things, such as pursue study, but Francis was having second thoughts, and for good reason. In the next generation, the order would produce men who were known less for their poverty, humility, service or Christ-likeness, and more for their great learning. A few examples are: Alexander of Hales, the 'Irrefragible Doctor'; Bonaventure, the 'Seraphic Doctor'; Roger Bacon, the 'Admirable Doctor'; Ockham, the 'Invincible Doctor' and Duns Scotus, the famous rival of Thomas Aquinas.

Shifting gears, Francis then moves into direct admonitions: 'Let the brothers be careful not to receive in any way churches or poor dwellings or anything built for them unless they are according to the holy poverty we have promised in the Rule.' In fact, the order had gradually begun accepting some churches and residences, and Francis had tacitly agreed to these exceptions. But, again, he was questioning his former flexibility.

> 'Francis saw many rushing for positions of authority. Despising their arrogance, he strove by his own example to call them back from such sickness.'
>
> **Thomas of Celano, *The Life of St Francis*, 1228–29**

Furthermore, says Francis, 'I strictly command all the brothers through obedience, where they may be, not to dare to ask any letter from the Roman Curia . . . whether for a church or another place or under the pretext of preaching or the persecution of their bodies.' Again, this is a matter which Francis had, through his silence, let slide.

He also tells the brothers to recite the daily Office according to the Rule. And any who do not are to be brought before the nearest custodian who, in turn, will 'keep him securely day and night as a man in chains' and 'personally deliver him into the hands of his minister'. The minister, in turn, 'would guard him as a prisoner' until he can be handed over to the Protector of the Order.

Though Francis says that he is not writing 'another Rule', he does say that the brothers are 'bound through obedience not to add to or take away from these words'. Then he adds, 'And let them always have this writing with them together with the Rule'. In other words, this document was the key to interpreting the Rule. 'I strictly command all my cleric and lay brothers, through obedience,' he says, 'not to place any gloss upon the Rule or upon these words, saying, "They should be understood in this way."'

It is clear that Francis felt that the order was softening, that its vision was fuzzy and that the brothers were settling into a reasonable, ordered life of moderate devotion. Francis, no doubt, also realized that he himself was being slighted. His pleas are punctuated by the repeated phrase 'through obedience', a desperate attempt to bring the brothers back into conformity by the force of his personality. As it turned out, this was an exercise in futility. The order simply could not sustain his pure vision without his saintly presence. Mere mortals were simply incapable of living day by day with the intensity that his ideals demanded.

Ultimately, Francis recognized the futility of his *Testament* because, during this same period, he told a story that captured the irony of his rejection by his order. The story illustrates Francis's longing for utter self-denial which, paradoxically, led Francis to experience a type of joy that few people have known. It is in the very rejection of his ideals that his personal aspirations were fulfilled. A fourteenth-century manuscript contains a condensed version of a longer version recorded in *The Little Flowers of St Francis*:

One day at Saint Mary [of the Angels], Francis called Brother Leo and said, 'Brother Leo, write this down.'

He answered, 'I'm ready.'

'Write what true joy is,' he said. 'A messenger comes and says that all the masters of theology in Paris have joined the order – write: that is not true joy. Or all the prelates beyond the mountains – archbishops and bishops, or the king of France and the king of England – write: that is not true joy. Or that my friars have gone to the unbelievers and have converted all of them to the faith; or that I have so much grace from God that I heal the sick and I perform many miracles. I tell you all that true joy is not all those things.'

'But what is true joy?'

'I am returning from Perugia, and I am coming here at night, in the dark. It is wintertime and wet and muddy and so cold that icicles form at the edges of my habit and keep striking my legs, and blood flows from such wounds. And I come to the gate, all covered with mud and cold and ice, and after I have knocked and called for a long time, a friar comes and asks, "Who are you?"

'I answer, "Brother Francis."

'And he says, "Go away. This is not a decent time to be going about. You can't come in."

'And when I insist again, he replies, "Go away. You are a simple and un-educated fellow. From now on, don't stay with us any more. We are so many and so important that we don't need you."

'But I stand at the gate and say, "For the love of God, let me come in to-night."

'And he answers, "I won't. Go to the Crosier's Place [lepers' hospital] and ask there."

'I tell you that if I kept patience and was not upset – that is true joy and true virtue and salvation of the soul.'

So, despite the fact that his order seemed to be saying, 'We don't need you', Francis was dying in joy. At the end, in fact, it was this very joy that further scandalized his brothers.

He had been brought to the bishop's palace in Assisi in late summer 1226 and, when he experienced violent attacks of pain, he asked the brothers to sing to him 'The Canticle of Brother Sun', both night and day. When Elias, among others, heard about this, he told Francis that it was unseemly for him to be rejoicing like this. People were talking. He scolded Francis: a saint, which the people considered him to be, should be preparing for his death in a more solemn and holy fashion.

Francis patiently asked him to indulge him in this, 'For by the grace and assistance of the Holy Spirit, I am so united and conjoined to my Lord that by his mercy I may rightly rejoice in him, the Most High.'

Even that was not enough for Francis; it was at this time that he added the stanza about death to his 'Canticle':

Praised be you, my Lord, through our Sister Bodily Death,
    from whom no living man can escape
Woe to those who die in mortal sin.
Blessed are those whom death will find in Your most holy will,
    for the second death shall do them no harm.

When Francis felt that death was imminent, he asked to be carried to the Portiuncula. Halfway down the slope from Assisi, he told his bearers to stop so that he could bless his hometown. He was finally put down in a hut a few metres from the chapel of St Mary of the Angels. In honour of Lady Poverty, he asked to be placed on the ground naked but, finally, at the insistence of the brothers, he agreed to return to his bed. He absolved and blessed the brothers, listened to readings from the Gospel of John and had the brothers sing his 'Canticle' again.

Then, on 3 October, as Thomas of Celano describes it, 'The most holy soul was released from the flesh, and it was absorbed into the abyss of light, his body fell asleep in the Lord.'

One brother thought that he saw the soul of Francis rise to heaven, 'like a star but as big as the moon, with the brilliance of the sun, and carried up upon a small white cloud'. Others later said that a great flock of birds descended on the hut, circling and singing with 'unusual joy'.

'Naked he lingered before the bishop at the beginning of his conversion; and for this reason, at the end of his life, he wanted to leave this world naked.'

Bonaventure, *The Major Legend of St Francis*, 1260–63

CHAPTER 21
THE MODERN MEDIEVAL MAN

The following spring, Francis's longtime mentor, Cardinal Ugolino, became Pope Gregory IX. As one of his first acts, he pushed Francis's canonization through the necessary bureaucratic hoops, so that Francis was made an official saint in July 1228 – less than two years after his death. In May 1230, Francis's remains were moved from the San Giorgio Church to a new basilica: Basilica San Francesco (the Church of St Francis), built under the direction of Brother Elias.

Elias had been replaced as the order's head in 1227, but Gregory gave him the job of building an appropriate basilica in Francis's honour. To many followers, the grand, ornate building that emerged was anything but appropriate. Many brothers were shocked, not only at the imposing

---

Medieval burial

Before Christianity took root in Europe, a variety of burial customs was practised. The Jutes, like the Romans before them, buried their remains. The Angles, Saxons and Scandinavians cremated the body. After the arrival of Christianity, cremation was abandoned in favour of burial, so that the dead might have bodies to meet the Lord on Judgment Day. Furthermore, no longer were the deceased buried with grave goods, such as weapons, jewellery or coins, since none of this was thought to be necessary in the afterlife.

The rich were the only class which could afford elaborately carved stone coffins but, by the end of the Middle Ages, wooden coffins had become the norm for all classes.

Francis's death presented some special difficulties. Everyone knew that Francis was headed for sainthood. The temptation to raid his tomb and steal his bones as relics would be almost irresistible. So Elias and Gregory went to great lengths to bury his tomb deep within the Basilica San Franceso – under a slab of granite gravel and 10 welded bands of iron, an 86-kilogram grill and, finally, a 91-kilogram rock. The plan worked. The coffin was not discovered and unearthed until the beginning of the nineteenth century.

structure, but at how Elias had badgered provincials to raise money to build it. It was, they felt, an utter contradiction of everything Francis stood for.

On the other hand, Gregory and Elias were not alone in admiring the basilica. Many other brothers thought it a shrine worthy of their holy founder. Nor were they scandalized, as some were, when Gregory named it (and not the humble St Mary's) as the 'head and mother' of the order.

These developments only widened a split in the order that Francis saw coming. His *Testament* was an attempt to get all the brothers to commit

The medieval cathedral

Francis's era saw the rise of Gothic architecture and the beginning of many of Europe's grandest architectural projects. The Basilica San Francesco in Assisi was not a grand project such as Chartres or Rouen, but it was inspired by cathedrals such as these.

The scale of these building projects pushed medieval architecture to its limits. Massive amounts of material were required. Ely Cathedral in England took more than 363,000 kilograms of wood and stone to finish. Whole forests were felled in France to complete some projects. Eighteen-metre-long beams were imported from Scandinavia. Stone for the Norwich Cathedral was shipped from 483 kilometres away (making the cost of shipping twice the price of the stone itself).

New machinery had to be constructed. To lift heavy carved stones high up a cathedral roof, workers used winches, windlasses and a 'great wheel' – a wooden wheel which was large enough for one or two men to stand inside.

The amount of detailed work seemed unending. Although some stained-glass windows were as high as 18 metres, they still had to be made up of pieces no larger than 20 centimetres wide or high. Cathedrals included dozens, if not hundreds, of sculptures – Chartres Cathedral today has more than 2,000.

And then there was the patience required; some cathedrals took more than 100 years to build, and some bishops spent their entire tenure holding church services in the middle of a huge construction site. Yet, despite the architectural and financial challenges, during one 400-year period, Europe saw the construction of some 500 cathedrals.

themselves again to strict poverty. Now the new minister general, John Parenti, tried to take up the dying Francis's cause. He appealed to Gregory to make *The Testament* binding on the order.

Gregory saw no future in that. He believed that Francis's radical vision could not be sustained, and that strict adherence to *The Testament* would undermine the future growth and stability of the order. So he announced that the more moderate Rule of 1223 would be the standard. Furthermore, he said, money could now be held on behalf of the order, and friars were to be allowed books and other personal effects. They would also be permitted to use and live in large and permanent buildings.

> *'I have done what is mine to do; may Christ teach you what you are to do.'*
>
> **Francis to his brothers on his deathbed**

Franciscan divisions

The subsequent history of the order is both complex and bitter. The rift between the champions of strict poverty – soon called the 'Spirituals' – and the moderates widened. By 1317, the Spirituals had become such an irritant to church authorities that they were excommunicated as heretics. Some were arrested and burned at the stake.

This did not solve the Franciscan dilemma: how were ordinary mortals to sustain an order founded on the ideals of a saintly personality? In the 1330s, some friars south of Assisi again took up a 'stricter observance' of the Rule. Avoiding some of the extremist rhetoric of the Spirituals, they managed to gain papal recognition for their efforts in 1415. In 1443, they were given their own minister general and, in 1517, they were separated from the main Franciscan body (known as the 'Conventuals'), and are today known as 'Observants'.

> *'Today we take it for granted that if you are deeply committed to the gospel, you will go into the world to serve. That assumption is due in large measure to Francis's ministry.'*
>
> **Conrad Hawkins OFM, St Bonaventure University, New York, *Christian History Magazine*, 1994**

But, by 1525, some Observants began to question the purity of their order, and Matteo da Basci led a movement to live by Francis's Rule more literally. In 1529, the pope permitted them also to become an independent order, the Capuchins, an order that today emphasizes contemplative prayer.

Today, these three orders combined make up the largest order in the Roman Catholic Church. Added to this are the Order of St Clare, the Episcopalian Franciscan Orders and the Order of secular Franciscans in many denominations. The overall numbers are not overly impressive, totalling in the tens of thousands – some Pentecostal congregations in Korea and Brazil are larger. But numbers are not everything. Francis continues to have an influence beyond the devotion of his formal adherents.

Unfortunately, this influence is narrow in scope. For the larger world, Francis has become a statue to be placed in gardens or, more seriously, the patron saint of two modern movements – those of peace and ecology. Very few people today show much interest in Francis's deep personal faith, his call to strict poverty or his absolute devotion to the Roman Catholic Church. In fact, many Catholics in the peace and ecology movements, who regularly name Francis as their champion, pride themselves in rebelling against the established church, showing nothing but disdain for the hierarchy – a fact which their patron saint would deplore.

> 'Beyond the romantic clichés about St Francis, one discovers a person who, for all of his transparent attractiveness, is complex to the point of enigma.'
>
> **Lawrence S. Cunningham,** *St Francis of Assisi*, 1981

This selective admiration is reinforced by the popularity of two poems, which people believe best summarize Francis's life and thought. Unfortunately, in both instances, the real Francis is misrepresented.

One is his 'Canticle of Brother Sun'. In this case, modern readers show a remarkable ability to skip over the opening stanza:

Most High, all-powerful, good Lord,
    yours are the praises, the glory, the honour, and all blessing.
To you alone, Most High, do they belong,
    and no man is worthy to mention your name.

And they remain deaf to the repeated references to God throughout. In other words, the poem in their minds is an ode to the wonders of nature. Francis becomes, for them, merely a troubadour of the environment. This is despite the poem's clear intention to glorify not creation, but the Creator.

The other poem that has gained popularity since the twentieth century goes like this:

Lord, make me an instrument of your peace.
Where there is hatred, let me sow love;
*   where there is injury, pardon;*
where there is doubt, faith;
*   where there is despair, hope;*
where there is darkness, light;
*   where there is sadness, joy.*

O Divine Master, grant that I may not so much seek to be
*   consoled as to console;*
*   to be understood as to understand;*
to be loved as to love;
*   for it is in giving that we receive;*
it is in pardoning that we are pardoned;
*   it is in dying that we are born again to eternal life.*

Most readers assume that these words come from Francis himself. Not quite. Though he expressed many of these sentiments in his life, he never did so in this form. As far as we can tell, it was first composed at a Catholic eucharistic congress that met in Chicago, Illinois, in 1925. To be sure, it represents one theme of Francis's life and teachings – but only one.

Thus we come to the unhappy conclusion that the Francis who is remembered and adored today is not the Francis who walked the Umbrian roads in the thirteenth century. But this is not surprising. The real Francis makes every age a tad uncomfortable. The Francis who calls us to peace and respect for creation – causes we readily sign up for – is the same Francis who challenges our age, as he did his own age, by speaking and living against our most vexing sins.

In a secular age, when talk of God is awkward or rigidly privatized, stands the deeply pious Francis, whose God-intoxication drove everything he did. In a materialistic world, where the meaning and measure of life is counted by the things we buy and the experiences we enjoy, the barefoot, raggedly robed Francis calls us to simplicity and poverty. In cultures drowning in rampant individualism, in which we baulk at submitting to anything outside the self, Francis tells us to abandon our lives in complete obedience to something bigger than ourselves.

In short, Francis would instil in us, as he tried to instil in his contemporaries, profound gratitude and humility – towards God, our world and even the flawed institutions that have nurtured us. In the end, although our modern world wishes to discard so much of Francis into the rubbish bin of history, it is the medieval Francis who shows the modern world a better way.

CHRONOLOGY

Summer or autumn 1181 Giovanni di Pietro di Bernardone is born and baptized in Assisi; the child is renamed Francesco by his father.

1190 Francis attends the parish school at San Giorgio.

1193 Chiara di Favarone (Clare) is born to a noble Assisi family.

1199–1200 Civil war in Assisi; destruction of feudal nobles' castles. Some Assisi families (including Clare's) move to Perugia.

November 1202 War between Perugia and Assisi; Assisi defeated at the Battle of Collestrada. Francis spends a year in prison in Perugia, until ransomed by his father.

1204 Francis is slowly healed of the illness contracted in prison.

Spring 1205 Francis sets out for war in Apulia but returns the next day after receiving a vision in Spoleto. This is the beginning of his gradual conversion.

Autumn to winter 1205 Francis receives the message of the crucifix of San Damiano. He is mocked by fellow Assisians. He prays and meditates in countryside caves.

January or February 1206 Francis's conflict with his father ends with a trial before Bishop Guido.

Spring 1206 Francis nurses leprosy victims in Gubbio. From summer through winter, he repairs San Damiano, San Pietro and the Portiuncula.

24 February 1208 Francis hears the Gospel of St Mathias Mass. He changes from hermit's habit to that of barefoot preacher; he begins to preach.

Spring 1208 Bernard, Peter Catanii and Giles join Francis at the Portiuncula; they embark on their first mission. By the end of the year, four more join the order.

Early 1209 When the group returns from another mission, another four recruits join them, bringing the total to 12 (including Francis).

Spring 1209 Francis writes a brief Rule and obtains informal approval for his order from Pope Innocent III. On their return, the brothers stay briefly Rivo Torto.

1209/10 The friars move to the Portiuncula.

Night of 18–19 March 1212 (Palm Sunday) Francis receives Clare at the Portiuncula; she moves to San Damiano in May.

1213 Francis receives the gift of Mount Verna, which he uses as a hermitage.

1213–14 or 1214–15 Francis travels to Spain and back.

November 1215 Francis is in Rome for the Fourth Lateran Council. He meets Dominic.

Summer 1216 Honorius III is elected pope upon Innocent III's death. The new pope gives Francis the Portiuncula Indulgence.

5 May 1217 Five thousand brothers convene at the Pentecost general chapter at the Portiuncula. The first Franciscan missions take place in Germany, Tunis and Syria.

1219 After the general chapter, another overseas mission is inaugurated. Francis sails from Ancona for Acre and Damietta. He crosses crusader battle lines to preach to the Muslim sultan.

1220 The first Franciscan martyrs are killed, in Morocco. Francis goes to Acre and Holy Land. Cardinal Hugolin appointed Protector of the Order

1220 Francis resigns as head of his order. He appoints Peter Catanii as vicar.

1221 Elias becomes vicar after Peter Catanii's death. The Rule of the Third Order is approved by Honorius III.

1221–22 Francis goes on a preaching tour in southern Italy.

15 August 1222 Francis preaches in Bologna.

Early 1223 Francis composes the Second Rule. The Rule is discussed at the June general chapter. Pope Honorius III approves it in November.

24–25 December 1223 Francis celebrates the Christmas crèche Midnight Mass at Greccio.

15 August–29 September 1224 Francis fasts at La Verna and receives the stigmata.

December 1224–February 1225 A weakened Francis rides a donkey to make a preaching tour in Umbria and the Marches.

Early 1225 Nearly blind from an eye problem, Francis is cared for by Clare at San Damiano. Francis composes 'The Canticle of Brother Sun'. He reconciles the feuding bishop and *podesta* of Assisi.

Summer 1225 to summer 1226 Francis travels. He receives various treatments for his various illnesses, to no avail.

September 1226 Knowing his death is imminent, Francis insists on being carried to the Portiuncula. He dies on 3 October and is buried the next day at San Giorgio Church.

19 March 1227 His friend Hugolin becomes Pope Gregory IX.

16 July 1228 Gregory IX canonizes St Francis.

25 May 1230 Francis's remains are moved to his new basilica, Basilica San Francesco in Assisi.

(Adapted from Omer Englebert, *St Francis of Assisi A Biography*, Franciscan Herald Press, 1965, pp. 393–96, and Joanne Schatzlein, 'Francis of Assisi 1181–1226: The Christian History Timeline' in *Christian History*, Issue 21, No. 2, spring 1994, pp. 26–27.)

FURTHER READING

Augustine and His World

Gerald Bonner, *St Augustine of Hippo: Life and Controversies* (London: SCM Press, 1963, rev. ed. Norwich: Canterbury Press, 1986).

Peter Brown, *Augustine of Hippo: A Biography* (London: Faber, 1967, rev. ed. 2000).

Averil Cameron, *The Later Roman Empire* (Cambridge, MA: Harvard University Press, 1993).

Henry Chadwick, *Augustine* (Oxford: Oxford University Press, 1986).

Henry Chadwick, *Augustine: A Very Short Introduction* (Oxford: Oxford University Press, 2001).

Mary T. Clark, *Augustine* (London: Geoffrey Chapman, 1994).

Allan D. Fitzgerald O.S.A. (general editor), *Augustine through the Ages: An Encyclopedia* (Grand Rapids, MI and Cambridge, MA: Eerdmans, 1999).

Carol Harrison, *Augustine: Christian Truth and Fractured Humanity* (Oxford: Oxford University Press, 2000).

Serge Lancel, *St Augustine*, Paris: Fayard, 1999, English translation: Antonia Nevill (London: SCM Press, 2002).

Robert A. Markus, *Saeculum: History and Society in the Theology of St Augustine* (Cambridge: Cambridge University Press, 1970, rev. ed. 1989).

Paul Monceaux, *Histoire litteraire de l'Afrique chrétienne* (Brussels: Culture et Civilisation, 1966).

James J. O'Donnell, *Augustine: Conferences*, 3 volumes (Oxford: Oxford University Press, 1992).

John J. O'Meara, *The Young Augustine: The Growth of St Augustine's Mind up to His Conversion* (London: Longmans, 1954, rev. ed. 1980).

Richard Price, *Augustine* (London: Harper Collins, 1996).

John Rist, *Augustine* (Cambridge: Cambridge University Press, 1994).

Colin Wells, *The Roman Empire* (London: Fontana, 1992).

Garry Wills, *Saint Augustine* (London: Orion, 2000).

Websites

James J. O'Donnell's website at: www .georgetown.edu/faculty/jod/augustine

Francis of Assisi and His World

Primary sources

Regis J. Armstrong, J.A. Wayne Hellmann and William Short (eds), *Francis of Assisi: Early Documents*, Volume 1, *The Saint* (New York: New City Press, 1999).

Regis J. Armstrong, J.A. Wayne Hellmann and William Short (eds), *Francis of Assisi: Early Documents*, Volume 2, *The Founder* (New York: New City Press, 2000).

Regis J. Armstrong and Ignatius Brady (eds and trs), *Francis and Clare: The Complete Works* (New York: Paulist Press, 1982).

Martin Habig, *St Francis of Assisi, Writings and Early Biographies: English Omnibus of the Sources for the Life of St Francis* (Chicago, IL: Franciscan Press, 1991).

Biographies

Omer Englebert, *St Francis of Assisi: A Biography* (Chicago, IL: Franciscan Herald Press, 1965).

Arnaldo Fortini, *Francis of Assisi*, tr. Helen Moak (New York: Crossroad, 1992).

Julian Green, *God's Fool: The Life and Times of Francis of Assisi* (San Francisco, CA: Harper, 1985).

Adrian House, *Francis of Assisi: A Revolutionary Life*, Mahwah (Mahwah, NJ: Hidden Spring, 2000, 2001).

Johannes Jörgensen, *St Francis of Assisi: A Biography*, tr. T. O'Conor Sloan (New York: Doubleday, 1955 [1912]).

Michael Robson, *St Francis of Assisi: The Legend and the Life* (London: Geoffrey Chapman, 1997).

Paul Sabatier, *Life of St Francis of Assisi*, tr. Louise Seymour Houghton (New York: Scribners, 1905).

Reflective interpretations of Francis

G.K. Chesterton, *St Francis of Assisi* (New York: Doubleday, 1924, 1957).

Roy M. Gasnick (ed.), *The Francis Book: 800 Years with the Saint from Assisi* (New York: Macmillan, 1980).

Nikos Kazantzakis, *St Francis: A Novel* (New York: Simon and Schuster, 1962).

Valerie Martin, *Salvation: Scenes from the Life of St Francis* (New York: Knopf, 2001).

Gerard Thomas Straub, *The Sun and Moon Over Assisi: A Personal Encounter with Francis and Clare* (New York: Saint Anthony Messenger Press, 2000).

Middle Ages, miscellany

Adrian H. Bredero, *Christendom and Christianity in the Middle Ages* (Grand Rapids, MI: Eerdmans, 1984, 1986).

Christopher Dawson, *Religion and the Rise of Western Culture* (New York: Doubleday, 1957).

Frances Gies, *The Knight in History* (San Francisco, CA: Harper & Row, 1984).

J.R.H. Moorman, *A History of the Franciscan Order from its Origins to the Year 1517* (Oxford: Clarendon Press, 1968).

R.W. Southern, *Western Society and Church in the Middle Ages* (London: Penguin, 1993).

André Vauchez, *The Laity in the Middle Ages: Religious Beliefs and Devotional Practices*, ed. and tr. Daniel E. Bornstein (South Bend, IN: Notre Dame, 1993).

INDEX

Francis of Assisi and His World

F

Lightning Source UK Ltd.
Milton Keynes UK
UKHW021427020719
345426UK00005B/167/P

9 781912 552245